STRANGE CLEVER TURNS

Remarkable Speciality Acts in Variety, Vaudeville and Sideshows at the Turn of the 20th Century as seen by their Contemporaries

COMPILED BY
CHARLIE HOLLAND

HOLLAND & PALMER
London

For Amy

Thanks for their help to Caroline, Betty and Vivitext

A CIP record for this book is available from the British Library

First Published in 1998 by
HOLLAND & PALMER
22 Gilbert Road
London SE11 4NL

ISBN 0 9532373 03

CONTENTS

The Alhambra, Leicester Square in its opening year 1860, with proscenium arch and stage. The audience capacity was 3,500. Following a fire in 1882 it was swiftly rebuilt and reopened in 1883

PALACES OF VARIETY

While jugglers, acrobats, magicians and other speciality acts have amazed and entertained audiences throughout time, events in the late 19th century conspired to allow the extraordinary and fabulous performers in this book, literally, a world of opportunity. Take as an example the subject of one of the magazine articles reproduced here, a young American juggler named W.C. Fields – many years before he became one of the most famous film comedians. In December 1900 Fields boarded a steamship bound for Europe. Aged just twenty, he already had three years of vaudeville touring experience behind him and was eager for the new opportunities and challenges that Europe had to offer.

On 1 January 1901 he started a month's run at the Wintergarten in Berlin after which he travelled to London for a three-week booking at the Palace Theatre of Varieties in Leicester Square. From London he went north to Birmingham, Leeds, where he topped the bill for the first time, and Bradford. In late April he was back in Germany, in Leipzig, then spent May at the Folies Bergère in Paris. Come July he was in England again, at the Blackpool Tower Circus, before returning to America. In August he opened at Keith's vaudeville theatre in New York before going on to Providence, Toronto, Pittsburgh, Cincinnati, Chicago, St Louis, back to Chicago, Indianapolis, Toledo and Buffalo - his last engagement in that year.

The Wintergarten, Palace Theatre, Folies Bergère and Keith's were top venues in the top cities of the world: they epitomised modern popular entertainment. And while shows in different countries had their own national characteristics and titles - vaudeville in America, music hall in Britain, café concert in France, variété in Germany - they all presented a succession of various acts. The best of the speciality acts, particularly those not dependent on language, could perform worldwide.

Britain was enjoying the benefits of its empire, America had recovered from its Civil War, and around the world the rewards of the industrial revolution were reaching people thanks to the major technological advances that had taken place. Much of the population had moved from the countryside to live and work in cities - London had swelled from over one million inhabitants in 1815 to almost six million in the 1890s - and there was a huge market for entertainment. In those days, with film in its absolute infancy and radio and television still a long way off, entrepreneurs enthusiastically met the demand, building magnificent venues for variety shows, devising touring circuits and providing work for thousands of performers.

Railways and steamships provided largely reliable, safe and quick methods of transport, enabling performers to travel from city to city and from continent to continent. Bookings could be arranged by electric telegraph and the telephone, methods of communication which had developed during the second half of the 19th century as electricity started to be put to practical use. By the end of the century numerous cables had been laid across the Atlantic Ocean, making rapid communication between Europe and America possible. Electric lighting, which was beginning to replace gas in the more prosperous homes, was adopted even more readily in public buildings, especially theatres. One of the earliest all-electric theatres in England was the Matcham designed Hackney Empire that opened in 1901 as part of the Stoll music hall circuit. Acts as well as the venues were quick to incorporate modern technology, as can be seen in the article entitled 'A Curious Electrical Display'.

By the 1890s, developments in photography and printing allowed magazines to reproduce photographic images. The Strand Magazine and Pearson's Magazine were amongst the most popular, publishing new stories, such as Arthur Conan Doyle's 'The Hound of the Baskervilles' and H.G. Wells's 'The War of the Worlds', alongside illustrated articles on photogenic subjects as diverse as natural history, scientific discoveries and popular entertainers. The articles in this book were published between 1894 and 1904, during the prime of music hall, variety and vaudeville.

MUSIC HALL AND VARIETY IN ENGLAND

Music hall evolved in stages, from amateur entertainment provided by singers and comics to amuse clients eating and drinking in public houses and supper rooms, through to purpose-built halls offering food and drink accompanied by a wide variety of professional entertainment, ending with a variety of professional entertainment performed on stage before a conventional auditorium.

An enterprising publican called Charles Morton is credited with creating the first true music hall when he opened the Canterbury Hall in Lambeth, south London, in 1852. The purpose-built hall seated 700 men and, most unusually for the time, women. There was a platform for entertainers to perform on and a chairman to oversee the proceedings. As well as earning money from the sale of food and drink, Morton introduced the practice of charging for admission. His new venture was so successful that after only two years he rebuilt it as a 1500-seat hall.

The concept quickly caught on with the opening of halls in London's West End such as the Alhambra, Pavilion and Empire and later the Palace, Hippodrome and Coliseum. The West End halls were exceptional in the same way as the West End and Broadway theatres of today are, attracting out-of-town audiences to lavish productions. In competition with each other, halls developed their own individual styles and added other entertainments to the bill of singers, comics and musicians. Plays were not produced in music halls. Venues could obtain either a Theatre Licence, which allowed the performance of plays but not eating and drinking in the auditorium, or a Music and Dancing Licence which did not permit drama but did allow eating and drinking in the hall, which was more profitable for the owner.

Many of the acts featured in this book were seen in one of the longest established, largest and grandest music halls in London - the Alhambra in Leicester Square (which was the model for the Folies Bergère in Paris). Originally opened in 1854 as the Royal Panopticon of Science and Art, the building became a circus in 1856 and was converted into a music hall with a proscenium arch and stage and renamed The Alhambra in 1860. Léotard, the 'daring young man on the flying trapeze', about whom more can be found in the chapter on aerialists, performed here shortly afterwards. By the time the performers in this book were appearing there it had been rebuilt, following a fire in December 1882. Instead of seating their patrons at tables, theatres now tended to have tip-up seats and a ledge for your glass, and the title Variety had gained in popularity.

The Royal English Opera House opened in 1891 but failed and became The Palace Theatre of Varieties a year later. Charles Morton was its manager in 1901 when W.C. Fields first appeared there as one of seventeen acts on the bill, which included singers, cyclists, a mimic, a card magician, a hypnotist, the orchestra (its programme featuring a selection from Wagner's Lohengrin), a clown with his menagerie, a troupe of Russian dancers and singers and the latest Biograph moving pictures. The first Royal Variety Performance was held here in 1912, in the presence of King George V and Queen Mary. Two of the performers in this book were featured, Paul Cinquevalli and David Devant, but the biggest music hall star of the time, Marie Lloyd, was omitted, probably because her act was too risqué.

In the three decades up to 1912 music halls and theatres were opened at a rapid rate around the country by entrepreneurs such as Oswald Stoll and Edward Moss, creating circuits for the variety performer to tour throughout the year. At its peak the Moss Empires Circuit controlled thirty-three theatres around the country. A typical variety bill, with two shows a day, would run, following an overture by the orchestra:

1. Dancing duo
2. Ventriloquist
3. Cycling act
4. Comedian
5. Roller skating act
   Interval
6 Return of the dancing duo
7. Small time speciality act such as a paper tearer
8. Straight musical act
9. Star turn comic/comedienne
10. Visual speciality such as a juggler or Biograph (silent short film)

Variety gradually became less fashionable as talking motion pictures and the radio were developed. The advent of television in the 1950s was the final challenge and by the 1960s most of the old theatres were shut and many demolished.

AMERICAN VAUDEVILLE

Variety entertainment had long been presented in beer halls to all-male audiences, and had tended to be low quality and vulgar. In October 1881 a variety performer called Tony Pastor opened Tony Pastor's New Fourteenth Street Theatre in New York and set the stage for Vaudeville. He wanted to attract women as well as men, and was the first to offer clean, wholesome variety entertainment in a theatre without alcoholic drinks and the accompanying vulgarity. As so often happens, another entrepreneur was to make a fortune from this new idea.

In 1883 a showman, Benjamin Franklin Keith, established a dime museum in Boston. In the mid-nineteenth century, when going to see plays at the theatre was generally not socially acceptable, nearly every city boasted at least one privately owned museum and these were often the main and most popular cultural attractions of their day, showing everything from the wonders of natural history to waxwork figures; painted panoramas to scientific demonstrations. Profit as well as education was the motive, and the attractions in attached 'lecture theatres' could be classified as what we now call edutainment.

Following the success of his dime museum, in March 1884 Keith opened B.F. Keith's Theatre in Boston, presenting two shows a day and introducing the term Vaudeville. The theatre was an immediate success, encouraging him to open more. In 1885 he found a business partner, Edward F. Albee, and the two set about establishing a vaudeville empire. In the big theatres shows remained twice daily, but in smaller ones continuous vaudeville became the norm, with shows running from the morning to 10.30pm. Most acts would appear two or three times during the day, and audience members could stay for as long as they chose.

In spring 1900 Keith and Albee established the Vaudeville Managers' Association representing more than fifty leading vaudeville theatres to arrange the routes, salaries and dates of performers. Theatres gained quality acts and performers gained guaranteed tours. The Keith Circuit controlled many of the best vaudeville theatres in the east and worked in close association with the Orpheum Circuit which controlled many of the best west and south of Chicago.

In preparing a bill, the theatre manager would have to consider late arrivals and early leavers among the audience, the need for sets and equipment to be laid out and removed, and the demands placed on the orchestra in addition to the appropriate rhythm of the show for its audience. A typical bill in a two-a-day show in a major city could be made up like this, following an overture by the orchestra:

1. an acrobatic or similar 'dumb' act on full stage which will make a good impression but not be spoiled by latecomers seeking their seats
2. a song and dance number, in front of the first curtain ("in one"), to settle the audience and prepare it for show
3. a comedy dramatic sketch on full stage with special scenery and lots of costumes and lighting effects, to wake up the audience
4. a smart comedy talking act, in one to allow for the scenery to be struck and the next act to be set, as the first big punch of the show
5. a big musical act, full stage
   Interval
6. a strong comedy speciality act, in one, to maintain the interest gained
7. a comedy or drama with a big name, full stage
8. a top comedian, the headliner of the bill, in one
9. a big sight act such as animals or trapeze artists, full stage.

As with variety in England, technological advances in entertainment diverted audiences from vaudeville, and the Great Depression of the 1930s marked the final decline.

THE HUMAN BILLIARD-TABLE

AND OTHER GREAT JUGGLERS

Paul Cinquevalli, the subject of the article 'The Greatest Juggler in the World', was the inspiration for many other jugglers. Born in 1859, he became a star of the halls, as his selection for the 1912 Royal Variety Performance shows, but with the outbreak of the First World War in 1914, the fickle British public turned against him. Although he had lived in Britain for twenty years and entertained the King and Queen, he had been born in Prussia.

Paul Cinquevalli with cannon-ball

The diversity of dangerous tricks and original ones that Cinquevalli performed set him apart from other jugglers, and gained him the nickname The Human Billiard-Table. One of the jugglers he is said to have impressed was the young W.C. Fields, who was himself to create a sensational billiard-table routine a couple of years on from the act featured here (in an article which suffers from having appeared originally in a poorly printed weekly magazine).

A 1934 movie *The Old Fashioned Way* includes Fields's juggling routine, almost complete, and the billiard-table act. The table, with a mirror arranged so that the audience could see the balls, had gimmicks including rounded cushions that allowed balls to bounce back to Fields and a mechanism that allowed all the balls to be potted in one stroke.

Fields started out with a tramp character, one of several different styles that were popular. There were strongmen jugglers, such as Paul Conchas featured here and Paul Spadoni in a later chapter, restaurant jugglers and gentlemen jugglers, plus the more gymnastic swingers of Indian Clubs, from which juggling clubs, lighter and balanced to spin well, were evolved.

Juggling had certainly come a long way from its early days, which, on the evidence of drawings found in the ancient Egyptian Beni-Hasan tombs, were at least 4,000 years ago.

The Greatest Juggler in the World.

BY WILLIAM G. FITZGERALD.

SOME men were born to explore: others to write, or paint, or fight. Paul Cinquevalli was born to juggle. As a boy at school he would throw his slate and pencil high into the air, catch the pencil first, and then swiftly draw the letter "A" in three lightning strokes, while yet the slate was in the air.

Therefore it is not to be wondered at that the boy presently ran away from home with a professional gymnast, whose discerning eye saw a fortune in the little fellow. And Paul, by the way, adopted the name of his new guardian.

Soon he made a name, and his father, reversing the parable, came to him and fell upon his neck.

Although rather below medium height, Paul Cinquevalli possesses enormous strength; his patience, too, is almost incredible, and his vigilance unceasing.

The feat depicted in the first photograph calls for all these things. The juggler comes on to the stage wearing the spiked helmet, and carrying four sections of a jointed pole. The tub is then brought on. He would bring it on himself only it's a thing one can't carry about conveniently; it is a family tub, and weighs 44lb. The juggler places it on one section of the pole, and makes it spin. When its velocity is great, he commences to lengthen the pole by fitting the other sections: and at last the lower end of the pole is resting on his shoulder, whilst the tub is revolving madly some 25ft. above his head.

Even so far, this is no ordinary feat of nerve and strength: but what follows would be absolutely incredible were it not that multitudes have seen it done. Raising one hand, Cinquevalli deliberately dashes away the pole from beneath the tub, causing the latter to fall in a perfectly straight line. The great juggler braces himself for a tremendous effort, and after judging the centre, he dexterously catches the huge tub on the spike of his helmet. And there the tub keeps revolving. But only consider the thing. A 44lb. tub falling 25ft. on to a man's head! "If I am only two or three inches out of the centre," said Mr. Cinquevalli to me, "the tub sends me flying across the stage, and nearly breaks my neck with its whirling impact."

CATCHING THE TUB ON THE SPIKE OF THE HELMET.

Once, at Lyons, that tub hurled Mr. Cinquevalli twenty feet from where he stood; and to-day one may see the scars inflicted at various times by its murderous rim.

The wonderful balancing feat shown in the next photo. is the most difficult in even Cinquevalli's *repertoire;* it took him *eight years* to perfect. A glass is held in his mouth. In the glass is a billiard ball, on which is balanced an ordinary cue. On top of the cue are balanced two other billiard balls, one on top of the other. After eighteen months' weary practice he could maintain the lot in position for one, two, or three seconds—"then my will gave way, and I gave it up." Later on, in Chicago, he again attempted this feat, but found he couldn't do it at all, solely because—as he afterwards found out—there was some heavy machinery working in the basement of the house in which he lodged. He moved to San Francisco, and recommenced practice with some success.

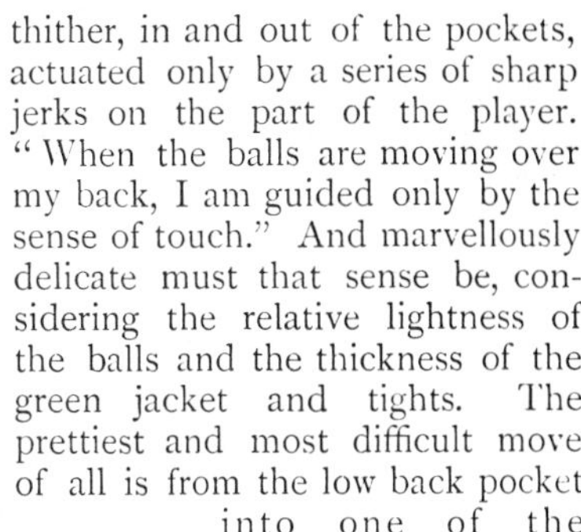

BALANCING THE BILLIARD BALLS (MOST DIFFICULT FEAT EVER EXECUTED.)

It sounds idiotic to say that anyone could do this if the billiard balls were flattened; of course he could. Times beyond number has Mr. Cinquevalli been called upon in various parts of the world to decide bets arising out of this very feat. "It's an utter impossibility," one man will say; "he uses wax or something." But he doesn't.

In these two photos. Cinquevalli is seen in a queer garment. This is his "billiard table" jacket, which was made to his order by a Regent Street tailor. Briefly, he plays an orthodox, scientific game of billiards on his own sinewy person. The jacket is of real billiard cloth, with five beautifully-made pockets of cord and brass wire. The sixth "pocket" is the juggler's own right ear, and his forehead is "spot." His arms and knees serve as cushions, and wonderful cushions they are.

Roberts or Peall would consider the whole game wonderful. "I play an ordinary game of 'fifty up,'" says Mr. Cinquevalli. "Cannons are made in the air. There is a pocket on each shoulder, two in front, and one at the bottom of my back."

The game is a very miracle of neatness and skill. The balls fly into the air, cannon, and then descend, only to glide hither and thither, in and out of the pockets, actuated only by a series of sharp jerks on the part of the player. "When the balls are moving over my back, I am guided only by the sense of touch." And marvellously delicate must that sense be, considering the relative lightness of the balls and the thickness of the green jacket and tights. The prettiest and most difficult move of all is from the low back pocket into one of the shoulder pockets. The ball doesn't seem to know where to go; it runs along hesitatingly, but at last it recognises its destination, and seeks it with a comical little spurt.

Mr. Cinquevalli tells me that the next trick is one involving real danger. A 48lb. cannon-ball is pitched to him, and he catches it on the edge of a dinner-plate. Now, the plate may have flaws in its composition, causing it to shiver to atoms in the juggler's hand and cut him severely, as, indeed, has often been the case. I asked Mr. Cinquevalli how far the cannon-ball might be thrown in this feat. "The farther the better," he replied;

THE HUMAN BILLIARD TABLE.

CATCHING A 48LB. CANNON-BALL ON THE EDGE OF A PLATE.

"for then I have more time to judge where it will descend. In most cases, however," he went on, "my assistant is not strong enough to pitch it very far—as you may imagine."

He is an extraordinary man, this Cinquevalli. He might have his big tub suspended with fine wire, his billiard balls slightly flattened, and his cannon-ball hollow, or made of wood—such as his imitators use. Only, personally, he despises such professional chicanery. Once he saw a Japanese juggler throw up a weighted worsted ball and catch it dead on his forehead. He suggested using an ordinary tennis-ball instead, and he offered one. The Japanese juggler laughed and took it airily. Every time the tennis-ball came down it struck the man's forehead at a different angle, and rebounded a ridiculous distance. After half an hour's practice, that Japanese juggler said the thing was impossible. Now, Cinquevalli literally knows not this word as applied to a juggling feat, so he took home with him that identical tennis-ball, and practised daily for exactly *four months*. He does it easily now. The ball descends, rebounds, and is caught again and again, until it is coaxed down inert.

An amazing feat of quickness and dexterity is next shown. Cinquevalli holds in his left hand a blow-pipe, loaded with a small dart, whilst in the right he juggles a heavy knife, a fork, and a turnip. All at once the fork is thrown high into the air, followed by the turnip. Some fraction of time before the ascending turnip meets the prongs of the descending fork, the blow-pipe is used and the dart embedded in the turnip. A moment later, the united three are received on the blade of the knife, and the juggler claims his applause.

A MARVELLOUS FEAT WITH PUFF AND DART, FORK AND TURNIP.

This beautiful feat grew out of another. At supper in St. Petersburg, one night, Mr. Cinquevalli's host asked him to do something for the company's entertainment. He protested he had no apparatus, whereupon the host (resourceful man!) handed him a knife and fork and a potato that had been boiled in its "jacket" — as every potato should be, by the way.

The famous juggler juggled these things aimlessly for a time until the new trick came to him like a flash. Rising like one inspired, he continued to throw up the three articles, higher and higher.

Suddenly, whilst the potato was falling, Cinquevalli sliced it in halves by a swift movement, and then instantly received each half on the point of knife and fork. He suceeeded first time, in fact; but when he began seriously to practise the feat, he realized its extreme difficulty of achievement. The potato could never be depended upon. According to its texture, it would either fall perpendicularly or else evince a sudden briskness on being halved, which would cause it to

"RAINY DAY UMBRELLA" TRICK—THE LEMONADE BOTTLE DESCENDING.

glance off at peculiar angles. It was only after using almost as many sacks of potatoes as would mitigate an Indian (or Irish) famine, that the juggler was able to combat the vagaries of the erratic tuber.

It will be seen that Mr. Cinquevalli juggles with very homely articles, and gets ideas for new feats in very curious ways. Take the clever and diverting feat shown in the next two photos. "One summer I was up the Thames picnicking with a party of friends. At Marlow we left the launch, and on the bank there we spread the cloth. Later, I commenced juggling as usual with everything within reach—sardine-boxes, glasses, serviettes, and so on. Then I picked up an umbrella, and presently a bottle half full of lemonade. After juggling these in various ways, I threw up the bottle, opened the umbrella while it was descending, and received it upon the ferrule, while it poured out its contents." Of course, this added a new trick to Mr. Cinquevalli's list.

He only lives to juggle. Once he dropped a half-crown; it fell on to his felt slipper. Without stooping to pick it up, he gave his foot a jerk, and lo! the coin flew into his eye as an eye-glass. When this was done he jerked his slipper upwards from his foot, and it instantly stood meekly, toe upwards, on his massive head.

He has sustained injuries innumerable, and almost any one of these would have induced an ordinary man to seek a less dangerous and trying calling. In his

THE SHOWER.

acrobatic days he was doing a wire-walking act in a circus at Odessa. The weight of snow burst the canvas roof and descended into the arena like an avalanche. Of course it swept the wire-walker with it. He fell on to a lady's lap, breaking both her legs; she died, and her guiltless slayer was laid up for weeks.

A very effective feat is depicted in the next two photos. here shown. It is something of a physical phenomenon, but we needn't enter into that. Mr. Cinquevalli's assistant holds two open razors, and from these are suspended a couple of loops of twisted paper, made before the audience. In the loops is hung a broom-handle.

BREAKING A BROOM-HANDLE RESTING IN PAPER LOOPS ON RAZOR-EDGES—"READY."

The juggler then takes a heavy oak stick, and sharply strikes the broom-handle, breaking it in halves, but without in any way injuring the paper loops that are hung on the razor-edges. Sometimes the trick is varied by placing the broom-handle on two clay-pipes, these pipes being smoked, more or less placidly, by a couple of assistants.

Mr. Cinquevalli performed this interesting feat before a brilliant gathering at Marlborough House, in 1886. The Prince himself was greatly struck with it, and asked the juggler to repeat it again and again, in order that he himself might select razors, broom-handle, and striking stick, and also make the paper loops.

This well-known entertainer has for many years practised the extremely difficult art of doing several things at once, until now one may see him at home writing an important business letter with one hand, juggling three plates with the other, and at the same time carrying on an animated conversation with two different people.

One result of incessant practice in this direction is the successful accomplishment of feats like the one next shown. Here we

THE FEAT ACCOMPLISHED.

FOUR SEPARATE MOVEMENTS AT ONE TIME.

Elsewhere I remarked that at all times Mr. Cinquevalli is on the look-out for new tricks. I'm afraid he is often something of a trial in the house. The "afternoon tea" feat was actually invented at that cosy, attractive meal, and a remarkably neat trick it is. He juggles first of all with a cup, a saucer, a lump of sugar, and a teapot *half full of tea.* Suddenly the cup descends as if by magic into the saucer, the laggard sugar joins the cup a second later, and before you could count three Mr. Cinquevalli is gallantly pouring out "a nice hot cup"—not indeed for one fair lady, but for a mixed multitude.

THE "AFTERNOON TEA" FEAT—JUGGLING.

see Mr. Cinquevalli juggling plates with one hand, and keeping a basin revolving on a stick with the other, whilst his powerful head is performing a trick of extraordinary delicacy. On his forehead is balanced a lighted candle, and in his mouth he has an unlighted cigarette in a holder. By certain movements of the jaws the cigarette goes back to the candle, and is lighted and smoked for a while. At length, it is ejected by blowing through the holder, and the latter then inclines again towards the candle, which it extinguishes—that is to say, Mr. Cinquevalli blows through it once more. And, remember, during all this both arms are occupied in different juggling actions.

Here is, perhaps, the juggler's riskiest feat. He first of all balances two pieces of gas-piping—one on his forehead, the other on his chin. On the former is placed the 48lb. cannon-ball, which the juggler has to transfer to the other piece of piping without using his hands

Slowly the fore-head piece inclines forward until it touches the great ball. It slips under it, and then

THE AFTERNOON TEA FEAT—"A NICE HOT CUP."

TRANSFERRING THE CANNON-BALL—A TICKLISH MOMENT.

There is hardly a trick that has not its own story. I asked Mr. Cinquevalli how he came to do the extremely difficult feat seen in the next photo.—difficult if only on account of the sheer physical strength called into play.

"Years ago," he said, "I was engaged at Koster and Biall's famous theatre, in Thirty-fourth Street, New York. Every day, on my way to the theatre, I had to pass the shop of a wealthy cooper. One morning he greeted me as usual, and said: 'Say, I saw yer last night, and it were fairly marv'lous—right, straight marv'lous.' Then he pointed to some 18lb. casks, and said: 'Could you juggle them, now?' I said I could, whereupon he declared with rapture that he would make me a set of three, if I would use them. And I use that very set now."

But Cinquevalli can juggle with anything. He juggles a cannon-ball, an egg, a bottle, and a scrap of paper all together; which is amazingly difficult.

JUGGLING THREE CASKS.

by some extraordinarily delicate movements, it begins to take the weight off the other section of piping. The crucial moment is when the ball is exactly between the two; it is so apt to slip down between them. Obviously, the time for getting out of the way is not great. The 48lb. cannon-ball has only to descend 15in., and Mr. Cinquevalli's head is held well back, as you may see in the photo.

What, then, does he do when it slips? Well, somehow he knows when it is going wrong; he feels it. Quick as thought he turns his face aside, and receives the ball on the side of his neck. Only once or twice has the ball had the best of the incredibly brief race, and then Mr. Cinquevalli couldn't take solid food for days, so sore and stiff were his jaws.

No feat illustrates the man's astonishing instinct for his work so well as the one next seen. He was practising the catching of the tennis-ball on his forehead when he chanced to drop one of the balls. As it rebounded, he jumped upon it and struck it in the air, first with the sole of one foot and then with the other.

This led up to the extraordinarily clever war-dance, which Mr. Cinquevalli executes on the stage, having beneath his feet some tennis-balls. Of course, the steps of the dance are wholly controlled by the upward rebound of the balls, and as

THE "WAR DANCE" WITH TENNIS-BALLS.

this rebound is never twice the same, the dance is proportionately eccentric and diverting. Try this for yourself with two tennis-balls, and you will most certainly realize the apparent impossibility of a sustained dance.

Cinquevalli possesses amazing strength, though no one would think so who met him in the street. Look at the next photo. The juggler has raised his assistant—table, chair, and all—and placed the whole in his mouth, whilst he juggles three balls with evident *nonchalance*. The assistant weighs 10st. 6lb.; the chair 22lb., and the table 15lb. And this in a man's mouth!

The genesis of this remarkable feat was a wager, made in a café in Paris. Cinquevalli was there recognised one day by a gentleman, who betted 500 francs that the juggler could not lift him in the chair above his head. Simply that—no holding the chair in the mouth. The challenge was accepted, and Mr. Cinquevalli retired to practise with a terrified waiter. In a few minutes he came in and won the wager, though with a tremendous effort. "I couldn't hold the gentleman quite at arms' length above my head," he remarked, naïvely, "because he was in such a hurry to get down. Besides, on that occasion the chair was none too strong."

The next photograph shows how complete is the great juggler's command over three separate movements executed at the same time. He juggles some hats with one hand, and holds in the other an inverted straw hat, whirling on a stick. On his forehead is balanced another stick, surmounted by an unfashionable hat.

Mr. Cinquevalli has juggled with his great cannon-ball for many years, but the law of gravitation still renders it a dangerous professional companion. It does not turn upon and rend him, but it sometimes descends upon and cripples him. Tame it may be for a long time, but it breaks out now and then. The photo. reproduced shows a perfectly appalling

JUGGLING UNDER DIFFICULTIES.

THREE INDEPENDENT MOVEMENTS.

feat, done for the first time in Providence, U.S.A. The manner of it is this: The 48lb. cannon-ball is hoisted up 40ft., measured distance. It rests on a collapsible shelf at this height, and the shelf is controlled by a string, acting on a bolt.

Immediately beneath the ball is placed a big, strong table. The string is jerked: down comes the cannon-ball and smashes that table into firewood. And then Cinquevalli takes the place of the table. The feat calls for great strength, iron nerve, and wonderful skill of judgment. If the stage lights get into the juggler's eyes, the ball will, perhaps, strike him an inch or two out of the proper place—the lower part of the back of the neck—and then he sees stars, and gets "pins and needles" most shockingly. If the deviation were to run to three or four inches, it would mean certain death.

CANNON-BALL FALLS 40FT. ON TO MR. CINQUEVALLI'S NECK, AFTER DEMOLISHING BIG TABLE.

A Curious Electrical Display.

By Harold J. Shepstone.

A CURIOUS and ingenious method of entertaining the public by the aid of electricity has certainly been introduced by Mr. George W. Patterson, of Chicago. This gentleman has devised a means of swinging electrically-lighted Indian clubs in such a way as to produce startling, yet beautiful, spectacular effects. Although this kind of electrical display with Indian clubs is entirely new so far as the public is concerned, Mr. Patterson has given much time and thought to the subject, and his entertainments have not reached their present high degree of excellence and novelty without a great deal of patient study of that vast and marvellous subject which we call electricity.

Until very recently Mr. Patterson used to give displays with Indian clubs to which flaming torches were attached. It was the success which attended these entertainments that led him to devise a means for obtaining a more elaborate and effective display. The only thing which could possibly help him to obtain this end was electricity, and that he has succeeded in his endeavours is well evidenced from our set of unique photographs, which illustrate some of his pretty spectacular effects.

In our first photograph we are introduced to Mr. Patterson and all the paraphernalia necessary to an entertainment. One of the greatest difficulties which this electrical entertainer has had to face was the securing of a portable battery of high voltage and light weight. For some time past Mr. Patterson has been unable to give his performances except in halls and houses wired for electrical illumination ; now, however, this drawback has been overcome, and Mr. Patterson can amuse the public with his electrical illuminations in any hall or theatre, and also give exhibitions of his skill in private houses and other places. This has been rendered easy of accomplishment by a storage battery which he has himself designed and built. This battery, which has evoked much comment from eminent electricians, who have been struck with its wonderful powers, is seen in our photograph. It weighs 35lb., has thirty-two volts normal, and a capacity of ten ampères at about twenty-five volts. It is of such convenient size that it can be easily carried by one person.

If one looks carefully into our view, they will detect the small electric lamps which decorate the Indian clubs. These clubs are made in two parts, the split being lengthwise. A flexible cable of five wires leads into the club handles through a rubber tube, the wiring being cleverly concealed. Three series of eight three-candle-power miniature lamps are set in small, specially turned brass sockets, the length of the club, so the lamps stand out at right angles to its surface. As the little globes are coloured, no fewer than six series of different colours are obtained when the current is turned on.

From a] MR. PATTERSON AND HIS APPARATUS. [*Photograph.*

From a] A SIMPLE EFFECT. [*Photograph.*

ornamented with strips of silver. Another pair, which may be detected in our first photograph, are those designed to represent the American flag. Each of these latter contains a music-box. The torch clubs Mr. Patterson made himself. They are of regular shape, with long handles, painted with pegamoid or aluminium paint, giving them the appearance of silver. At the ends are fixed wire screens of spherical shape, filled with asbestos fibre, which is saturated with gasoline before using. These make brilliant effects in the dark, and will burn nicely for about five minutes. Mr. Patterson claims that they are the only pair of the kind in the world, and are entirely safe, whereas the ordinary torch club is not, as cotton is used instead of asbestos. In some of the halls and concert-rooms of Chicago where he has given performances, Mr. Patterson has swung his clubs before a conical mirror reflector, which acted as a powerful footlight, and also threw upon the wall behind him the shadow of a giant club-swinger.

A pretty design produced by lighted clubs

To give a display the room is darkened, of course, and Mr. Patterson, taking his stand in front of the audience, turns on the current and swings the clubs with the most wonderful results. In the next photograph, which is one of a series of Mr. Patterson's numerous "figures," we notice two distinct "O's," with a very thick outer circle or ring. This larger circle is produced by a thirty-two candle-power, fifty volt lamp which is usually run on 110 volts, fixed to the tip of each club. Some idea of the power of these two lights, which are necessary to make the figures, may be gauged from the fact that they are too dazzling for the naked eye when lighted and stationary, and are so powerful that they are capable of illuminating an entire church or public hall of average size. The smaller circles of light shown in our illustration are the reflections of the miniature lamps on the body of the clubs.

In addition to this pair of electrically-lighted clubs, Mr. Patterson also uses fancy ones in his displays, made of black wood and

From a] A PRETTY DESIGN. [*Photograph.*

From a] AN ARTISTIC EFFECT. [Photograph.

they are swung quickly, while the grace and style of the whole effect speak volumes for Mr. Patterson's ability as a club-swinger. His club-swinging has rightly been termed "poetry in motion."

Our photographs, it may be added, were taken while Mr. Patterson was swinging his clubs at ordinary speed, by the light of the incandescent lamps studded on the clubs. The time of the exposure was from five to ten seconds. Great credit is undoubtedly due to the photographer who has furnished us with practically exact miniature facsimiles of the various displays. The only thing we can complain of is that we are not treated to the numerous other electrical features which go to make up an ordinary performance. There is the telephone, for instance, with megaphone attachment, through which Mr. Patterson sings from a distant room.

Then there is also the electrical storm, which lacks nothing but buckets of water to

in a darkened hall is seen in our third photograph. The clubs are always swung to music, so that the effect to the audience is still more pleasing. The patterns or figures which may be obtained by the swinging of the clubs are almost infinite in variety. The lights on the clubs are under the control of an operator behind the scenes, who turns on and off the lights of both clubs by means of a switchboard.

Mr. Patterson is a recognised expert in the swinging of Indian clubs, which we can well believe after glancing at the illustrations which accompany this article. He is thoroughly at home with a pair of these wooden implements hovering around his head, and makes a novel picture as the large yet graceful circles of light flash all round him. In order to produce such a charming picture as seen in our next photograph, the clubs, of course, have to be swung fairly rapidly. Indeed, it would be impossible to obtain so many circles with one pair of clubs unless

From a] A COMPLICATION. [Photograph.

From a] A "RUNNING FIGURE." [*Photograph.*

which is so prominently seen on the table in our first illustration. As the storm abates the more cheerful tune of "Anchored" is heard through the disturbed elements. No sooner is quietude restored than a perfect double rainbow gradually appears across the hall, and is dissolved by a water rheostat by sending the rays of a single-loop filament incandescent lamp through a prism. The colours come out beautifully; when at their brightest the lamp is run greatly over voltage. By turning the lamp slightly, so that the filament is not in direct line with the prism, lights from two points strike the prism, producing two rainbows, as sometimes seen in the sky. This part of the performance is greatly appreciated by the audience, so realistic are all the details of a thunderstorm carried out.

make it complete. The storm begins with distant heat lightning, simulated by well-distributed Geissler tubes, gradually increasing to the fiercest of chain or "zig-zag" lightning, with corresponding gradation of thunder, the latter being produced in the usual manner by a "thunder-sheet" of iron. The nearer lightning is produced by the direct arching of carbons in Mr. Patterson's hands. The arc is struck in a small box from which the light is thrown by a lens through a cardboard disc having lightning forms cut into it. The disc can be revolved to any form and the light flashed out in any direction. The effect, as may be imagined, is very startling, especially as it is accompanied by the fiercest thunder, and a sound of dashing rain, the latter being produced by skilfully manipulating a circular vessel into which peas are constantly poured.

To add to the terrors of the scene Mr. Patterson laughingly sings "The Lightning King" through the megaphone, the horn of

However novel thunderstorms made to order may sound, Mr. Patterson is not yet fully satisfied that he has reached the limit of his powers as an electrical entertainer, and has great hopes of producing more startling novelties before very long. In addition to the thunderstorm there are other curious and ingenious electrical displays, which it would be impossible to describe here.

One of his great plans is to produce ozone electrically, and blow it gently among his audience by means of electric fans. With the aid of an atomizer and apple blossom perfume he believes he can reproduce the genuine air of a country orchard. Should this new wizard of electricity ever come to London and give exhibitions of his wonderful skill as a conjuring electrician, those who long for a breath of country air need only go to one of Mr. Patterson's performances, close his eyes, and imagine beautiful blossoms and graceful trees, as he drinks in the sweet perfume of a distant country orchard.

The Most Extraordinary Dinner on Earth.

By Albert H. Broadwell. Photographs by A. J. Johnson.

AN ELDERLY GENTLEMAN AND A PREPOSSESSING LADY ENTER THE DINING-ROOM.

WAITERS are proverbially clever; in fact, they are mostly too clever for anything or anybody. The man who ever gets the better of a waiter has yet to be found. Not that waiters are not human after all, and who would blame them?—but they have a sublime way of juggling with your change, and in such a way, too, that would have you believe that coppers were withdrawn from circulation for the time being.

There are two waiters *par excellence* who claim special notice at our hands at present. There is no half-and-half way about them; they take the cake, the biscuit, the pancake, the bun, the wedding cake, and the champion cake all in one. There is a swing about them that is pleasing—at a distance! They catch and throw, and juggle and throw, and catch and throw again; sometimes they miss, and then there's a crash and a bang, and the fragments of plates and glasses fly like chaff in the wind.

They are stage waiters, and form part of a group of four clever performers who go by the name of The Rambler Troupe, and their ramblings have taken them to most parts of the habitable globe, to the intense enjoyment of thousands of people.

It has been the writer's good fortune to witness the Ramblers' clever act at the Alhambra Theatre, Leicester Square, and he has much pleasure in acknowledging herewith the courteous assistance of Messrs. Dundas Slater and E. A. Pickering, the able

CATCHES THE VISITOR'S HAT ON HIS HEAD.

THE GUEST LAYS HIS CIGAR ON A TABLE.

managers of one of the best places of amusement in London, in obtaining this photographic interview for the special benefit of STRAND readers.

The photographs as shown in this article are exact reproductions of the doings that take place on the stage; it is a pity that much of the actual movement is lost, but then we cannot claim to run cinematograph pictures through the pages of a magazine. These snap-shots, however, will convey in some measure the marvellous proceedings which take place in the course of this the most extraordinary dinner on earth.

An elderly gentleman and a lady of prepossessing appearance enter the dining-room of a restaurant. They are received by two waiters of the most approved and up-to-date type; their names, *pro tem.*, will be Garçon No. 1 and Garçon No. 2. Garçon No. 1 takes upon himself the onerous task of unloading the happy pair of their coats, stick, and fan; with an artful twist he throws up the gentleman's hat (whilst the latter isn't looking) and catches it on the back of his head in the most comical manner. These preliminaries are shown in our pictures on the preceding page.

Now, however, they are entering upon a more serious phase of the business. It is proverbially difficult to do two things properly at one and the same time, so that our worthy guest places a half-smoked Havana of the finest brand upon the edge of a small table close by. The waiters spot this, of course, and there's a rush for the coveted weed.

Garçon No. 2 makes a dash, but misses. Garçon No. 1 quickly picks up table and all and by an artful twist, and an equally artful jerk, he throws the cigar up into the air and catches it in his open mouth with the consummate skill of an expert juggler. Result: Consternation of Garçon No. 2.

GARCON NO. 1 THROWS THE CIGAR FROM THE TABLE INTO HIS MOUTH.

UP GO THE LAMPS —

In the meantime our guests have taken their places, but somehow the pretty but cumbersome standard lamps, with their gorgeous shades of flaming red silk, are found to be in the way.

"Here, garçon, remove those lamps, will you?"

"Yes, sir," comes from both attendants, simultaneously, and no sooner said than done: quicker than lightning those lamps fly right up to the ceiling and are caught again and placed aside, to the horror and amazement of the diners!

It is the waiters' turn to be startled, however, for no sooner have they returned with the necessaries "to follow" than the lady does a little juggling of her own.

—AND THE KNIVES, FORKS, AND SPOONS.

—AND THE SERVIETTES—

Up go the serviettes, to the consternation of Garçons 1 and 2, who are fairly caught at their own game.

The example seems contagious; certain gentlemen have opinions of their own about themselves, and they are often prone to think that, if one of the

ENTER THE SOUP!

IT SPINS ON THE HANDLE OF THE SOUP LADLE.

weaker sex should happen to be on the high road to supremacy, she should be quickly suppressed or put into her proper place; so up go the gentleman's knives and forks and spoons in a rush. He has quite forgotten his dinner: he *will* show his fair partner that *she* is by no means the only pebble on the beach. No, there are others, and he is one of them. But, lo! *her* knives and *her* spoons and *her* forks follow *his* knives, *his* spoons, and *his* forks in rapid succession. In fact, it is a case of a knife for a knife and a spoon for a spoon!

The waiters are happy: here at last they have met with a pair worthy of their steel! No. 1 is jubilant; No. 2 tries to look like it.

"Enough, enough; soup, waiter, do you hear? Bring the soup, or I'll wipe the floor with you."

"Clear or thick?"

"*Clear*, and be quick about it," comes the stinging reply.

There is a lull

EXIT THE SOUP!

THE COINS DISAPPEAR INTO HIS WAISTCOAT POCKET.

and a hush, a dead silence creeps over an overstrung audience. What-*ever* is going to happen now?

Whoop—brr—bang! Enter the soup! It flies from one side of the room to the other, from one pair of hands into another pair of hands. Flop! Has he missed it? No, he smiles and bows and scrapes and "Clear or thick, madam?" in a whisper, follows what promised to be an exciting episode. It is an anti-climax such as we meet with every day.

The lid is removed and a cloud of steam rises to the ceiling. It is soup, real soup, and spectators gaze aghast. After all, "the proof of the soup is in the steaming."

Whoop—brr—bang! Out goes the soup! Back it flies the way it came, over the heads of the guests on to the very tip of the soup ladle, where it whirrs and twists fast enough to be turned into ice-cream, if only the motion lasted long enough.

The dinner proper is nearly over by this time, and the bill is duly presented. With a flourish and much twisting of the silver dish in his right hand Garçon No. 2 approaches timidly. He nearly drops the dish on to the gentleman's head, recovers himself in time, smiles, and gets a splendid tip for the quiet way in which he and his friend have performed their duties.

Proverbially suspicious, Garçon No. 1 approaches from behind and is on the point of seizing what seems to him a fair share of the profits, when, with a dexterous jerk, up go the coins, to disappear, in a glittering shower, into the waistcoat pocket of Garçon No. 2.

It seems that juggling, like many other diseases, is contagious in the extreme. I knew a young fellow, smart in his way, who would insist upon showing me how to spirit a penny by means of a handkerchief, an overcoat, a silk hat, and a perambulator. He was so engrossed in finding the latter that I conveniently disappeared, and soon breathed once

THE BOTTLES KEEP TIME TO A WALTZ.

TWENTY ORANGES ON THE MOVE.

more the fresh air of my old-world suburban rose-garden. I used to think that juggling as a fine art might pay, but I gave it up after that.

Not so our friends; but, then, they are professionals. Watch their bottle performance and listen to the tick-tack, bang-bang, tick-tack, bang-bang as the lower edges of their bottles keep time on the edge of the dining table to the tune of a popular waltz.

Not content with juggling all the available bottles, they unite in thorough good fellowship, and we see them enjoying themselves with oranges, of all things! Twenty oranges are on the move in rhythmical progression, and a very pretty sight it is too.

These are quickly put by, though, and now comes one of the most extraordinary features of the evening. True to their profession our waiters, assisted by their guests, quickly proceed in clearing the remains of the feast, and here Garçon No. 1 comes in with a vengeance. His late guests and Garçon No. 2 have before them two piles of plates, numbering something like a hundred altogether. These have evidently to be transferred from one table to another. Whirr—whizz—whirr—whizz—follow each other for quite thirty seconds, while the plates fly from one table to another with amazing swiftness.

REMOVING THE PLATES.

Garçon No. 1 catches them in their flight and places them on the table before him, without missing so much as a solitary one.

It is awful to contemplate what might happen should the unfortunate man miss a couple, or even one, of the delicate missiles as they come in quick succession.

The bottles are gone, the fruit is gone, the plates are gone: there are only the tables, and chairs, and lamps, and flowers left. Hurrah! Up goes a chair, then a table, then a lamp, and a bouquet. Then more chairs and more tables, and more lamps and more bouquets. They fly all over the room. The air is thick with them. Yet not one is missed. They all come back to their owners in due course. The Ramblers are clever — very clever, in fact, and they are genuinely funny and amusing.

There is a menu provided, but this, of course, is for private circulation only. We caught a glimpse of it, and glimpses are all you can reasonably expect, considering the rate at which these good people dine. We here give a few of the items that form part of the bill of fare provided for the occasion:—

Hors d'Œuvres.
Sardines on the Wing. Slippery Olives.
Anchovies quickly.
Soup.
First clear, then thick, à la whoop—brr—bang—flop!
Fish.
Poisson d'avril à la flying salmon.
Entrées.
Anyhow on toast.
Joint.
Roast beef, mashed out of shape à la squashed.
Roast.
Flying roosters à la Lee-Metford.
Bullet-proof Yorkshire pudding.
Salad.
Let-us-go! and other kinds ad lib.
Sweets.
Blanc mange all over the place.
Cheese.
Emilezola. Petits Suisses. Stilton à la Hurry.
Glaces.
Bombs Glencoe and Modder. Shrapnel Special.
Coffee quick as lightning, etc.

"THE AIR IS THICK WITH THEM."

HOOP-ROLLING EXTRAORDINARY

By H. J. Holmes.

Most of us became interested in the art of hoop-rolling whilst yet we were of very tender years. The wildest dreams of childhood's ambition, however, rarely exceeded a desire to practise the art under fairly favourable conditions. Beyond this, we sought no great honours in the hoop, which was finally relegated to the nursery museum in favour of the more exciting pastimes of cricket and football.

Possibly the first person who grasped the possibilities of the hoop under scientific manipulation was Mr. William Everhart, an American gymnast-juggler. Seven years ago he introduced a pair of hoops into his performance. It did not take him long to see that the little bit of hoop-juggling stood out very strongly in the favour of the public. He thereupon determined to enlarge his opportunities for displaying dexterity in that direction. The result was that hoop-rolling, as practised by him, became one of the most amazing performances imaginable. Hoops in the hands of Everhart are as billiard balls manipulated by Cinquevalli. He can make them do almost anything but talk.

Yet there is nothing that Everhart does, remarkable though his performance is to the eyes of onlookers, that a scientist or mathematician could not explain and demonstrate satisfactorily. A strong arm, an unerring eye, and a knowledge of the laws of motion and gravitation have succeeded in astonishing all who see his performance.

Hoop-rolling in the hands of any smart athlete can undoubtedly be made one of the most bewildering of entertainments. At the same time, it is one of the finest exercises for every muscle of the human frame. And the outfit is so simple! Half-a-dozen hoops will suffice.

Everhart uses about a dozen hoops 18in. in diameter and $1\frac{1}{8}$in. wide, concave outside, very similar to the rims used in the manufacture of American bicycle wheels. This form of hoop gives considerable advantage in manipulation. The material used is hickory wood, which possesses the double virtue of toughness and lightness.

The first exercise in the art of scientific hoop-rolling, as practised by the inventor, is the shooting forward of three hoops, in rapid succession, upon the platform or floor. In leaving the hand, each hoop is given a backward twist. An optical illusion will make most spectators believe that the hoops *roll* forward. This is not so. They slide, covering a distance of from three to five yards according to the strength of the throw. Presently the backward revolutionary movement begins to tell, and the hoops roll back to the manipulator.

As the first hoop returns the toe of the right shoe is ready to catch it. It runs quickly up the leg, body, and out upon the arm, until it is dexterously caught around the right wrist, where it continues to revolve at high speed. A similar movement of the left foot brings the second hoop to the left wrist, whilst the third is caught by the toe and revolves around the lifted right instep. In this way the three hoops are kept in eccentric motion at once. The exercise is repeated, but this time the performer balances a fourth hoop, spinning at high speed, upon his forehead, whilst he throws, catches, and keeps in motion, as before, the other three.

Mr. Everhart keeping four hoops in motion.

In the feat illustrated on the preceding page, six hoops are used. With a quick back twist, one is tossed into the air, caught on the outstretched right wrist, and, moved by the reversed impetus given it, rolls along the arm, across the back of the neck from right to left shoulder, and outwards upon the left arm and hand, by which it is grasped, twisted, dropped, and re-crosses ready for the right hand to pick up and repeat the former movement.

Short though the time is for the first hoop to "go the round," before it reaches the performer's right hand for the second time, all the six hoops have been sent on a similar journey, and in this way they are kept in continual motion along the right arm, across the shoulders, out on the left arm, and round again. The difficulty of the feat is obvious. Were not the "pace" of each hoop kept exactly the same, so that every hoop arrives at its proper place at the proper moment, disaster would certainly happen.

An extremely neat exercise is that in which four hoops are thrown forward from the hand of the manipulator, and given the backward twist which is so puzzling to the spectator. Each hoop is shot to a different point; as it returns, it is neatly lifted by the toe of the shoe, caught in the right hand, whence it passes over the corresponding shoulder, down the arched back into the left hand, by which it is again thrown forward to repeat its journey.

As the performer has to shift his position to meet each hoop as it returns from a different point, he has a most busy time of it!

The finish of this exercise is remarkable. As the hoops return at increased speed after the last throw forward, they are caught successively on the right toe, and roll up along the entire length of the body, from breast to chin and forehead, being finally dropped alternately into the right and left hands.

In this trick four hoops are thrown forward, each to a different point, with a back-twist. Each, as it returns, is lifted by the performer's toe, is caught in the right hand and set rolling down the back into the left hand, by which it is again thrown forward, to repeat its journey.

We illustrate another remarkable feat. A strong cord is gripped in the teeth of an assistant at a distance of thirty or forty feet, according to the available space. The other end of the cord is grasped in the right hand of the operator. The latter throws four hoops in quick succession into the air and towards the further end of the cord, now drawn as rigid as possible. As each hoop leaves his hand, the magic backward twist is given it. Rushing through the air, the hoop drops on the floor and bounds upwards, to drop again precisely on the waiting cord, when it immediately starts rolling towards the thrower's end.

As soon as it reaches his hand it is again thrown as before, the other three hoops in the meantime accomplishing a similar little journey. For some time the rolling hoops are kept going, rarely failing to catch the cord at the right moment.

The concave form of the hoops helps considerably in the roll backwards, but a very calculating eye and accurate throw are necessary to insure the desired meeting of hoop and cord.

Here is the most bewildering feat of the entire series in Everhart's repertoire. Two hoops are thrown in the usual way with reverse motion, but in different directions.

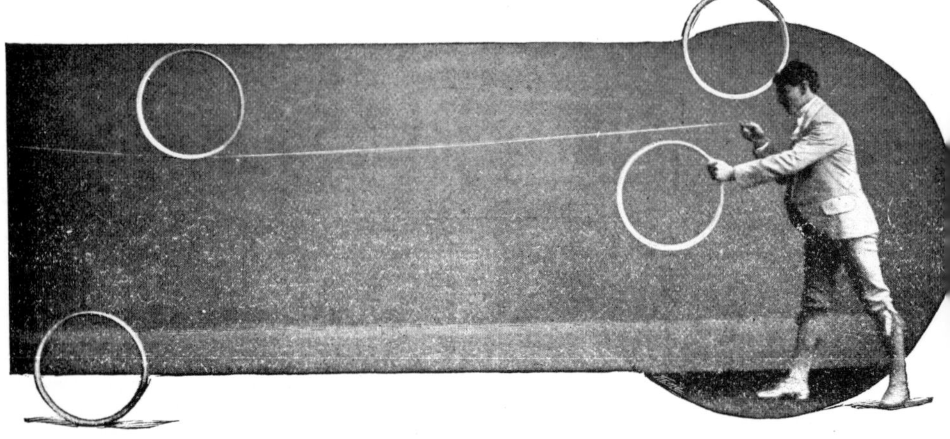

In this extremely clever feat, four hoops, in turn, are thrown forward with a backward twist. Each, on striking the ground, jumps into the air, is caught on the string, and runs back to the performer—jumping on his head—to be thrown again by his left hand.

In this trick Mr. Everhart throws five hoops, in rapid succession, against his assistant's back. Each jumps forward over the assistant's shoulder, on to the ground, and then runs between his and the performer's legs.

They slide along until a distance of ten feet separates them, and then roll towards each other.

At the moment when they are passing parallel, their edges almost grazing, another hoop—half an inch less in diameter—which in the meantime has been thrown after the others, but at right angles to their course, passes through its larger brethren, the three continuing to roll to their respective points. This feat is accomplished not once only, but many times.

The accuracy exhibited in throwing the hoops to insure all three crossing a given point at one moment, whilst rolling from three different directions, is nothing short of marvellous, especially as the in-passing hoop is only half an inch smaller than those through which it rolls, and must pass through cleanly, otherwise all would come to grief.

In a much simpler feat, five hoops are kept rolling from the back of an assistant on to the ground in such a way that they twist back, run through the assistant's and the performer's legs, to be picked up by the latter, and thrown again in the same way, following one another in bewildering repetition.

Hoop-rolling with a vengeance is displayed in the following feat. The operator stands at one point and sends, in rapid succession, seven hoops on a tour that involves a journey of from 100ft. to 150ft. according to the available elbow-room. Each hoop must be started at the same angle, and with the same impetus, to insure its return to the very spot whence it was set in motion.

Mathematicians would have no difficulty in stating the exact angle at which a hoop should travel at a certain speed to reach the spot whence it started after a circular tour of 100 feet. But much has to be taken into consideration, and certain allowances made for the surface over which the hoop passes; a nail, or other projection, or a dip, or a rise may upset

Juggling with four hoops.

the most careful calculations, with disastrous results to a large circle of touring hoops.

Force of throw and quickness of eye have much to do with the successful issue of the feat. The circle is kept in perfect formation for minutes by a mere touch of the finger as the hoops pass the manipulator. In the last journey or two, he lifts each hoop as it comes to his hand, and throws it over his shoulders, yet the circle is still maintained in its former precision!

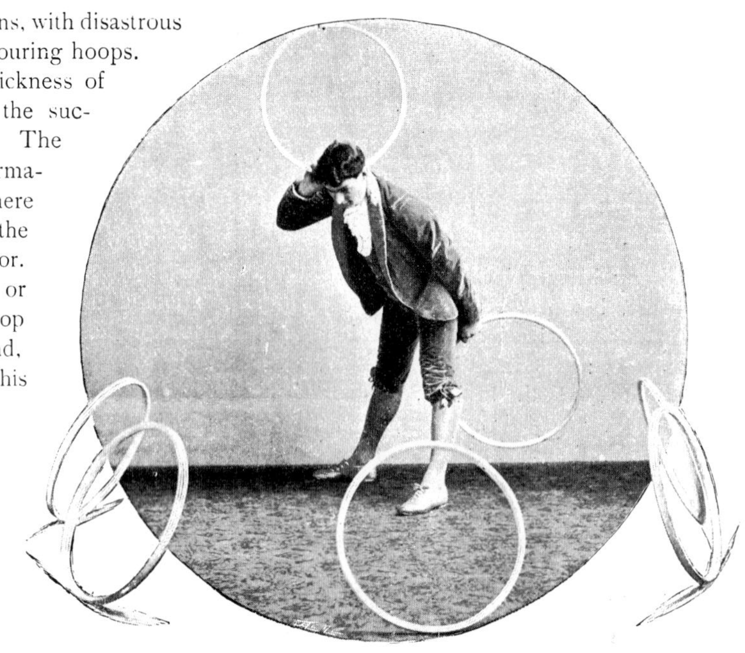

This extraordinary trick consists in throwing seven hoops in rapid succession so that they run round the performer in a circle. As each hoop passes the performer, it is caught and thrown over his shoulder, to continue its journey.

Another striking exercise is the throwing, with the usual backward twist, and in rapid succession, of six hoops to a distance of ten to fifteen feet. It takes a strong arm to slide a hoop so far against the backward twist that would send it rolling in an opposite direction. Starting from a common centre, the hoops are so manipulated that in due course they have travelled to and from every point of the compass.

This exercise is concluded by catching each hoop, as it returns, on the point of a cane, up which it rolls to the holder's body, chin, nose, and brow, to the top of the head, then on down the back, where it is caught by the left hand.

Thus far has the art of hoop-rolling progressed. It is bound to advance, for even now many are taking it up with enthusiasm, and we may expect in the near future to see something still more extraordinary than the feats which are dealt with in this article.

The tramp leaves his tattered seal-skin as security

The Tramp Juggler arrives

Get out of my way. How can I do this?

A TRAMP JUGGLER

A NEW AND CLEVER "TURN" AT THE PALACE THEATRE

I THOUGHT I knew him directly I saw him. This, said I, was his second visit to the Palace Theatre. Apparently he had made some alterations in his "act," for certain features were new to me. But I felt confident about the personality—it did not seem possible to make any mistake about the figure—such a figure! Clothes—old, torn, loose and unclean; boots—big and bulging; hat—an artistic wreck. And the face! Hirsute and blotchy, with a ludicrous expression of countenance that was most diverting. Yes, I thought that must be my shabby old friend back again. And with this conviction firmly established in my mind I sat through and enjoyed the performance, none the less because my thoughts were reminiscent.

Subsequently came the awakening! Later in the evening, stumbling across a friend of mine, I remarked about this turn, calling his attention to the fact that it was rather different in detail to that presented on a previous occasion. "That cannot be," said he, "for this is the first time it has been seen in this country, and has been at the Palace only a week." I am neither a pugnacious nor a self-assertive man, but I felt monstrously inclined to take up an attitude of firmness in this matter. I suspected that he was deliberately attempting to deceive me. Yet was he not, for correct he was. It was an entirely new turn, but so like a previous one in many respects that I excused myself for mistaking them. It was yet another of the apparently extensively patronised type of tramp which appears to be indigenous to American vaudeville entertainments. It is always the same: hairy and florid face, seedy attire, grotesque movements. Sometimes it is a juggler, at others a cyclist, anon a musician. Take Ritchie, Harragan and Fields—the last-named the subject of this article—place them in a row, and lo! "Tom, Dick and Harry!" As like as three peas.

The fake cigar-box trick—One!

The fake cigar-box trick—Two! Bravo

The fake cigar-box trick—Three! Ah! Sold again!

Juggling with balls

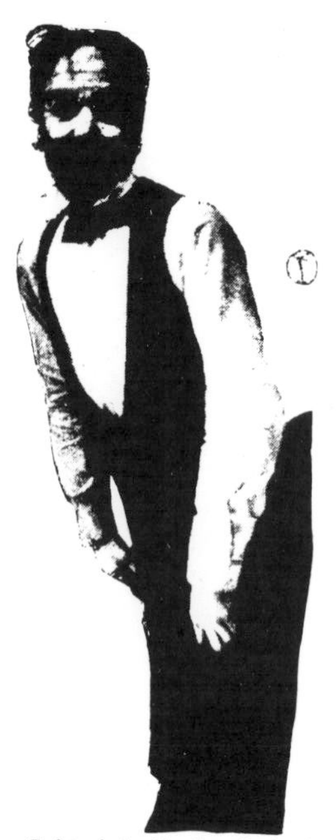

Going into the handy back pocket

Going into the handy back pocket

In the "business" of the latest of these bedraggled gentlemen there is much that is new, and the act, taken as a whole, is worthy of some sort of distinction in dress. I do not think it advantageous for an artist to be closely associated in "get-up" with another, however prominent either or both may be.

Mr. Fields, who is assisted in a measure by a young and attractive lady, does not crowd the stage with apparatus. In fact, there is little to be seen when the curtain goes up. Just a small table on which are a few cigar-boxes. The latter, however, supply an opportunity for some really remarkable tricks in dexterity which set at nought all laws of gravitation. Mr. Fields takes six or eight of the boxes and holds them together horizontally between his hands; he then proceeds to detach them one at a time by hitting them sharply on the top, retaining the horizontal position till they have all been dislodged. He does it with such speed and precision that it appears as easy as amorously saluting your hand. He can also as readily readjust them, and with such neatness that the boxes would appear to be coated with an adhesive substance. That, however, I assure you, is not the case, for the only "deception" which Mr. Fields brings to bear upon his tricks is incessant practice, which, as we all know through the medium of proverbial philosophy, makes perfect in almost anything.

One of the tricks which Mr. Fields performs is *not* clever, but is certainly very funny. And thereby hangs a tale.

The change hat trick—One

With one kick a hat lands on the tramp's head, a cigar in his mouth, and a brush in his back pocket

The change hat trick—Two

The description first, then the tale. The juggler produces from his table a few cigar-boxes, reposing one on top of the other in the orthodox manner. He makes a great show of preparing for a *coup*, something to really startle you; and does, in fact, perform what you believe to be a really remarkable feat of manipulation. Anyway, you applaud vigorously, and are sorry for it afterwards. I freely admit I did applaud and was sorry; annoyed, almost savage. I was within an ace of blushing, a thing I have not known myself to do for many years.

Well, with a sudden twist of the wrist the boxes are shot into the air and come to rest end on end. Then, when the applause is at its loudest the juggler allows the boxes to fall over, but not to the ground. They are fastened together *with string!*

At a theatre in Germany, on one occasion, Mr Fields informed me, in a chat I subsequently had with him, that this innocent deception created quite an amusing "situation." It was taken in earnest by some distinguished friends in front, who made themselves prominent by the generous measure and quality of their applause. When the "fake" was revealed and the laugh came, the embarrassment of the appreciative folk was so great that they beat a hasty retreat.

Until I saw Mr Fields I did not know that tennis balls could be made to perform such remarkable and such a variety of evolutions. He gets them into the most extraordinary positions, employing both hands and feet in their manipulation. They fly about all over his body, resting now and again in the most inconceivable places, with a maximum of movement to a minimum of effort. He will bring them to the closest possible quarters, still revolving – the balls, not the juggler – and expand again into a long-distance aim with perfect ease and smoothness. I do not know whether there is any professional jealousy between Mr Fields and Mr Renshaw.

Another very good trick is with two tall hats, a black and a white, both more or less dilapidated. One the juggler places on his head and the other on his outstretched foot. Simultaneously he jerks the latter up on to his head, and drops the former on to his foot. Like all good tricks it looks very simple, and isn't. Then he turns his attention to a hat, a cigar and a whisk brush. For this he utilises a large pocket at the back of his trousers, just below the waist. he tosses the articles about in a similar manner to the tennis balls, and finally gets the hat on to his head, the cigar into his mouth, and the brush into his back pocket.

Mr Fields is unconventional in many things, not the least striking of these being the way he ignites a match on the side of his face.

SEE-SAW WITH A 350-LB. KRUPP SHELL.
Taking a running leap, the performer alights with great force on his end of the board, which hurls the projectile into the air.

A HEAVY-WEIGHT JUGGLER.

By Édouard Charles.

JUGGLERS are common enough on the stage; the name of those who make pretty and clever play with anything varying in weight from a cigarette-paper to a pony-trap, and in shape from an umbrella to a table, is legion. In fact, ordinary clever acts of this kind are so common that they have almost ceased to draw, and certainly never "bring down the house" as in days gone by.

But there remains one man whose turn is undoubtedly novel. It never fails to hold the audience spellbound, thrill it as with an electric current, and draw for its performer appreciative enthusiasm. The reason of this is to be found in the fact that the juggling act of Paul Conchas is the most remarkable in the world, for he does not juggle with commonplace objects, contenting himself with nothing lighter than Krupp shells that turn the scales at over three hundredweight, and such awkward and heavy things as gun-carriages and Maxim guns!

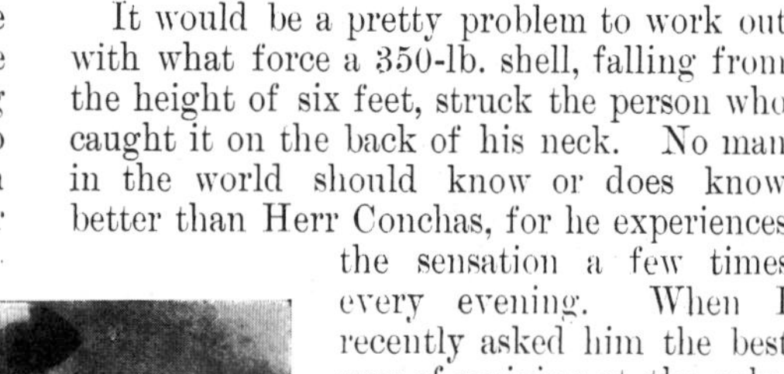

It would be a pretty problem to work out with what force a 350-lb. shell, falling from the height of six feet, struck the person who caught it on the back of his neck. No man in the world should know or does know better than Herr Conchas, for he experiences the sensation a few times every evening. When I recently asked him the best way of arriving at the solution of the problem, he shook his head sadly and said the only way he could think of was that I should do the trick myself. He assured me my curiosity would be fully satisfied; moreover, that I could depend on getting the correct answer first time! He was even considerate enough to offer to lend me the shells he uses himself, so that there would be no doubt about the matter. Not possessing a cast-iron neck or a head for figures, I must leave readers to work out the answer for themselves. Conchas will oblige them at any time with the loan of a shell.

HE THEN CATCHES IT ON HIS BACK.

So far as Conchas is concerned, these heavy shells

might be nothing more than soap-bubbles; a snowflake falling on the back of his neck would certainly cause him more discomfort than the 350-lb. projectile, though it would not hit him so hard. In performing the hair-raising feat of catching Krupp shells, as illustrated in our photographs, he takes a strong stick, six feet in length, into the slightly grooved top of which he lifts the shell. Most men cannot even do this. Then inch by inch he raises the stick until he can get it on to his forehead; there he balances the load. This in itself is a striking performance.

For thirty seconds, perhaps, he stands getting his breath, while he gazes at the shell above. Suddenly he gives the stick a blow that knocks it spinning across the stage, and down comes the three-hundredweight of solid steel. He watches it as it falls, watches till the very last instant, when it seems inevitable that the shell must smash flat his face, then he swiftly bends his head. There is a thud that sounds all over the house as the shell strikes flesh, for a second it seems that the man must be borne down by the force of the contact, and he sways a bit; but he stands firm, and then with a herculean effort he casts the shell behind him on to the stage, where it leaves its signature an inch deep.

CHANGING THE POSITION OF A 350-LB. KRUPP SHELL FROM THE LOWER STICK TO THE HIGHER ONE, AND VICE VERSA.

CONCHAS RAISES A 350-LB. SHELL AND BALANCES IT ON HIS FOREHEAD. THEN, KNOCKING THE STICK AWAY, HE—

What would happen if the shell were caught half an inch lower on the neck than it should be, or if Conchas did not duck at exactly the right moment, is no problem; there certainly would be no Conchas! In the one case it would catch the top of his spinal cord and break his neck, in the other it would pulp his skull. That is as the onlooker sees it; but there is little real danger, for just ere the shell reaches its destination, Conchas throws up the wonderfully developed muscles of his shoulders, and so prevents the shell from falling on his vertebræ, and from this momentary rest it rolls into the groove of the neck.

A remarkably difficult trick, calling for more than ordinary strength and courage, is illustrated in our first two photographs. In this a heavy Krupp shell is placed on one end of a board that acts as a see-saw. The performance of the feat is well-nigh as sensational as that previously described, though the tension on the nerves of beholders is not so acute.

The shell in position, Conchas makes a running leap and lands on the opposite end of the board, the result of the impetus being to hurl the shell into the air towards him when he alights on the ground. The next moment a sounding thwack announces that he has caught the weighty projectile on the small of his back !

When Conchas conceived the idea of this performance, he did not start right away practising with three-hundredweight shells. His first shell was a wooden one weighing no more than a couple of pounds, and he started by dropping it from the height of a couple of feet. For two years he continued practising, gradually increasing the height and weight, until a two-hundredweight shell had no terrors for him. Then he made his *début*. During his probationary period he received more hard knocks than he has ever had since, and often he had to give up for days on end, so bruised and swollen did his neck and back become ; but he has never met with anything approaching a serious mishap.

IN THIS REMARKABLE FEAT WITH THREE 56-LB. CANNON BALLS, THE SOLID SPHERES ARE BALANCED AS HERE SHOWN. THEN, THE SUPPORT BEING KNOCKED AWAY, THEY—

Another exceedingly clever trick is that in which two sticks are used. He takes this couple of sticks grooved at their tops, but not more than a foot in height. Placing the shell on one stick, he balances it on his forehead ; the other stick he leans against the first, its foot being on his chin. Then he deftly rolls the shell from the one stick to the other, a feat calling for absolute equilibrium and finesse of neck movement. A miss in this act would assuredly flatten his features.

GETS READY TO RECEIVE THE SHELL ON THE NECK, WATCHING ITS DESCENT UNTIL THE LAST MOMENT.

After Krupp shells he turns to a gun-carriage, a most ungainly object to balance. He takes it to pieces and fixes it together so that on the wheel, which he rests on his forehead, the axle stands upright, supporting at its top the other wheel, revolving.

The whole weighs just under 300 lb., and while the top wheel is turning rapidly in one direction, he spins the bottom one on his head in the opposite direction. The nastiest accident that ever occurred to him resulted from the breaking of the axle one evening. The top wheel smashed his head, and he took an eight weeks' rest in hospital.

Juggling with awkward, heavy things is his delight ; and another of the feats he performs consists in lifting a twelve-stone man who is seated at an awning-covered table on a chair, and carrying the collection round the stage, balancing the whole by one leg of the chair. The act works all right if the man in the chair looks after his part of the business, which is to assist in the balancing while pretending to evince dismay at his exalted position ; if he does not, there are great and unexpected possibilities in it. They were fully developed one night at a Continental theatre, for man, table, and chair went over the footlights with a suddenness as startling as it was unpleasant to everybody concerned, particularly the orchestra and the

ARE CAUGHT IN THIS FASHION.

man in the chair. It took several minutes to sort out t'other from which, but fortunately the result was nothing more serious than a couple of smashed violins.

Concerning this particular trick Conchas tells an amusing story. During one of his visits to Buenos Ayres, a young man in the audience loudly proclaimed his disbelief in the genuineness of the weight of the combination as declared by the performer. The sceptical individual himself weighed a matter of twelve stone, and challenged Conchas to lift him with the table—even going so far in his enthusiasm as to wager *mein Herr* a case to a bottle of sparkling champagne that he couldn't do it. Though it was rather above the weight Conchas was lifting, he readily took him on.

The sequel was amusing for everyone but the confident person. He took his seat in the chair and was hoisted aloft. He was carried around the stage, and admitted himself convinced. He had paid twelve bottles to go up, but he had not bargained for the descent. He reluctantly paid another dozen to avoid coming down with a rattle!

JUGGLING WITH SIX 56-LB. CANNON-BALLS.

Conchas also juggles with two loaded rifles of regulation weight—which he fires off as he catches—and a couple of bayonets; he parades around the stage with a soldier on his chin, and the soldier beats a drum the while; he also catches in the back of the neck 56-lb. cannon-balls that are hurled at him by his assistant. Missing would mean attending a funeral at which he would play the most important part. A trick that he has erased from his list was the catching of cannon-balls in a scooped-out, padded, brass helmet, which he wore on his head; and the balls were fired from a real cannon, with a charge of powder behind them!

Conchas well recalls the first time he tried it. Never had he practised it ere he performed in public, for though he

LOADED RIFLES FIRED AS CAUGHT.

AS A CONTRAST, THE PERFORMER JUGGLES WITH FIVE MILITARY CAPS.

had tried his best to do so, he could not get his courage up to sticking-point. Still, he was billed to appear in this act, and appear he had to. As an instance of the staying power a contract gives one, the non-fulfilment of which contract would mean heavy damages *contre lui*, it only remains to be stated that Conchas on the eventful night took his courage in both hands, put on his cup-fitted hat of brass, and made his bow on the stage. It was arranged that the gun should be fired at the word "Three!" from him. Hitherto he had never been able to give voice to it. He did not know what to expect when the ball struck him, but he preferred an accident, or even death, to laughter, which failure would have provoked; so he got past "One!" on to "Two!" and then after a moment's pause, "Three!" and ere he knew it the cannon-ball was in the helmet, and rounds of applause were ringing in his ears. He confesses it was the most trying ordeal of his life; and though he caught cannon-balls with his head for years afterwards, he never experienced such an uncomfortable five minutes as on that premier occasion.

He has retained, however, several sensational tricks with steel balls weighing no less than 56 lb. apiece. With cannon-balls of this weight he can juggle as easily as with light military caps. He juggles with six of the former—that is to say, with a matter of 3 cwt. of solid metal; then does the same thing with five military caps, whose aggregate weight is not more than two-and-a-half or three pounds. It is a contrast with a vengeance, and serves to show how keenly his judgment of weight and his sense of calculation in the matter of the impetus to be imparted to the differing objects has been developed.

He also catches cannon-balls that are thrown to him by an assistant from a distance of some feet—not in the hand, but just behind the head. He watches their coming as they rapidly pour upon him, ducks his head just in time to catch the foremost, hurls it behind into the wings, and is ready for the next. But probably his smartest feat with these weighty spheres is that in which he raises a trio of them on a three-forked stick, and balances the lot on his teeth, well above his head. They constitute 1½ cwt. of metal, bear in mind. Then he knocks the support away, bends his body, throws forward his head, and puts up his arms, and down come the balls—one on the neck, another on his right shoulder, and the third on his left.

THE JONES-HILLIARD BICYCLE SENSATION

The first convenient and practical mode of personal transport for the urban masses came of age in the 1890s - the bicycle. Its popularity was marked in the halls by the introduction of acts featuring this fantastic machine.

In the 1870s and 1880s cycling had been a sporting hobby for young, athletic men willing to risk their necks sitting above the five-foot front wheel of the Ordinary, better known as the Penny Farthing. The big wheel was necessary for achieving any kind of speed, since the cranks of the pedal were connected directly to the axle of the wheel (as on a unicycle). The bigger the wheel, subject to the length of your leg, the faster you could go. However, to add to the difficulties of mounting and dismounting, the position of the rider was such that if the wheel hit an obstacle the rider was likely to be sent flying over the top.

In the mid-1880s the Safety came along - essentially the bicycle as we know it today. Gearing up the rear wheel and driving it with a chain set meant that a big wheel was no longer needed for the bicycle to be capable of being ridden fast. Then in 1889 The Pneumatic Tyre Company was set up to produce the bright idea of a Scottish vet called John Boyd Dunlop. Now comfort was available as well as speed and safety, and bicycle sales boomed.

For the rich another mode of transport had arrived; the motor car. In 1890 commercial production of motor cars was begun by Karl Benz and in 1896 Henry Ford built his first car in America. By 1905 there were over 18,000 vehicles on Britain's roads, and in America a woman called Octavie LaTour was looping-the-loop in a car. By 1914 the number of vehicles in Britain had risen to over 350,000 of which around half were cars and half motor cycles.

Within a decade of the invention of the safety bicycle Wilbur Wright made the first aeroplane flight, and in 1909 Louis Blériot flew across the English Channel.

Singular Cycle Tricks.

Mr. and Mrs. Valdare changing from side to side.

By Merriden Howard.

Beyond doubt there has never before been a time when so many people were bent upon the same task as there are to-day determined to gain the upper hand over the ordinary safety bicycle. But it nevertheless appears to defy subjugation. Apart from Mr. and Mrs. Valdare, there does not seem anyone who has a mastery that is never gainsaid over a front-steering machine.

Certainly it is trick riding pure and simple which these young Americans make their speciality, but to watch them ride becomes almost aggravating, since it has the effect of causing one's own ideas of excellence to appear so paltry. I confess I should have been almost glad to discover some trickery in their machines when I went to examine them in that mysterious region behind the stage of the Alhambra theatre, where they made their first appearance.

But there was nothing. The machines are of average weight and similar in appearance to thousands of other American Clevelands that are manufactured every year, with one trifling exception. The bicycle ridden by Mr. Valdare is provided with a double saddle to afford a footing for his wife in one of the eccentric performances they do together.

The front wheel is allowed rather less freedom than is usual with road work, and the tyres are blown out as fully as possible without incurring the risk of an explosion when ridden in the hot atmosphere of a theatre.

In saying that there is nothing which the Valdares do that would be impossible to any other cyclist I am not depreciating their work. On the contrary, the credit to them is all the greater, since their pre-eminence is due chiefly to the fact that they are apparently endowed to an unusual extent with that genius which is the infinite capacity of taking pains, and in this particular case, a good many bruises, too.

Perhaps the most remarkable fact in connection with these two riders, whose work in England has aroused so much interest, is that before her marriage, some three years ago, Mrs. Valdare had never ridden a bicycle nor appeared at all in public. In the first week of her honeymoon she commenced to learn, and in one hour's lesson was able to ride by herself. Three weeks later she took part in her husband's performance!

Valdare himself commenced his cycling career in 1888 on an old-fashioned high machine. He was then fourteen years old, and used to ride through the streets of Denver,

U.S.A., from his home to school on one wheel, having dispensed with the other as superfluous.

The manager of some travelling circus noticed the boy and persuaded him to join his troupe. On the old high machines, however, trick riding was comparatively easy. It was only when the safety suddenly became the craze that Valdare saw his opportunity of venturing on an absolutely new field. The difficulties of fancy riding on a safety are so much greater than on an ordinary that no comparison can be made. Both the Valdares practise two to three hours a day to keep proficient at their work. But in spite of everything they can never be sure that all their tricks will be successful.

As is nearly always the case with performances such as the Valdares give, a comparatively easy trick is quite as likely to appeal to the public as one to which they have devoted week after week of practice to accomplish. The most difficult performance that Valdare takes part in is riding his machine with the front wheel taken off altogether. He does this standing on the pedals, stooping slightly to hold the steering-head tube in both hands, the body thrown forward at an angle of at least ten degrees in front of an imaginary line drawn from the axle upwards. In this position lies the secret which it took the best part of a year to discover and appreciate.

If you balance a stick on your hand and then move the hand quickly in one direction, what is the

12 miles an hour on a rearing bicycle.

A ride on the back wheel.

An interlude in a ride: climbing through the diamond frame.

Not at all discouraged at such unrelenting failure he continued practising, and at last succeeded in keeping his balance during one entire revolution of the pedals. It was not in itself a great result for so much practice, but in that moment he discovered the secret of the exact position that was necessary. Within a week he could

result? The stick at once falls backwards. But give the stick a decided forward slant and if your hand travels fast enough it will remain fixedly in that position.

To carry this principle into operation when you represent the stick, however, requires considerable presence of mind. An irresistible impulse seizes you to jump forward and get clear of the dismantled machine on which you are mounted. For my own part I may safely say that I shall never master even the preliminary step of trusting myself to the mercies of such an irresponsible conveyance.

For months Valdare attempted to conquer this trick, holding to a rope fastened by means of a pulley wheel to a rail running along the ceiling. The result of this, however, was to swing him round and round in a circle. Ultimately he decided to dispense with any mechanical assistance, and trust to his own powers of balance. His idea now became to mount from a table, but for three weeks he made the attempt, and the whole of that time never rode a foot.

Bicycling backwards.

The vaulting act.

that some supernatural agency is preventing the bicycles from falling.

The trick which entails the greatest strain physically is that in which Valdare draws the front wheel by sheer strength from the ground and rides along gaily with his machine pawing the air like a rearing horse.

Once in Cincinnati he rode one third of a mile in this extraordinary position in 1min. $17\frac{3}{5}$sec. Until he dismounted he had no idea what the strain had been. The moment his feet touched the ground they gave way as if every muscle had been paralysed.

To climb through the diamond frame of his machine is another amusement in which Valdare in- mount confidently from his table without any apparent effort.

It is not an unnatural opinion that no one in his right mind would ever wish to ride a machine in that way except on the stage. But it is just this riding on a stage that requires the greatest skill. The space being limited to a diameter of about twenty feet, the performer is perpetually riding round a curve. The stage, too, drops considerably towards the footlights, and is made rough and uneven at the back by iron slides which cross from one wing to another.

There is literally no position which is impossible to the Valdares on their machines. They climb over them and through them and round them until you begin to think

Mrs. Valdare dismounting and mounting again without touching the ground.

Pyramid riding without using the handles.

dulges. It can be done by anyone who cares to imitate his movements, provided they possess the heaven-sent gift of patience.

Valdare commences by standing on the left pedal with the left foot, and swinging the right leg to the same side he thrusts it through the frame, sinking down till head and shoulders are even with the front wheel on the left side. Then with both hands grasping the tyre of the front wheel, which is turned at right angles, he swings the head and body back on a level with the frame. Now the head is put through, and the easier half of the trick is accomplished.

He has still to come up on the farther side, and to do this must shift his hands from the wheel to the handle-bars. Thrusting the right shoulder well forward, he grasps the left handle with the left hand from the right side of the machine keeping the right hand still on the front wheel. Then he lies well forward and straightens up, swinging the left foot over the saddle, and taking care the while not to put too much weight on the right-hand pedal, since there is nothing to prevent the machine starting backwards and throwing out the balance. What could be more simple?

I have described the riding on one wheel as the most difficult trick which Valdare performs, but it is little more so than to mount a machine without touching any part of it but the pedals. This can only be accomplished by dismounting when the bicycle has acquired considerable momentum, and running beside it till the left pedal is down, springing up with a light touch on it into the saddle.

The terrible risk of accident which such performances as these suggest are nothing to the Valdares; for neither of them has ever suffered from any serious injury through riding. Bruises, especially on the ankle, are naturally common enough, and the little lady cyclist's chief grievance is the hard task of always looking pleasant when things happen which, in private, would make every kind of grimace allowable.

A matter of balance.

Valdare has met with one really dangerous accident in his life. It was in a trick which he still practises, not on a bicycle, but on the wheel of an ordinary American carriage. Starting from a platform ten or fifteen feet from the ground, he rides down a ladder, keeping a footing on the narrow hub. The first time he attempted this feat the incline of the ladder was so great that the wheel left it altogether, and with one tremendous bound brought him to the floor.

Were he given enough space this intrepid rider would substitute a bicycle for the carriage wheel, but to attempt this on the Alhambra stage would alarmingly increase the rate of mortality among the orchestra. At the Milwaukee Exposition, however, he rode down a flight of 112 steps on his machine. He weighed then, as he does now, 118lb.

It would be a mistake to suppose that a trick on a cycle is mastered once and for all like a trick with cards. To do them justice they ought not to be described as tricks at all, but as exhibitions of skill. There are several pretty exhibitions which Mrs. Valdare gives alone. In one she mounts her machine with her back turned to the handle-bars and rides it thus round and round, sometimes steering with one hand, sometimes folding both arms before her.

Mr. Valdare steering with his foot

In another, keeping her left foot on its pedal the whole time, she swings her right leg over, and placing it on the brim of the wheel, lowers the machine till it rests on the right pedal. From this posture, and without ever touching the ground herself, she draws the machine to an upright position again, and starts off as if there had been no interlude whatever.

And riding at full speed she will now and then spin her front wheel round like a teetotum, without wavering an inch out of her course.

More showy even than this, however, is the way in which she rides, standing first on one pedal and then on the other keeping both legs always on the same side of the machine, or another trick in which she and her husband swing round and round each other, changing from one side of the machine to the other, while as if by magic it continues to run diligently about the stage.

Valdare can ride with his wife on his shoulder, even with a third person to cap the human pyramid, and still circle round or balance the machine in the centre of the stage as the fancy comes. But more dangerous than this is, after working up a great pace on the machine, to stand on the saddle with one foot, and with the other resting on the handle-bar, to guide the bicycle while his intrepid partner climbs up behind.

Now Valdare will be racing round, finding an imaginary seat in front of the handle-bar, and working the pedals from there; now his wife will have turned her machine upside down, and without putting foot to the ground, have mounted the pedals, and, balancing there, will be working this ceaseless treadmill with as little ostentation as if it were not something which one person out of ten thousand could not do.

The Jones-Hilliard Bicycle Sensation.

By Tertius Carr.

Illustrations from Photographs by A. J. Johnson.

I WAS standing at the door of the London Pavilion the other day chatting to my friend, Mr. Frank Glenister, when he suddenly turned to me and said: "By-the-bye, have you been to see my show on the cycle-track?"

"What's that?" I answered.

"Why, the Jones-Hilliard bicycle sensation, with Charlie Jones, the ex-champion of Australia and New Zealand, in the chair—at least, not exactly in the chair, but on the seat."

I confessed that although inclination would make me a constant spectator of his marvellous collection of varieties, yet time and business had so far kept me away.

"Never mind," said he, "come in to-night, and if your blood doesn't curdle and your eyeballs hang out like a pair of ripe cherries, don't call me a showman again."

Well, I went, I saw, and I was conquered. I kept my eyesight, and the red corpuscles still flow genially through my system. But what a show! Certainly, as regards the art of cycling, the most striking thing the world has ever seen.

MR. CHARLES JONES, THE SENSATIONAL CYCLIST.
From a Photo. by H. Pawson, Blackpool.

Hearing that Charlie Jones was a New Zealander I had an indistinct notion that I was going to see a native Maori doing the ordinary business on a trick bicycle, and as I sat in the stalls I felt no particular anxiety one way or the other, but when the curtain went up on what appeared to be a gigantic soup-plate with the edges shaved off and part of the front sliced out like a Wedgwood card-basket, I began to wonder. Then I found that the redoubtable

THE TRACK, AS SEEN FROM THE DRESS CIRCLE.

Charlie Jones was no Maori at all, but a well-set-up, fine-trained specimen of British manhood, clean cut in his limbs and as lissom as a panther. After the show was over, by dint of persuasion I was "taken round" and introduced; hence this story.

To return to our soup-plate. We were told that, in order to show the absolute control he had over his machine, he would ride it at full speed round the track, and that without The ex-champion was to ride round the card-basket, standing on the upper or right-hand side of the machine with his left leg passed through the frame, the frame of the bicycle, *bien entendu!* He did it, and never turned a hair, and the bicycle looked none the worse.

By this time we had begun to settle down, and when we heard that he would ride round that rumbling, grinding, crashing track seated side-saddle, using one foot only and disdain-

THE TRACK, AS SEEN FROM THE STALLS.

using his hands or his handle-bar. Now, considering the fact that this said track, or soup-plate, or card-basket, is only 18ft. in diameter, and that its sides rise at an angle of 60deg. and are only 5ft. in width, we in the stalls smiled gently at one another, because to us it was perfectly evident that the pretty gentleman in the white shirt-front had been telling us a tarradiddle.

But, no; in a brace of shakes there was Charlie Jones scorching round that track with his hands spread out and arms upraised, and the soup-plate was shivering and rattling and groaning, and we were holding on tight to the arms of our seats, wishing that our feet were in stirrups and screwed to the floor. But there was no time to settle down, for out comes our lecturer with another story—we half believed it this time, but only half.

ing his handle-bar, we thoroughly believed our informant and only waited to see Charlie Jones break his neck.

Slowly at first and then with a wild rush he was on the track—whiz—whoosh! round he went, the gallery boys yelling and sedate stalls applauding vigorously. Our hands had got loose from the seat-arms by this time.

Our friend in evening dress, who up to this time had kept us strictly informed on every point of interest, now came to the front and looked round the house with an expression of sadness. "I am empowered to challenge anyone in the world to ride the ex-champion on the Jones-Hilliard track for £50 a-side." There were no takers. I asked him afterwards why he was so sad, and he told me that it arose from a long-continued

RIDING WITHOUT HANDS ON HANDLE-BAR.

intensity of our excitement.

"Thirty miles an hour and without his handle-bar; no power of guidance over his machine save his wonderful balance. See it before you believe it." Thus our friend. Thirty miles an hour! Whoop, whizz, and away; faster, and faster, and faster still! He no longer looks like a man on a bicycle: he is a blurred line drawn round the track, and the track groans and protests and then, yah! our hearts are in our mouths and we catch at our breath as if we had swallowed a fly, for, in mid-career, he has made one wild jump from his machine, and is standing smiling and bowing in the middle of the card-basket.

disappointment. He was always hoping against hope that somebody would come forward to make Jones stretch himself, but no one had succeeded yet. I felt almost inclined to oblige him, but when I looked over the edge of that awful soup-plate I thought of my loving wife and precious children, and crept wearily away.

"He will dress himself in ordinary street-going costume, he will ride at full speed round the track, he will light a cigarette, and he will—in short, he will undress"; this from our sad-eyed friend. The ex-champion of Australia and New Zealand did all these things, and we once again stamped and split our gloves in the

RIDING SIDE-SADDLE.

RIDING WITH LEG THROUGH FRAME.

and a pleasant wit; he looks after the business arrangements, whilst Charlie Jones saves as much of his neck and other parts as possible. He was sitting on the basket, and as the two chairs were occupied with a miscellaneous collection of uncouth garments of varied colours he offered me a share of it. The share was small, but then he is a man of large stature and ample beam, but gentle withal. I sat beside him.

At once I plunged *in medias res.* "Tell me, Mr. Jones, are you a born Australian or are you a native of New Zealand?"

"Neither," he replied. "My foot is on my native heath; my name's—'Jones.' I am London born--but ask Hilliard, he'll tell you all about it while I finish dressing."

I turned to Mr. Hilliard, and information came rolling from him.

"When Jones was two years of age his people emigrated, first to Australia, and later to New Zealand, where they disposed their Lares and Penates in Christchurch. He took to cycling when he was twenty years of age, and rode one of those old fire-escape machines known as

Then they led me trembling to the personal interview I referred to above.

A three-cornered room with red walls, a mat, two chairs, a table, a looking-glass, a square basket, and a collection of mysterious colours and cosmetics on the mantelpiece, with a washstand in the corner. Present: "Charlie" Jones, Mr. Harold Hilliard, and myself. Mr. Harold Hilliard is Charlie Jones's partner and co-inventor. He is a big man with a genial cast of countenance

REMOVING HANDLE-BAR WHILE RIDING AT FULL SPEED.

ordinaries. Three months later fortune provided him with one of the modern safeties, and at his first attempt he broke the New Zealand record for road-racing. Three months after he carried off five races in succession at Kirwee, and then he was put on the scratch mark. In 1894 he won the Ten-Mile Championship of New Zealand, besides several provincial contests.

"On September 8th of the same year, at Moor Park, Sydney, he carried off the Ten-Mile Championship of Australia. In 1896 he came to England with a view of riding for the World's Amateur Championship, and for some months he trained at Wood Green for that purpose, but on the score that he had rendered himself a professional he was refused his license as an amateur, and so perforce he entered the professional ranks and started lowering records, which he has done successfully."

REMOVING CLOTHES AT FULL SPEED.

Mr. Hilliard stopped, but my thirst for information overbore my natural timidity. I turned to the ex-champion and asked: "Have you ever done anything else than lower records and do impossible feats on nerve-breaking tracks?"

He took the towel out his mouth and said: "Ask my partner Hilliard."

Again I turned. "Yes," said Mr. Hilliard, "he is an expert revolver shot, and he plays the cornet; he can make a watch—he hasn't tried to mend mine, but that's by the way—and he can make or mend a bicycle as well as he can ride and end them; and I believe that on one or two occasions he illustrated the local edition of the New Zealand *War Cry*. No, it did not kill the Salvation Army in the Colony, but I believe it lowered its tone. It became more gentle and modest after that trial."

"There's one thing I should like to tell you, Mr. Carr," said Mr. Jones. "Thirty-seven years ago, at the Agricultural Hall, my father scorched round the track at the enormous and unheard-of speed of eight miles an hour and created a record. He rode what we call to-day a 'bone-shaker,' with iron tyres and wooden wheels. The handle-bars were about 7in. across, and you kicked forward at the pedals like a shot rabbit. So, you see, the disease is hereditary. My brother, too, has been bitten, and although he only rode three races in his life, he won them all. It was somewhere up-country in New Zealand, and a more motley collection of machines and riders I never saw. My brother was riding my light racer, and the others disported themselves on bicycles of every known age, type, and quality. He won the five-mile race by a mile, and then turned back to look for the others. Yes, we are a racy and racing family."

ACROBATS, AERIALISTS AND THE KING OF CONTORTIONISTS

The first English superstar of modern entertainment was the singer Charles Leybourne who invented the character of Champagne Charlie, a city swell 'good at any time of day or night, boys, for a spree'. In the 1860s and 1870s he wrote and performed many hits One, based on a sensational new act, was called 'The daring young man on the flying trapeze'.

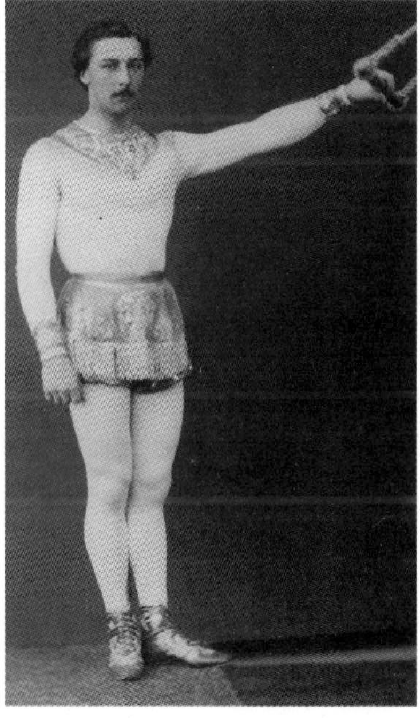

Jules Léotard

One day in the late 1850s, a young Frenchman, whose father owned a gymnasium and swimming pool, realised that if he attached pairs of the cords that opened and closed the ventilators in the roof above the pool to wooden batons he could swing out from one baton to the next. The daring young man who invented the flying trapeze made his debut in 1859, at the age of twenty-one, at the Cirque Napoléon in Paris. His act delighted the public. Dishes in fashionable restaurants were named after him, and even today we remember him by an article of gymnastic clothing. His name was Léotard and he toured Europe to great acclaim with his new act. He appeared for the first time in London at the Alhambra, Leicester Square, shortly after it opened in 1860, receiving the enormous sum of £180 a week. Unfortunately his success was to be short lived as he died of smallpox just ten years after his Paris debut.

Leotard's act was not Flying Trapeze as we know it today. He flew solo from one bar to another, including a somersault between the trapezes, over a long mattress. Having a catcher to fly to and return from, and performing over a safety net, were introduced in the 1870s. By the 1880s textbooks of gymnastics included instruction on use of the trapeze, alongside the parallel bars, horizontal bar, vaulting horse and rings.

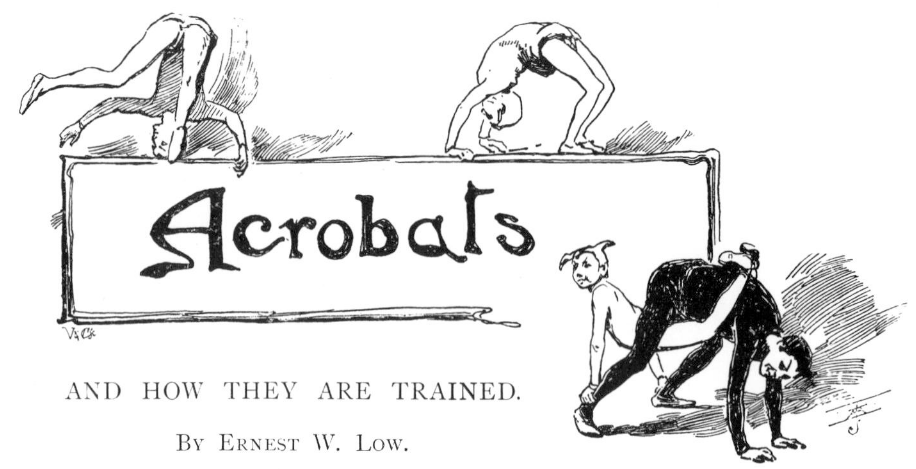

Acrobats

AND HOW THEY ARE TRAINED.

By Ernest W. Low.

THE taste of the public as regards its amusements is proverbially fickle, and many of the performances which were hailed with enthusiasm by the audiences of only a few years ago, would to-day be received with a very languid show of approval, if, indeed, they did not evoke positive hostility. Particularly marked has the change been in the case of "variety entertainments," and all the more striking, therefore, is the fact that there is still a class of artists whose hold upon the affections of the spectators is still as great as of yore.

We never seem to get tired of watching the evolutions of acrobats; there is a magnetic influence in feats demanding nerve and agility which is well-nigh perennial; it appeals to those of all classes and all ages, to the horny-handed son of toil as well as the man about town; alike to the middle-aged paterfamilias and his boisterous boys and girls home for the holidays.

No doubt, the *soupçon* of danger which attaches to these feats (which, as a matter of fact, is much slighter than is commonly supposed) may, in a measure, account for their never-failing popularity; but the tendency of late years has rather been in the direction of discountenancing the exploits which had nothing but their audacity to commend them. Public opinion has altered towards this as towards everything else, and nowadays the performers who rank highest in favour are those whose feats excel in strength, agility, and grace, of which the latter is by no means the least potent factor.

Very few out of the thousands who enjoy witnessing performances of this description have more than the very faintest idea as to "How it's all done." The question is constantly put by an inquisitive child to his parent, much to the latter's perplexity, who, being unwilling to acknowledge his ignorance, launches out into the most fallacious statements in his endeavour to enlighten the mind of the awestruck child concerning the life of an acrobat "behind the scenes."

Personally, I can even now recall to mind what a harrowing picture used to be drawn for my delectation of the tortures endured by the hapless young people, no older than myself, whose wonderful feats I had witnessed at the Crystal Palace with unfeigned wonderment and delight. Stories of little boys having their spines broken at the age of two (to make them supple!), of little, writhing creatures condemned to stand for hours daily with one leg strapped up, and of a multitude of other horrors, were impressed upon my youthful mind, with the result that many a sleepless night did I pass after these occasional outings.

No doubt my experience is not unique, and perhaps even to-day there are people who believe that an acrobat's training cannot be successfully carried through without a certain amount of hardship and cruelty. Indeed, to my shame be it said, until very recently some lingering doubts on the subject still occupied my mind, and they were only thoroughly dispelled after I had had the opportunity of personally witnessing the methods of the several celebrated performers who have been kind enough to place the knowledge, gained from long experience, at my disposal for the benefit of the readers of THE STRAND MAGAZINE.

Few men are better qualified to speak on the ups and downs of an acrobat's life than Mr. Henry Balcombe, or "Ara," of the "Ara, Zebra, and Vora" trio. At the present time their performance mainly consists of balancing feats, amongst these being one which "Ara" claims to have originated. Exceedingly difficult it looks. "Ara" balances himself on his hands upon a small pedestal, and supports on his neck "Zebra," who in turn bears "Vora" upon his shoulders.

But although the trio's exhibition is of this character just now, there is hardly a branch of the profession which "Ara" has not had a turn at. Certainly, he and his brother Arthur ("Zebra") have been through the mill. They were apprenticed in 1875, at the respective ages of nine and six, to the Jackley troupe, and the following nine years of their lives were spent entirely abroad, and it can be understood that during this time life was not all *couleur de rose* for the two little Balcombes. Still, they learnt all that was to be learned in their calling, and although they acknowledge that many hardships had to be undergone unknown to latter-day apprentices, they have never regretted having been brought up in so hard a school.

"ARA, ZEBRA, AND VORA."

There were scarcely any music-halls in those days, and travelling troupes had to depend upon finding concert-halls at various places they halted at, or, failing this, go through their performance in the open. Often as not, too, if business were bad, the hapless little apprentices would fare badly, not infrequently being really ill-treated. There is not much fear of anything of this sort nowadays, as the law has taken these little performers under its protecting wing, and a master not carrying out his duties as set forth in the terms of apprenticeship, would soon find himself called upon to answer for his conduct.

A few years after finishing their apprenticeship, the two young Balcombes struck off for themselves, their originality being apparent in their choice of professional names, which they selected by taking the first and last letters of the alphabet, so as to run no risk of clashing with other professionals. Then they commenced a most successful tour, visiting all the principal cities of Europe, and winning golden laurels wherever they went — there being a peculiar quality of refinement about their work which is lacking in that of many otherwise clever combinations. The "Nonpareil Trio," as the show is now called, only dates back two or three years, with the accession to the troupe of the youngest sister of the celebrated "Mosers," who is now known as "Vora," but in private life is Mrs. Henry Balcombe. Like her husband, she has been virtually all her life in the business, for since her fifth birthday she had been taking part in the performances with her brothers and sisters; on the next page is a picture of the little mite as she appeared soon after making her first shy bow to the audience.

When I asked "Ara" to give me an idea of the way a youngster was taught from the very beginning, he told me that there was no royal road. The great thing to bear in mind is to learn to walk before you attempt to run. The great object of a child's early training is to make him strong and supple before attempting anything in the shape of difficult feats. For this purpose he is put through a variety of simple exercises no more difficult than what may be seen done at many a school gymnasium, but the great difference is, that the little professional has to *keep at it*, to steadily go on practising until the most intricate movements are done without effort.

First he is taught to bend his back slightly, and only slightly, for undue slackness in the muscles of the back unfits a man for the performance of many acrobatic feats.

Of course, I am not speaking of "contortionists" or "human snakes," with whom bending is the chief stock-in-trade. When the youngster can bend his back a little without straining, he goes on to learn "flip-flaps" and "hand-springs." "Flip-flap" is the name given to the evolution which consists of throwing the head back, placing the hands on the ground, and turning over to an upright position, and a "hand-spring" is the reverse of a "flip-flap." These and the "splits," which is too well known to need description, may almost be called the A B C of tumbling. When the learner has mastered flip-flaps and hand-springs, he is ready to attempt somersaults, back and front and side, and the more difficult "twisting somersault," which combines a complete vertical turn with a horizontal change of position.

VORA, AGE 5.

Whatever branch of ground-work the learner is going to take up, the rudiments of the art have to be first thoroughly mastered. To use "Ara's" own words: "Tumbling is the father of all ground acrobatics." And he was particularly emphatic in bidding me remember that everything must be attempted very gradually, and every feat, however simple, done over and over again, until it becomes second nature. If the learner is content with just being able to manage a trick, he will never shine in combined work in which quickness of movement and "style" are so essential to success. "Ara" said it was quite possible for a young fellow of sixteen or seventeen to become fairly proficient in one branch, but if a boy wanted to become an all-round performer, like himself, he ought to start not later than ten years old.

Even after a man becomes thoroughly proficient he cannot afford to "rest on his arms reversed"; if he does not continually practise and improve himself he will soon get stale. Performing, as he does now, three times a day, "Ara" has no need of additional exercise; but when abroad or in the provinces, and only appearing once in the evening, the mornings are regularly devoted to practising new tricks and general exercise for keeping in condition. He says he finds half an hour's *skipping* a splendid thing to keep the limbs supple and improve his breathing power.

"Ara's" long career has not been without its share of adventures and accidents, but, luckily, none of the latter have had any very serious results. As a lad, he was for some time doing the "Risley" business, which consists in one of the men lying on his back with his feet at right angles to the ground, on which human apparatus the lighter members of the troupe perform. Young "Ara," while doing a difficult somersault, was unlucky enough to slip, and, falling on the edge of the pad, broke his arm. Another fall, which might have been fraught with far more serious consequences, occurred at Rotterdam, when he fell off a high trapeze, owing to having forgotten the indispensable handkerchief, to wipe the perspiration off the bar. Although the fall was about 40ft., he got off scot-free. He landed in the laps of a lady and gentleman, and before the former had recovered from the faint caused by the shock, he was once more aloft and proceeded with his act, to the surprise and admiration of the spectators!

"Ara's" pluck and agility were once put to a noble use. Very few professional acrobats can boast that their training was the means of rescuing another from certain death, but this was the case with "Ara" when he was but a slip of a lad. While performing in a small village, a fire broke out opposite the hall, and just as the troupe arrived on the scene a woman came rushing down the stairs imploring someone to save her baby, which was asleep in a room on the first story. To climb upon one another's shoulders (or, technically, to make "three-man-high") was the work of a moment for three of the Jackley troupe, and young "Ara" was at the top. He could just get his hands upon the window-sill, but managed to pull himself up, brought the baby to the sill, and, resuming with difficulty his position on the shoulders of his companion, lowered his precious burden down to the ground and its anxious mother. One can quite understand

"ARA SAVES A BABY'S LIFE."

that the troupe had to stop in the place several days longer than had been intended, for the people came flocking in from the neighbouring villages in hundreds to see the boy who saved the baby.

Few people who visited Olympia a short time back can fail to have been struck by a troupe of acrobats who, fantastically attired as demons, went through some extraordinary movements on the top of high ladders. The leading spirit of the troupe is Mr. Conn Fredericks, who has made a spécialité of this ladder-balancing. He also originated the daring feat of riding a bicycle down the "chutes," which caused such a sensation at the time. He hails from the United States, and is a good example of the result of the American system of training. He was never apprenticed, but while very young started practising acrobatic tricks at a gymnasium, and embarked in the profession at the age of twelve, much to the horror of his people, who are all strict Quakers in Chicago, and regard those who frequent theatres and music-halls as on the high road to perdition. So, certainly, Conn Fredericks' talents cannot be attributed to heredity or early associations.

Like "Ara," he has had a turn at almost every sort of gymnastic work; in his time he has given performances of trapeze work, the horizontal bar, tumbling, pure and simple, rope-walking, besides his unique ladder act. He explained that tricks on the trapeze and horizontal bar are learned nowadays by the aid of a mechanical appliance called a "longe." This consists of a broad belt going round the gymnast's body, attached to which are two ropes running through pulleys.

When the learner attempts a new feat, he puts on the belt, a man takes hold of the end of each rope, and, should he miss, they immediately give a pull, when he swings harmlessly in the air. This device has saved many a broken neck, but it had not been invented when Conn Fredericks learned his trade, so at that time a man learning somersaults off the bar had to trust to luck and the services of a companion.

Again, in aerial work, nets were entirely unknown until recent years, and the trapeze performer, when he went up to his lofty perch, literally had his life in his hands. In this respect, then, the lot of the learner is far happier than it used to be. In spite of being brought up in what may be styled the heroic school, he doesn't believe in the system adopted by many of the English acrobats, who, he says, want to teach in too much of a hurry, instead of sending the pupils through a regular course, as they do in the States. The English performers go in for specializing.

THE FREDERICKS TROUPE—THE GREAT LADDER TRICK.
From a Photo. by A. M. Bliss & Co., Lewes.

For this reason he does not encourage his little son to do head balances. Conn Fredericks, junior, takes part in his father's Mephistophelian antics, and a most engaging little fellow he is. He is just twelve, and, according to his father, started tumbling at the age of two! He is a clever little chap, quite childish in his ways, and absolutely without any comprehension of the meaning of the word "fear." In fact, his daring is a source of anxiety to his father and mother, for they never know what he'll be up to when he's out of sight. Not many days ago he was discovered perched up on the girders at Olympia some 100ft. from the ground, and turned a deaf ear to the entreaties of the manager, who implored him to come down. And when he at last consented to come back to *terra firma*, it was only with much difficulty that he was dissuaded from sliding

THE FREDERICKS TROUPE—PRACTISING SOMERSAULT THROWING.

while it is rare to come across an American performer who cannot do all-round work.

There are several tricks which Mr. Fredericks disapproves of; balancing on the head is one which he thinks leads to very bad results. In fact, he assured me that men who continually do this feat, sooner or later suffer from brain trouble.

A performer named Thuer used to do this some years ago while swinging on a trapeze, and for a time he was a tremendous attraction, but finally he went out of his mind. Surely one trick he wanted to do was the most extraordinary that has ever been heard of. This is what he proposed to do. He was to stand on a trap-door, a rope, with a knot to come under his ear, to be placed around his neck, and then the trap was to be opened! Of course, he was never permitted to perform this gruesome act in public, but it is a fact that he practised it successfully, and managed a drop of 2ft. to 3ft. with impunity!

down one of the wires! He has only been taking part regularly in the work of the "Demon" troupe for the last two years, and doesn't express himself as very satisfied with that sort of work. He says he wants to be a comedian, and sometimes rebels against the acrobatic work; but when his father threatens to take another boy in his place, he soon comes round to a different frame of mind. His father doesn't give him too much work to do; like the majority of men who are masters of their craft, he believes in the beginner doing a little and doing it well.

THE FREDERICKS TROUPE.

THE FREDERICKS TROUPE.

Mr. Fredericks was for a long time travelling with Barnum's circus, and he says the most enthusiastic audiences he has ever had were those made up entirely of niggers in the Southern States. The coloured folk used to literally go mad over a circus, and it was no uncommon thing to see a whole family — husband, wife, with a baby in her arms, and a boy or girl, coming from a place miles away, all perched on the back of one unfortunate horse!

Undoubtedly the cleverest trapeze performer in existence is a member of the "Hanlon" troupe, who, as "Little Bob," caused a perfect furore some twenty years ago. "Little Bob" is not very big in stature now, but he has three boys, aged twelve, eleven, and four, whom he has set his heart upon teaching to follow in his footsteps. He himself has been a member of the most famous troupe known to the present generation.

First he was apprenticed to the original Hanlon-Lees, whose reputation was so greatly enhanced by the attractiveness of "Little Bob's" feats, and afterwards he was one of the celebrated Hanlon-Voltas with whom he

THE FREDERICKS TROUPE.

worked both the trapeze and the horizontal bars. He had an engagement with his troupe at the Alhambra recently, and I paid him a visit one morning, when I was enabled to watch him putting his boys through their paces. Needless to say, Mr. Edward Hanlon, the smallest one, aged four, has only just commenced, but he positively beamed with delight when "Little Bob" lifted him up to the bar, and he pulled up to his chest twice very sturdily.

THE YOUNGEST OF THE HANLONS.

As for the eldest boy, Robert, he is already no mean performer, and has appeared in St.

ROBERT HANLON.
1.—THE BACK PERCH.

Petersburg with his father. Their preliminary teaching bears out my previous information; they stand on their hands, do the splits, "legs and shoulders," before they are put on the trapeze. After learning a few simple feats on a trapeze near the ground, they are started on the high one.

The first thing to learn here is how to fall, so as to land properly in the net, for an awkward fall of 60ft. or 70ft. means broken limbs, if no worse. Then they are carefully taught how to judge the swing of the trapeze, whe to leave go, and how to catch the othe properly, and to land safely on the littl platform suspended in mid-air, which i technically known as the "perch."

ROBERT HANLON. 2.—SOMERSAULT FROM BAR TO BAR.

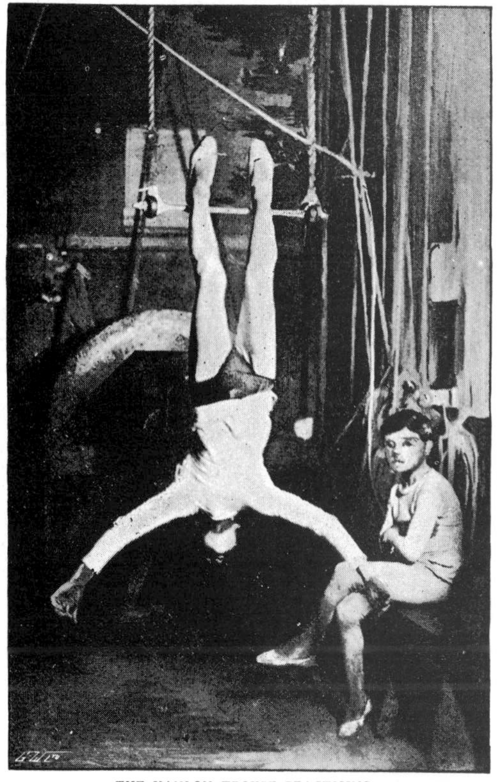

THE HANLON TROUPE PRACTISING.

THE HANLON TROUPE PRACTISING.

"Bob" is a very abstemious man; he never touches alcohol during the day, but he has no faith in dieting, and says he eats just what he fancies, and lets his boys do the same. He told me that there is comparatively little danger now about trapeze work so long as the apparatus is carefully looked to, but before the introduction of nets it was very different.

Many years ago, he had to be thrown from one man to another on the flying trapeze, and they practised the feat with half-a-dozen men holding a blanket, dodging about so as to keep under him and catch him if he missed his hold. On the other hand, bar work close to the ground is rather risky, for if a man slips, he is bound to hurt himself more or less. With all this, bad accidents are very rare considering the number of men engaged in the business.

THE HANLON TROUPE PRACTISING.

Taken all round, the life of an acrobat does not appear to be an altogether unenviable one. But even given the possession of all the necessary qualities, I should not recommend anyone to adopt the profession. To attain to mediocrity is not very difficult, but, like the great poet, the great acrobat is "nascitur non fit."

THE KING OF CONTORTIONISTS

By
LEVIN CARNAC.

Photos by Hana, Strand, London, and Chandler, Philadelphia.

IF you want to be pre-eminent in any particular line, you can do so by obeying one simple rule which, unfortunately, is a good deal easier to understand than to follow. It is just this: Go one better than the other fellow. That is what Señor Pablo Diaz did when he became, what I suppose he may be fairly called, the first contortionist of his day.

All other professional tanglers of the human form divine have contented themselves with getting into attitudes which apparently outrage all the laws of human anatomy either standing or lying on the stage, or at any rate while in some reliable contact with Mother Earth. On the other hand, gymnasts delight most in performing their gyrations at some greater or less distance above it, and between these two there is a mean which for Señor Diaz has proved a golden one.

He combined the two arts, made himself contortionist and gymnast in one, and in so doing raised himself, both literally and metaphorically, several feet above the surface of the stage, and a considerable distance above the next man in his profession, whoever that may be.

This was a distinctly happy idea, and one that must have needed almost as much originality of conception at the outset as it required perseverance and pluck in its subsequent execution. Of course one may wonder why no one thought of it before. Possibly many have done so, but the fact that Señor Diaz has no rival, shows at least that he is the only one who has successfully put it into practice.

Eminence of this kind is not achieved without very considerable assistance from Nature, which usually takes the form of an irresistible predilection for the kind of work which is to be excelled in, and it was thus with Señor Diaz. He is a Cuban by birth, his father is a Spaniard and his mother a Cubaña. The parental trade was shoemaking, and in this connection it may be remarked that Señor Diaz is, especially when he gets his spangled serpentine-looking tights on, a shining exception to the rule that the cobbler should stick to his last.

His parents, good, honest folk, thought in their old-fashioned style that "like father, like son," was a good enough rule in business, though it is possible that they may have been ignorant of the much-quoted aphorism. Not so, however, the youthful Pablo. Contortion, it would seem, was bred by some mysterious means in his supple bones, and in due course it came out in the still more supple flesh.

But withal, he was a dutiful and considerate son, and so, when he had reached the usually aspiring age of fourteen or thereabouts, and having already set his soul fixedly upon the sinuous glories of contortionism, he spared his parents the sorrow of prematurely learning the inevitable by going to bed dutifully at the usual hour, stopping awake till everybody was fast asleep, and then getting up and essaying to tie himself up in knots and twist himself into strange tangles on the floor of his bedroom.

Here, it may be granted, was the true enthusiasm which laughs at difficulties and makes jokes of apparent impossibilities. But not even such enthusiasm as this can achieve excellence without some sort of tuition or guidance, and how was the aspiring Pablo to get this? He had no money to pay masters, and even if he had had they might have demurred at the prospect of these secret and midnight séances.

But the will which is capable of twisting joints and muscles and vertebræ into shapes which would drive an intelligent chimpanzee mad with envy, was not to be easily daunted by such a trifle as this. In his birth-town of Sancti Spiritu there had been itinerant circuses, and he had had an opportunity of comparing what was actually done by the acrobats and contortionists in the arena with what they were represented doing on the circus posters. Out of this contrast he evolved what may be fairly described as a stroke of genius.

He ignored the performers and took the posters as his models!

No matter how wild had been the flight of imagination achieved by the

poster artist, he deliberately set himself to achieve its realisation—and he did it. There is even a certain amount of pathos in this, and it may be found in the contrast between the picture of the lonely boy in his little bedroom far away in Cuba, imitating the weird attitudes depicted on a flaring poster stuck up against the wall, and twisting his youthful limbs into unnatural postures by the light of a candle-end, and the first contortionist in the world going through his bewildering evolutions under the glare of the lime-light to the accompaniment of the applause of thousands of spectators.

It may not be one of the highest ambitions attainable by human industry and genius, but it is one consistently and honestly attained—and that, after all, is a good deal.

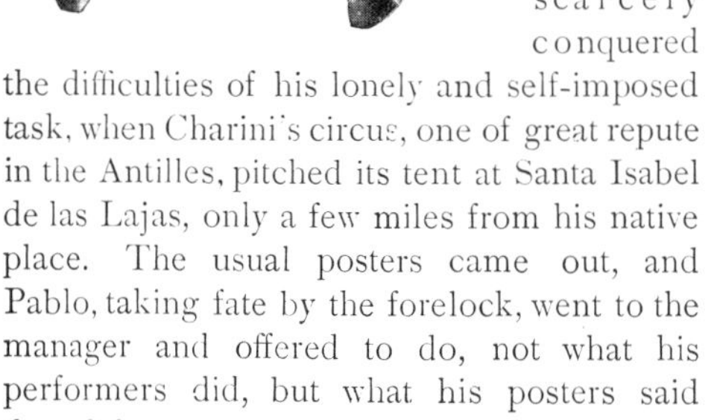

Pablo Diaz did not wait as long for his reward as a good many artists have to do, for he had scarcely conquered the difficulties of his lonely and self-imposed task, when Charini's circus, one of great repute in the Antilles, pitched its tent at Santa Isabel de las Lajas, only a few miles from his native place. The usual posters came out, and Pablo, taking fate by the forelock, went to the manager and offered to do, not what his performers did, but what his posters said they did.

Señor Charini, being a showman, knew something about the poster business. He knew, for instance, that the bills of a show are about as different from the actual performance as the placard of a halfpenny evening newspaper is from the news in it, and, with true professional incredulity, he took Pablo at his word—which Pablo promptly proved himself as good as, if not a trifle better than.

The result was an immediate engagement, and the commencement of a sinuous but distinguished career, which began in the Pearl of the Antilles, took him through the principal cities of Mexico, with the exception of the capital, to Yucatan and New York, and ended, so far as this present time of writing is concerned, at the Palace Theatre of Varieties, in Cambridge Circus, London, where, I suppose, he earns more in a week than his respected father does in fifty-two.

The distinctive feature in his performance is the fact that from the time he walks on to the stage to the time he walks off he never sets foot on it, save when he goes through the single-ring performance described hereafter. He swings himself up into his rings, and then proceeds to put himself through the apparently impossible gyrations, which the accompanying photographs will describe a good

deal more graphically than any printed words could.

The most difficult and trying of all his feats is the one represented on column one of page 576. It may not look so at first sight, but Señor Diaz says that it is, and he ought to know. If the supplest of my readers will try to put himself into anything like the same position, suspended in mid-air in a pair of rings, I don't think he will feel inclined to argue the question at any considerable length when he has got back to his normal posture.

In person Señor Diaz is a lithe, muscular man, standing five foot four and a half, and weighing a hundred and thirty-eight pounds. He is much more powerful in the mere muscular sense than one would imagine from a superficial look at him. In fact, by dint of careful and constant training he has managed to combine suppleness and strength in a very remarkable degree.

Naturally, this training must be hard and rigid. As a matter of fact, Señor Diaz earns his nightly triumphs by living the life of an ascetic during the day. In one sense no jockey ever trained harder for a big race than he does from year's end to year's end. When he gets up in the morning, about half-past eight or nine, he has a cup of tea and, perhaps, a biscuit or a piece of bread, and this has to last him till half-past three in the afternoon, when he eats the one meal that he takes in the twenty-four hours.

This meal has to be as small in quantity, and as nourishing in quality as possible, and, therefore, it usually consists for the most part of the very best beef-steak obtainable. There are two reasons for this. In the first place, his muscular strength must be maintained; and in the second place, he cannot go through his performance with a particle of undigested food in his system. From this fact may be gathered some faint conception of the extraordinary convolutions into which his internal economy has to be tortured, or at any rate twisted, during the course of his "turn,"—a phrase which, in this case, has more than its usual meaning.

It will easily be understood that a man cannot take such liberties as these with his external and

internal anatomy without paying a certain amount of penalty to outraged Nature. Although Señor Diaz is perfectly sound in wind and limb, and above the average of men in strength, his performance involves such a tremendous physical strain that when it is over, to use his own words, a child of seven could knock him down. The tax upon the heart is, of course, the worst, and sometimes this is so great that he comes down from his rings with blinded eyes, and with the blood singing so loudly in his ears that the applause of those, who know so little of the physical cost of the easily executed evolutions, sounds to him like faint and far-away thunder.

But although Señor Diaz has won his principal and most striking triumphs suspended between the flies and the stage, they are by no means his only ones, as a glance at the somewhat weird illustrations on this page and the preceding one will show. Presumably by way of a pleasant and diverting change, and possibly in a certain sense relaxation, he descends to the stage to transform himself into quite a special kind of Genius of the Ring.

This particular ring is only twelve inches in diameter, which is considerably less than the latitude of the Señor. It looks bigger in the first illustration on the last page, but that is due to a trick of the camera. He is holding it in front of him, and therefore it looks larger than it really is. It is noteworthy that he can put himself through this ring in just as many varieties of contortion as there are inches in its diameter.

Unfortunately only the different stages of going through can be illustrated here. The whole performance in the air and on the boards would make an excellent subject for a series of animated photographs, from which, I daresay, comfortable royalties might be derived, although there might be some little danger of the audiences suspecting that they were being made the victims of some sort of photographic jugglery.

For such a man, amusements and relaxations—save, of course, in the purely physical sense—must naturally be few. Massage, practice, and walking exercise about make the sum of them. I was thoughtless enough to ask him whether, like all Spanish-Americans, he did not take a good deal of his recreation in the saddle. He speedily undeceived me by explaining that the condition of his vertebral column is such that the motion of a horse would either reduce it to the state of a string of beads, or start it on such a performance on its own account as would result in his general disintegration.

His principal mental occupation is thinking out new tricks and contortions to substitute for his present ones when these shall have been imitated, should anyone manage to do so, and get himself successfully untied. It is his glory to be unique, and he proposes to remain so.

So far as English audiences are concerned—which Señor Diaz says are most difficult to please but not to startle—he was discovered by Mr. Charles Morton, to whose courtesy I am indebted for the introduction which has enabled me to place the above facts and photographs before the readers of PEARSON'S MAGAZINE.

The Champion Jumper of the World.

BY OSWALD NORTH.

IN many ways it is distinctly advantageous to be a successful professional jumper, but the business has its drawbacks. Foremost among these is the joker who seizes upon the obvious. Mr. John Higgins, the wonderful man whose feats are depicted in these pages, at one time kept an account of the witty fellows who assured him he was "born to rise in the world"; but he soon gave up in despair, so great was the number of these would-be wits.

The curious thing about Mr. Higgins is that he is considerably below medium stature, being but 5ft. 3¾in. in height. He is not yet twenty-six years of age, and comes from Blackburn—a district famous for the number and variety of athletes it has produced. Higgins's various feats are truly remarkable, whether considered merely as jumps, or as dramatic spectacles, ingeniously contrived and brilliantly executed. The photographs reproduced here were specially taken by our own artist on the stage of the Pavilion Theatre, in Piccadilly Circus.

In the first feat depicted our artist has successfully "snapped" Higgins in the very act of leaping over a horse sixteen hands high. It will be noticed that the athlete has several inches to spare. "There are horses *and* horses," remarked Mr. Higgins to the writer. "Some are so quiet that I really believe they would stand there without any attendant at their head. Others, however, are a real source of danger to me. Perhaps just as I am 'taking off,' the brute will rear high into the air; something like this once laid me up for weeks in Los Angeles, California."

As a rule, Mr. Higgins tests his horse nightly. He takes a run, but does not jump, merely bringing his feet down sharply close up to the animal, and dropping his dumbbells precisely as he does in flight. In this way he sees how the horse takes it, and acts accordingly.

But this is a magnificent jump, as will be evident to anyone who realizes the great height and broad back of a sixteen-hand horse. And yet Higgins asks no consideration for his own lack of inches. He announces himself ready to meet all comers who challenge his right to the proud title of Champion Jumper of the World. One of his longest jumps, by the way, was performed at his native place in 1895; it measured 14ft. 11½in. One of his highest was done at the Manhattan Athletic Club, New York, where he jumped over an obstacle more than 6ft. 3½in. high.

JUMPING OVER A HORSE SIXTEEN HANDS HIGH.

The next feat which Mr. Higgins is seen performing is one of a number of very extraordinary trick jumps. Clutching his dumb-bells as usual, the wonderful little man gives a few kangaroo-like leaps, and then rises into the air and alights right in the middle of a case of eggs! And yet not an egg is cracked, although the athlete is seen to linger in their midst for a moment and then rise gracefully over the back of the chair. We asked him how this was done. He said he couldn't tell; it was partly an effort of will. When he alighted for that fraction of a second on the eggs, he did not, of course, exercise a single ounce of his weight, but completed the jump by certain strenuous movements of his shoulders and the upper part of his body generally.

INTO A CASE OF EGGS WITHOUT BREAKING ANY.

Often people in the audience have doubted that the eggs were real eggs. But such persons are always courteously invited on to the stage, not merely to examine the eggs *after* the jump, but before, and during its accomplishment. Beyond all doubt, the thing is genuine —a really graceful and beautiful feat, calling for extraordinary agility and suppleness, and extremely careful judgment.

Jumping, as is more or less generally known, is one of the favourite recreations of our North Country youth. Many of the factory lads make small wagers of a shilling or so, and decide them at jumping contests held after hours in the country lanes. When a recognised champion arises, he is backed for comparatively large sums against the amateur champion of a neighbouring district, the stakes being contributed by a weekly levy paid to a regularly constituted treasurer. The winner of several of these higher events, sooner or later, attracts the notice of sporting men, and the next stage is professionalism. One grieves to say that local publicans also get hold of likely lads and arrange a series of contests with the view of encouraging, not the spirit of healthy emulation or even the spirit of athleticism, but merely the consumption of other spirits —and beer.

A really tremendous jump is seen in the accompanying photograph. It is over eleven ordinary cane-bottomed chairs. In pointing out to me the difficulty of this jump, Mr. Higgins remarked that he had to rise about five feet and "travel" fourteen. The characteristic which is most forcibly borne in upon the spectator is the astonishing cleanness of action and lack of apparent effort that distinguish these feats. Higgins does *not* believe

OVER ELEVEN CHAIRS.

in overtaxing himself. His various jumps are well within his power, and he always has some inches to spare—a fact which shows that he could accomplish still more difficult feats if he chose.

I have before me Higgins's athletic record; it is virtually one long list of victories. After "little things" innumerable came the crushing defeat of Temple Jones. This gentleman, a kind of knight of the athletic world, bore on his crest the proud title of champion hopper of the world. Now, it must be a grand thing to be a champion hopper, and therefore one sympathizes with Mr. Temple Jones, who was one night forced to hop into comparative obscurity, ten inches behind the rising star.

INTO A TUB OF WATER AND OUT AGAIN WITHOUT TOUCHING THE BOTTOM.

Next, Mr. Higgins had the temerity to challenge the redoubtable Joe Darby, himself the greatest jumper of his day. Joe was a bit staggered, for he was mindful of his own immense reputation, hardly won and long held. Moreover, he had heard ominous rumours about the new athlete. However, he was pushed into a corner, and a match was arranged, to be brought off on the Moorfield Ground, Failsworth (!), on July 22nd, 1893. Here is the newspaper report about the match, which, by the way, was for £100 and the Championship of the World:—

"The most important jumping match of late years was brought to a satisfactory conclusion on Saturday afternoon, the contestants being Joe Darby, of Dudley, and John Higgins, of Blackburn. Both men had undergone a special preparation for the match, which turned out very much one-sided. Higgins won in his first jump by 2ft. $\frac{1}{2}$in., and could easily have made it much more. The jump was a hop, two strides, and jump, and Higgins broke the world's record by 17in. This record had stood twenty-two years. Higgins thus fairly proved himself to be a long way in front of all other athletes at all-round jumping, and he is fairly entitled to the title of Champion Jumper of the World."

The next illustration shows another remarkably effective trick jump in the very act of being accomplished. Higgins is seen jumping over the back of a chair placed on a table, into a tub of water and out again without touching the bottom. That he does actually touch the surface of the water is evidenced by the splash. It will be noticed that merely to jump over the back of the chair is an extraordinary feat; and yet to this must be added the astonishing trick—performed in mid-air, be it remembered—of alighting on the water and then springing out again, without touching the bottom of the tub. No wonder this surprising jump should make a "splash," in more senses than one. Higgins has been all his life beating existing records and creating new ones. The first record that he made was at St. Helens, against John Larkin. This was "stand, hop-stride, cross-stride, and jump"; and Higgins covered 17yds. 10in.; then came two hops and jump, 38ft.; four hops and jump, 59ft.; two back jumps, 20ft. 7$\frac{1}{2}$in.; three standing jumps, 42ft. 2in.; and so on.

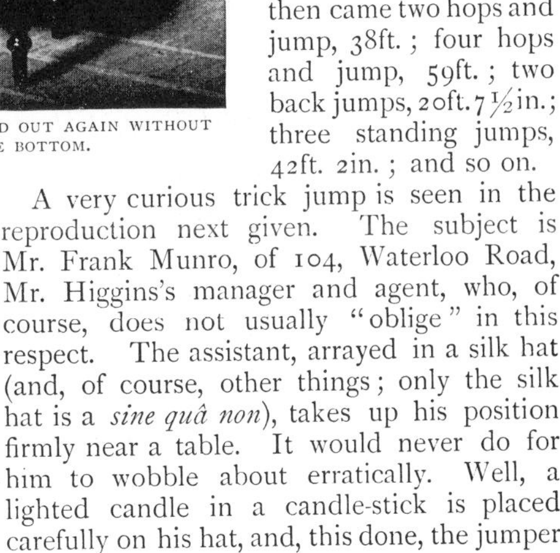

A very curious trick jump is seen in the reproduction next given. The subject is Mr. Frank Munro, of 104, Waterloo Road, Mr. Higgins's manager and agent, who, of course, does not usually "oblige" in this respect. The assistant, arrayed in a silk hat (and, of course, other things; only the silk hat is a *sine quâ non*), takes up his position firmly near a table. It would never do for him to wobble about erratically. Well, a lighted candle in a candle-stick is placed carefully on his hat, and, this done, the jumper retires some distance to take measurements with his eye.

The reproduction of the photo. fully explains this remarkable performance. It is, indeed, a tremendous jump from the other side of the table right up on to the candle with both feet together. The flame is extinguished with a quick movement of the foot from the ankle, and then the athlete sails gracefully down on to the stage.

EXTINGUISHING A CANDLE ON A MAN'S HAT.

In the photo. one dumb-bell dropped by Higgins in his flight is just about to drop on to the table. And these missiles certainly do fall around with alarming promiscuity. The stage at the Pavilion was fairly corrugated with deep dents from them, and they often disabled a chair or scared an incautious attendant nearly out of his wits.

Yet another candle-extinguishing feat forms the subject of the next reproduction. Six chairs are placed close together in a row, and on the seat of the sixth are deposited two lighted candles, in candle-sticks. Taking his dumb-bells and bounding hither and thither like a veritable Spring-Heeled Jack (he does this to keep himself in form), Higgins stands well away from the chair most remote from the candles, and takes in the situation with his keen eye. He next gives a few more skittish frolics, and then one, two, and up over the chairs with indescribable *élan*. He passes through the air with curious slowness, and actually alights gingerly on the lighted candles, which he carefully extinguishes, one with each foot. Having successfully accomplished this, the jumper seems to rise *off the tips of the candles* and alights gracefully on the ground, bowing to his admiring audience. Of course, the whole of the jump takes only two or three seconds, but it calls for marvellous nicety of judgment and delicacy of movement. Now and then it happens that Higgins only extinguishes one candle. In such cases he always performs the feat over again.

ANOTHER CANDLE-EXTINGUISHING FEAT.

Quite as difficult is the next extraordinary jump, which, however, is invariably performed with the same ease of movement and certainty of judgment which characterize all the feats attempted by Mr. Higgins. This wonderful man stands bold upright on an ordinary fire-brick, dumb-bells in hand, as we see him in the photo. Very well. After a few swings of his muscular arms, he rises lightly and alights for a moment with both feet together on a small stand, which is placed about eight feet away. Almost instantly he

TWO LONG AND DELICATE JUMPS.

rises again and takes another immense bound over a chair that stands rather more than another ten feet distant.

Obviously a useful accomplishment in cross-country races. Higgins has often taken part in these sports, clearing hedges and ditches and gates before which the boldest steeplechasers would shrink. And Mr. Higgins was once compelled to negotiate a six-foot paling at very short notice. As a matter of fact, an infuriated bull was the cause of this—and so ugly did that bull look, that Higgins declares to this day that he owes his life to his powers as a jumper.

Of course, Higgins went to the United States. Every individual who has made a great name in the entertainment world, here, does this. And Higgins's rivals even brought over a renowned American jumper who was to wrest the jumping crown—if there *is* a jumping crown—from the Englishman. The latter was challenged to try "three rises"—or hop, two strides, hop, two strides, and jump. His engagement list was full, however, and Higgins declined. The American sent letters to the sporting papers complaining about Higgins, and at last the latter met his trans-Atlantic rival. The match was, modestly enough, for £200 a side and "the championship of the planet." It was brought off at the Wellington Grounds, Bury, on September 29th, 1894, and Higgins won by 13½in.

Next we find the plucky little North Countryman carrying the war into his opponents' country. In other words, Higgins went off to the States again, travelled over 25,000 miles there, and defeated every athlete he met.

Mr. Higgins is next seen in the very act of ringing a bell in his flight—one of those bells you push down sharply. It is placed on a chair, which stands on a table, so that the mere jump, to say nothing about the bell-ringing, is worthy of notice. Of course, doubting Thomases have their say about this remarkably clever feat—"it is an electric bell, rung from the wings at the proper moment," and so on. Nothing but a close examination of the bell *in situ* will convince such people. A curious thing is that Higgins never practises. He considers his evening's work before the public

RINGING A BELL IN FLIGHT.

quite enough practice. Another remarkable thing is the way in which he has attained, after years of perseverance, his present position as champion all-round jumper. Fearlessly he has attacked professional and semi-professional men, who have made one particular kind of jump their speciality. For example, there was the match with Gregson, of Grimshaw Park, for £50 a side. The conditions were "stand, one cross, and four jumps." That Gregson was a specialist was evidenced by the betting, which was three to one *against* Higgins for the cross, and ten to one *on* him for the match. Higgins, however, won the cross by 1½in. and the jumps by *nine feet!*

In the photograph here reproduced we see Mr. Higgins taking a flying backward jump over a table and two chairs. The jumper stands several feet away from the chair, to which, of course, his back is turned. Swinging the dumb-bells, he throws his arms out behind him, and bounds backward to gain momentum. Resting for a second or so, he takes another terrific backward leap, and travels clean over the table and the other chair, having so calculated the distance and effort required as to be within, perhaps, a couple of inches of touching the seat of the farther chair as he descends.

This backward jump always appeals to an audience. "A forward jump, high or long," they seem to argue, "is all very well, no matter how big; but a leap backwards over a serious obstacle is a very different thing. A man may lose his nerve, or make an error of

A GREAT BACKWARD JUMP.

THE KANGAROO FEAT—OVER A RING OF CHAIRS.

judgment through not being able to see where he is going, and then there is a pretty bad fall before him—or rather behind him."

Even this wonderful "leap in the dark" is characterized by Higgins's neatness of style and ease of manner. He seems to rise from the stage with the elastic bound of an india-rubber ball, and he "travels" along in mid-air precisely as though he were gliding on an invisible wire. His legs are never sprawling apart, but always close together, and he smiles at all times as though he viewed his performance in the light of a mere pastime.

At Hull our champion jumper leaped over a horse 18 hands high; and at the Orpheum, San Francisco, he cleared two horses, each 17 hands. In November, 1895, he jumped over forty-five chairs in succession, placed in a ring, and each chair 10ft. from the other—a truly terrific feat of agility and endurance. The next photo. shows Mr. Higgins clearing a ring of chairs—a much smaller ring, of course, than the one just mentioned, or it would not have been photographable. The chairs are placed 10ft. apart, and Higgins braces himself for a great effort. The band plays a very slow march, and to keep time with the music the jumper regulates his prodigious bounds, the effect being peculiar in a very remarkable degree.

THE "HUMAN OBSTACLE."

What Mr. Higgins calls the "Human Obstacle Jump" is seen in the accompanying photo. We all know the Human Obstacle, but unfortunately we cannot all get clear of him with the ease and agility

OVER THE "HUMAN WALL."

displayed by Higgins. This is how the jump is arranged: Three gentlemen from the audience are invited upon the stage. Two take up positions about 5ft. apart, and the third extends himself rigidly crosswise, his head resting on the shoulders of one supporter, and his legs on the other. To maintain this position is a little trying. Few gentlemen are bursting to attempt it. Still, there is always someone thirsting for the fearful joy of a few moments' publicity.

The Human Wall is seen being negotiated in the next photo. reproduced here. This explains itself. Half-a-dozen gentlemen from the audience are brought on the stage and placed in a row. When the components of the "wall" appear to be a nervous lot, Higgins leaps over their heads from behind, but ordinarily he takes the jump with his men facing him. In the photo. it will be seen that the poor man over whose head the athlete is poised for a moment is shrinking half-unconsciously, lest a worse evil befall him. In this particular instance it may truly be said that "outsiders see most of the game." The men at each end know perfectly well that Higgins won't jump over *them*, so that they are really only ornamental adjuncts, and, as such, free to gaze at the jumper as much as they please.

This is a very effective feat. Sometimes it is varied by jumping over the wall endwise on, in which case it is extremely difficult to find a person willing to fill the onerous (and possibly dangerous) position occupied by the man at the end farthest from the jumper.

What may be called the athlete's most sensational jump is next shown. His victim for this occasion only was Mr. Frank Munro. As a rule, Higgins has to content himself with a paid underling as *corpus vile*,

ON TO A MAN'S FACE AND OFF AGAIN WITHOUT HURTING HIM.

unless there happens to be someone in the audience burning for distinction. A chair is placed on a table, and the assistant leans back with his elbows on the table and the back of his head resting on the seat of the chair.

When all is in readiness, and the audience suitably worked up, Higgins retires slowly to the other end of the stage. Here he dips his shoes into a preparation of lampblack and oil, so that "his mark" may be proof positive of successful accomplishment. Then giving the usual preliminary leaps, and carefully calculating distances with his eye, he bounds into the air, lingers for an infinitesimal period on his subject's face, and then descends to the stage on the other side. The ordeal past, the subject rises bashfully to take that share of the applause to which the big smuts on his nose and eyes entitle him.

The last illustration depicts Mr. Higgins's showiest feat—jumping over an ordinary brougham. There is a great fuss on the stage on the eve of this jump. Attendants run here and there. Some drag the brougham into its proper position, others spread an astonishing number of carpets, for the descent is very heavy.

Of course, Higgins does not leap off the ground clean over the carriage; no human being could do that. Observe the small table 2ft. 3in. high, which is placed close to the near hind wheel. Taking as great a run as the stage will allow, Higgins springs lightly on to the table, pauses for a moment, and then rises with an extraordinary bound right over—*and across*—the top of the brougham. One opines that the value of the carriage deteriorates nightly, mainly on account of those dumb-bells which are discarded in flight. Often they fall on the carriage and knock it about. Or one will fall on a lamp, and batter it somewhat. But it is a grand feat this jumping "over a full-sized brougham"—splendidly engineered so as to bring down the house the moment the "Human Kangaroo" alights on the carpets placed on the other side. Of course, a stumble or miscalculation may entail a broken limb. Such mishaps are among the "drawbacks" mentioned at the outset.

OVER A FULL-SIZED BROUGHAM.

UP A POLE.

BY FRANK HOLMFIELD.

Illustrations from Photographs by Foulsham and Banfield.

IN the world of entertainment there are many curious ways of earning a living, and one of the strangest I have ever witnessed is that of the man who climbs a twenty-foot pole, balanced on the chest of another, to perform a series of wonderful acrobatic feats, with only a slip of hand or foot between the performer and—well, at the very least, a bone-smashing fall!

Such is the description of the professional exhibition chosen by two American gymnasts known as De Witt and Burns, who, between them, recently succeeded in thrilling—with no uncertain thrill—the patrons of London's great palace of amusement, the Alhambra Theatre.

Sensational though the performance undoubtedly is, it is amusing withal, for the pair of smart young Americans are comedians of no small ability. So the thrilling part of their entertainment is intermingled with funny little quips and actions that arouse many a good, wholesome, hearty laugh, of which the hard-worked, brain-fagged Londoner stands so much in need.

It was not the first time that the patrons of variety theatres had seen a performer "up a pole," for this was a form of eccentricity favoured by a *troupe* which hails from the land of the chrysanthemums, and which I think appeared for the first time in England at the Alhambra.

But the shrewd Japanese boss always selects a slim and light member of his *troupe*—in fact, a boy—to go on the polar expedition, whereas the American explorer just tips the scale at 10 st. 2 lb.

A 20-ft. pole is of itself a by no means inconsiderable burden to rest confidingly on a man's bosom, end upwards, for a space of ten solid minutes. The "perch"—as they facetiously term it—used by the Yankees weighs 25 lb. Add to this a ten-stone man bumping and bouncing away to his heart's content, and it will be admitted that Mr. De Witt must be constructed on very sound muscular lines to be able to bear up this nightmare-like load. And when an appreciative audience insists on encores night after night, it may truly be conjectured that the man with the pole on his chest does not exactly enjoy himself as much as do the "kind friends in front."

The readers of this magazine who have not personally witnessed the remarkable performance are now given, thanks to the advancement of scientific photography, some vivid illustrations of several of the "acts," and I have to express my thanks to Mr. C. Dundas Slater for his courtesy in rendering it possible for the photographers to make use of their camera with such good effect in pictorially representing Mr. Burns's extraordinary feats whilst "up a pole."

First grasping the heavy pole with both hands, Mr. De Witt raises it to the perpendicular, and manipulates it with an amazing appearance of ease. He indulges in a little display of pole-juggling—just to get his hand in, as it were—at the same time losing no opportunity to "get in" a little bit of light comedy here and there—indeed, the whole performance takes the form of the quaintly humorous throughout.

Meanwhile the pole-bearer—apparently as strong as a polar bear—has placed the lower end of the 20-ft. "perch" into a kind of cup socket supported by a belt around his chest and waist. Balancing the pole without the aid of his hands, he places the latter behind his back to be used as a step.

With a quick, panther-like spring, the polar performer, who is behind the bearer, has landed one of his feet on the improvised foot-rest formed by his partner's hands, and hey, presto! he is half way up the 20-ft. pole almost before the audience are aware that he has left the stage.

Then ensues the remarkable series of acrobatic feats upon the pole. There is no exaggeration in stating that on the evening of the writer's visit those feats held the audience spellbound.

Poised on the point of the high pole, the performer seems quite at home. The rod—sturdy ash though it is—bends and quivers in response to the terrific strain caused by gyrations and lightning-like movements in all directions. At one moment the gymnast stretches out his body, without apparent effort, at right angles to the pole as it writhes, like a snake, under the strain. At the instant when it seems he must certainly crash to the boards below, he recovers his balance, only to dart out once again into a pose which one had formerly considered impossible even on the level of the stage. Every point of the compass is favoured by a feat of daring unsurpassed.

Twenty feet below, his partner is watching every movement of the agile athlete on that slender slip of timber, as the proverbial cat watches the mouse. The strain must be terrific, but the man at the base knows his business and has the confidence of the fearless gymnast above.

To the spectator it would appear, perhaps, that the balancing is accomplished chiefly by the various movements of the acrobat on top—that with him lies the responsibility of keeping the pole in its proper position.

This is not so.

Every little turn and twist, every stretch of arm and leg, every movement and pose

of the lithe body, must be carefully watched and acted upon by the man who bears the pole, and every bend compensated by a move on his part. *The balancing is done entirely from below; the whole responsibility for the safety of the man on the pole rests altogether on the shoulders of the bearer.* Watch him. An inch here, a foot there, a bend of the body yonder! Sometimes a full step to right or left is necessary. But the eyes of the spectators are attracted to the man above more than to him whose efforts keep the "perch" straight in mid-air, and they hardly notice these things—that the safety, the life of the man on the pole depends on the absence of falter or weakness of the bearer below. The gymnast, so high above, grips, by muscular hand, by supple leg, and by interlocked feet, that writhing pole. But will the pole remain staunch and upright under all the enormous weight which the rapid shifting about of a ten-stone body adds to that already bearing upon the chest of his trusty friend? Everyone knows that if you jump upon a pair of correctly weighted scales, you will pull down far more than your actual weight. In a like

manner does the jerking and bouncing of the man on the mast tell upon the one who has to bear the brunt.

The pole may bend like a twig, but no tremor shakes either performer. Well does each man know of a certain little episode which occurred to them in Louisville, Kentucky, seven years ago, when a tragedy was prevented by a seeming interference of Providence.

The story is worth relating. It tells of an act of infamy, born of envy and the hatred aroused by jealousy. Mr. De Witt and his partner were starring with a circus through the States. At Louisville the show opened to a house densely packed. At that time the pair were using a 30-ft. pole, having plenty of room aloft in the tent—in most halls the height of the stage permits only the shorter pole to be used.

Suddenly, whilst the man on the pole was performing one of his most sensational feats, an ominous "crack" was heard in the stillness of the vast audience, hushed by the daring feat they beheld. But an almost simultaneously uttered cry of horror went up at that moment. *The pole had broken in the middle.* Down crashed the doomed athlete from that dizzy distance of nearly thirty-three feet. Women fainted, and strong men had turned away their heads or closed their eyes. But they looked again when the cries of horror turned to wild "hurrahs" of joy. No ghastly sight of mangled remains lay there in the sawdust ring.

By what seemed little short of a miracle the gymnast had landed on his feet. He now stood grasping his partner's hands and smiling to the spectators.

The pole was examined at the broken part. When the cloth with which it was enwrapped was torn away, it was seen that the wood had been sawn partly through. When the extra strain came, it snapped across like a clay pipe-stem. It was the murderous work of a miscreant rival, who only escaped well-merited punishment from lack of sufficient evidence to satisfy a Kentuckian jury But that is another story.

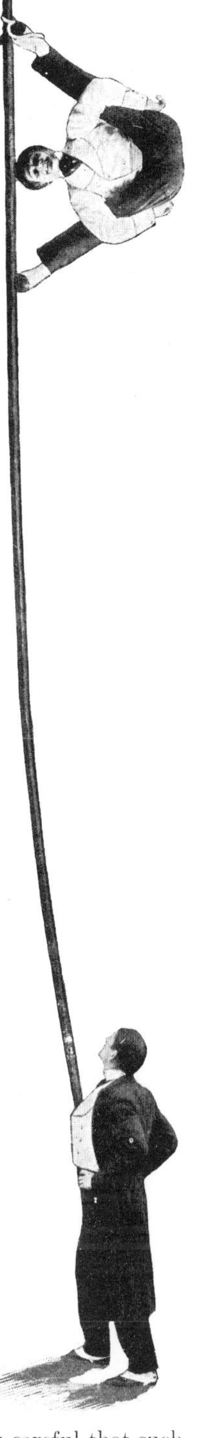

From the night of that miraculous escape, the pole is carefully examined and tested every evening before the performance. Both performers are now careful that such an event shall never occur again.

Perhaps the most sensational "act" of Messrs. De Witt and Burns's entertainment is the concluding one. The man on top has just finished one of his daring feats when he appears to make a slip, and slides, head downwards, at "falling" speed along the whole twenty-foot length of the pole, only missing crashing—seemingly—his skull against that of his partner by the eighth of an inch. He then calmly drops his feet upon the stage and—they go off.

Now and then a sceptic will arise to cast doubts on a genuine performance. In a big town in one of the Western States, a man of this class got up and asserted that the pole was supported from above in some mysterious way that he did not attempt to describe.

He was cordially invited upon the stage to form himself into a committee of inspection. He came up, asserting that he would "climb the bally pole" himself. He was offered every facility for doing so. He really could climb a bit, but he hadn't clambered up the pole more than half way when he was overcome with fright and bawled to Mr. De Witt to lower the pole to the stage.

"But I can't," replied the pole-bearer, with a smile towards the audience, "it's fixed on top, you know!"

"But I see it ain't," roared the converted sceptic. "Lower the pole, can't ye? I can't hold on any longer. If I let go, I'm a dead man!"

The audience fairly rocked with laughter at the fellow's antics and shouted—

"The monkey's got his stick at last!"

Keeping a keen eye on the miserable man above him, lest he should suddenly drop on his (Mr. De Witt's) head, the professional prolonged the agony for a minute or two longer, and finally allowed his victim to reach the boards in a terrible state of fright.

Amidst the gibes of the audience the disproved sceptic slunk off without a word further.

Amazing Tub Athletes

THE ART OF BARREL-JUMPING.

By Frank Holmfield.

In the hand-spring a young man's fancy lightly turns to thoughts of something new.

The circus and music-hall acrobat, except his entertainment be a good way out of the ordinary, is a drug in the market. The salary he commands is only equalled in extent by the rarity of engagements. It is only the man of some inventive genius who is able to hold his position and evade statuesque poses at Poverty Corner, where out of work "pro's" are not averse to picking up any odd turns an agent may offer them.

If the appreciative British public were imaginative enough to picture the risks incurred by many athletes and gymnasts in efforts to win applause, they would not, perhaps, enjoy their evening's entertainment so heartily. But men and women must live. A new "trick" of more than ordinary smartness is bound to capture kudos and the concomitant future engagements. So the inventive gymnast is always planning a "startler" of more or less effectiveness.

ACT I.—Jumping from the stage into the tub on the chair—turning a somersault in so doing—reaching the tub as it is vacated by another athlete, and thence to the stage on the other side.

Mr. William Deonzo is of that sort. It was the puzzling search after something new that made him think of the barrels of his childhood's days, when, in his father's cooper's shop, he played hide-and-seek in the recesses of

the paternal handiwork. He and his brother, when the idea of barrel-jumping first struck him, were only a pair of struggling American circus acrobats, working on Longfellow's blacksmith's system, "week in, week out." But in the barrels, as it were, they struck the

bung of fortune, and engagements flowed forth with gratifying regularity.

Deonzo's barrel-jumping act caught on. It was absolutely original. There was nothing like it anywhere. Although it took three years of hard and constant practice to perfect, the whole art of barrel-jumping made an impression on show-going folks. And, indeed, it is an amazing entertainment.

Through the courtesy of Mr. C. Dundas Slater, the popular manager of the Alhambra Theatre, the Editor of this magazine is enabled to present some striking illustrations of the wonderful performance of the Brothers Deonzo.

It is not surprising that the entertainment arouses

ACT II.—Jumping clean over five barrels—turning a somersault in mid-air on the way.

hearty and constant applause. Its novelty, and the remarkable agility and smartness displayed by the performers, raise it above the common level of music-hall turns.

It is by no means an easy task to effectively describe the various items which go to make up a really excellent quarter-of-an-hour's amusement.

A commendable feature of the performance is that the agile brothers go right through it at lightning speed, hardly giving the spectators time to recover from their astonishment at some wonderful feat, but immediately proceeding to accomplish another, still more marvellous than the preceding one.

The barrels, half-a-dozen of which are used, stand three feet in height and measure 26 inches at top and bottom, the latter being closed; they bulge three inches in the centre.

In the first Act a stack of three barrels is erected on the stage. One is placed on top of a second; another is placed on a chair. Into this barrel one of the athletes jumps, and stands facing his brother. At the word "Go!" the latter turns a somersault. At the same time the other performs a similar evolution out of the fourth barrel on the chair. So cleverly and smartly are the movements carried out, that just as the barrel on the table is vacated by one, the other brother lands into it, and out again, turning a somersault before touching the stage.

The second trick is illustrative of the great jumping capabilities of the brothers. Five barrels are

ACT III.—The two athletes jumping blindfolded from the stage into two tubs each, join each other in the fifth tub at the top of the pyramid.

placed in a row, the distance extending to thirteen feet. With a short run, one of the performers jumps clean over the lot, turning a somersault in mid-air and landing on his feet well beyond the fifth barrel! The gracefulness and ease with which the jump is accomplished add to the feat considerably.

And then comes a startler. Two tables are used — one, the smaller, being placed on another about eight feet long. In the centre of the higher table a barrel is placed; the total height from the stage being about ten feet. Below, on either side of the larger table, another barrel is set; whilst on the stage, on each side, are placed the fourth and fifth barrels.

Both performers are blindfolded, and their feet tied. They then take their positions on the outer side of the two lowest barrels. At the word "Go," each man jumps into one of the barrels on the stage, thence to the next barrel above, from this to the edge of the higher table, and finally both jump into the topmost barrel simultaneously. Each jumper moves with the other, as if worked by some invisible lever.

Now comes a really amazing series of jumps. Five barrels are placed as follows: One on the stage, one on a chair, another on one end of the table. In the centre of the table a full-sized man stands. Beyond him is another barrel, and a fifth on the stage. One of the performers is then carefully blindfolded, and his feet tied securely together. At the word "Go!" he jumps, first into the barrel standing on the stage, secondly into the one on the chair, thence to the third on the left-hand end of the table, whence he springs over the head of the man standing in the centre, and thus into the fourth barrel. He jumps from this to the fifth, on emerging from which he somersaults to the stage—all this blindfolded and with feet tied, be it remembered!

Under the circumstances, the man who stands in the centre of the table must have considerable confidence in the ability of the jumper—who must have still more confidence in himself to carry out so risky a feat. Marvellous to say, the blindfolded and feet-bound athlete accomplishes this bit of work as ably as if he were using his eyes, and with feet unbound, and rarely disturbs the barrels by so much as a hair's-breadth!

For the next feat, six barrels are left in a row, mouth upwards. Standing on one foot, the shorter performer jumps into the first barrel as cleanly as though it were double its size in girth and half the height. From the first barrel he rises as though impelled by some mysterious influence, for his legs

ACT IV.—Jumping blindfolded from the stage into two tubs—the second tub upon a chair—

scarcely seem to bend in the springing effort. He thus, as it were, in a single effort, passes from one barrel to the next, until he springs from the last one and turns a somersault, which lands him on the far side. All this is done without the slightest movement of the barrels, which remain as if fixed in immovable sockets to the stage.

The above feat is followed by one which may be said to improve upon it. The other brother springs from one barrel to another through the series of six, but instead of landing with both feet in the barrels, he performs a succession of hops, the right leg dropping into each barrel, the other outside, but not touching the stage.

Another astonishing feat is that in which one barrel is placed loosely on the right-hand end of a table. On the left end another barrel stands, unsecured, on a chair. The taller of the two brothers then springs from the stage into one of the barrels, the top of which stands six feet above the level of the jumper's feet. Landing in the barrel with beautiful ease, he in a second is out of it, clearing the distance separating the first from the second barrel and landing in the latter, only to once again spring out, and, turning a somersault, arrive on the stage apparently without any particular effort.

Six barrels are then placed in position along the stage, covering a length of fifteen feet. The taller of the brothers then accomplishes a straight jump over five of the barrels, and lands in the sixth without moving it an eighth of an inch from its place. As if he had alighted on a spring board inside the barrel, he has no sooner landed than he jumps again, rising out of the barrel as straight as a rocket. Whilst in the air, he turns a somersault, and finally lands on the stage a couple of feet beyond the last barrel.

As the opening at the top of the latter is only twenty-six inches in width, the cleanness of the jump is apparent, for the barrel never so much as shakes either when he drops inside or springs out again. When it is borne in mind that all the barrels are merely placed bottom downwards on the stage, without any fastening or wedging whatever, the wonderful agility which is necessary to perform this feat may be imagined.

ACT IV. (continued)—Thence into a third tub upon a table over a full-sized man, and so in and out of two other tubs to the stage again.

In their many journeys throughout the length and breadth of America the brothers Deonzo, who hail from Hamilton, Ohio, have met with many interesting adventures. Mr. William Deonzo asserts that all such have faded into insignificance compared with a little experience that happened to him on the occasion of the destruction of the Hotel Royal, in New York.

He awoke to find his room on the fourth floor full of suffocating smoke, and he could hear the crackling of the flames close at hand. Groping his way to the window, he looked

out in the hope that a fire escape would be handy. But nothing was there. Below him, from the windows of some of the third floor rooms, the flames spouted out. As he looked, a rope thrown from the sixth story shot past his window, and he saw a man endeavouring to descend. As this unfortunate victim slid past, the flames from the third floor burst towards him, burnt the rope, and hurled the poor fellow who clung to it to the pavement below.

Deonzo, sickened by the sight, turned away, and rushing to the door of his room, threw it open. The staircase was still intact, and he was hurriedly leaving the room, when he heard a series of soul-rending shrieks coming from the direction of his window. He rushed back and looked out. At the window to his right clung a young woman ghastly white and shrieking for help. From the smoke and flame issuing behind her, it was too plain that her escape inwards was cut off.

What could he do to save the poor creature? As his horror-stricken eyes gazed at her, he caught sight of the end of the rope down which the sixth story occupant had slidden to his awful fate. Deonzo was quick in making a decision.

Grasping the charred end of the rope, he formed a loop. Slipping his feet through, he swung, head downwards, out of his window. His acrobatic training stood him well in this adventure. He began a pendulum movement, which extended as he swung until he was able to reach the outside of the window to which the unfortunate lady was clinging. Grasping her around the waist, he swung backwards to his window. He was then enabled to place her in safety inside, and succeeded in following her. Getting out of the loop, rescuer and rescued eventually escaped down the stairs, but not a moment too soon, as immediately they reached the street the walls collapsed.

This thrilling rescue was witnessed by thousands of people who had gathered to see the great fire. Although Mr. Deonzo hurried away from the scene as soon as he reached the street below, for he was only half clad, he was followed by the excited crowd, who insisted on "chairing" him to the nearest hotel. He became the hero of the day. I have before me a cutting from a New York leading daily, in which this feat, with all the luridity of American journalism, is graphically described to the extent of nearly a column. The orthodox romance was not faithfully adhered to, however, in this instance. The rescued lady was NOT an heiress, nor did she fall in love with her rescuer and marry him. Mrs. Deonzo, I am sure, would have strongly objected to anything of the sort.

And this was not the only thrilling case of life-saving experienced by Mr. Deonzo.

A few years ago he happened to be

ACT V.—Hopping on one leg into six consecutive tubs without touching the stage.

standing on a railway station up-line platform in Cleveland, Ohio, waiting for an incoming train. Suddenly he heard a shout near him. "Go back!" was hurled at someone in a horrified shriek. He looked across at the opposite platform. Almost in the act of stepping from the down platform, by the steps provided for the use of railway servants only, was an elderly lady, evidently in a flutter lest she should miss the up train then due. She had got on the wrong platform, and in her haste to get across in time, she was courting certain death. Only a few hundred yards away, dashing along at the rate of fifty miles an hour, came a down express. The old lady, in her excitement, was quite unaware of the terrible death that threatened her, and her right foot was almost off the platform when something happened. Had she stepped on the rails she would have been cut to pieces.

Deonzo saved her. As she was about to step down, something struck her with such force as to hurl her flying backwards against the platform boundary.

She lay there gasping, wondering, angry at being thus so rudely treated. And as she lay there the express train dashed through—she was only saved from a horrible death by the quick act of a daring athlete.

When Mr. Deonzo saw her there, on the verge of annihilation, without a soul near to pull her back in time, an inspiration rushed through his mind. It was fully twenty feet from the edge of the up to the down platform. There was no time to reflect. He simply acted. A short run, and he was shooting through the air, straight for the old woman. He struck her full tilt, and knocked the breath out of her body—but he saved her life, although he nearly lost his own, as the rebound almost cast him under the wheels of the incoming express. By a great effort, however, he managed to recover his balance and was safe.

But, as a result of his plucky rescue, he lost his train and had to wait nearly four hours for the next.

A dash of humour was introduced into the incident as soon as the old lady

ACT VI.—Jumping from the stage into a tub, on a table 3 ft. high—thence into a second tub, and via a somersault on to the stage again.

recovered her breath. She insisted that she had been murderously assaulted by Mr. Deonzo and actually gave him in charge of the police! She would not hear the explana-

tions of those who saw the whole thing. No; she would teach her assailant a lesson.

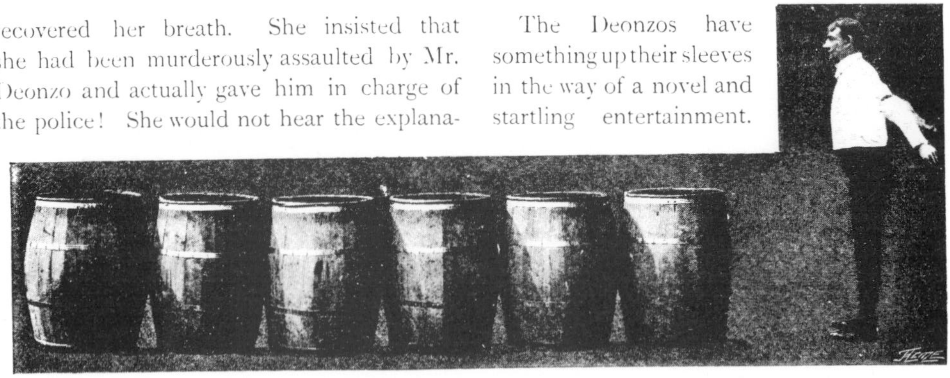

"He has saved you from a terrible death," they urged.

"Nonsense," she replied, "I could have got across in time!"

She was inexorable, and the "coppers" marched Mr.

Deonzo to the police-station. It was only after an immense amount of persuasion that she saw how ungrateful she had been, and withdrew the charge, but not until Mr. Deonzo had apologised profusely for saving her life!

The Deonzos have something up their sleeves in the way of a novel and startling entertainment. I must not say too much. But there is a wild horse, a barrel, and a man in it, and it will create a sensation such as is seldom experienced in show circles.

The numerous photographs illustrating this article were taken by the well-known Press photographers, Messrs. Foulsham & Banfield, of 95, Wigmore Street, Cavendish Square, London, W.

ACT VII.—Jumping over five barrels—into the sixth—turning a somersault, and finally landing on the stage.

THE BALANCE WONDERFUL.

SOME REMARKABLE EXHIBITIONS OF MUSCLE.

By H. J. Holmes.

NO branch of athletics demands more arduous and careful training than the art of balancing in its highest form. Patience, perseverance, and pluck are traits most necessary in the characters of those who aim at perfection in the difficult feats forming the subject of this article.

The severest critic must admit that a very trying course of practice is rendered imperative in the case of the muscular young lady who performs the striking, indeed startling, feat of sitting upon her own head whilst grasping with her teeth the top of a slender silver bar fixed some dozen feet above the level of a platform, and upon which slight support she balances herself and spins like a teetotum in mid air; and the young gentleman who calmly proceeds to balance upon his chin the full-sized dogcart which has conveyed him to the scene of his exploit certainly could not accomplish such a remarkable instance of equipoise without a tremendous amount of careful preparation.

Of course there are degrees in the art of balancing. Who amongst us, for instance, has not essayed in more youthful and frivolous days to set the parental walking-cane or the family broomhandle wobbling about in the air without visible means of support beyond the flattened nose-tip of the aspiring Cinquevalli? And has not a certain highly respectable dean stated that he used to seek solace from the carking cares of curacy by balancing, in the same manner, every cigar he smoked before lighting up? It is, however, with the higher reaches—if I may say so—of equipoise that I have to deal.

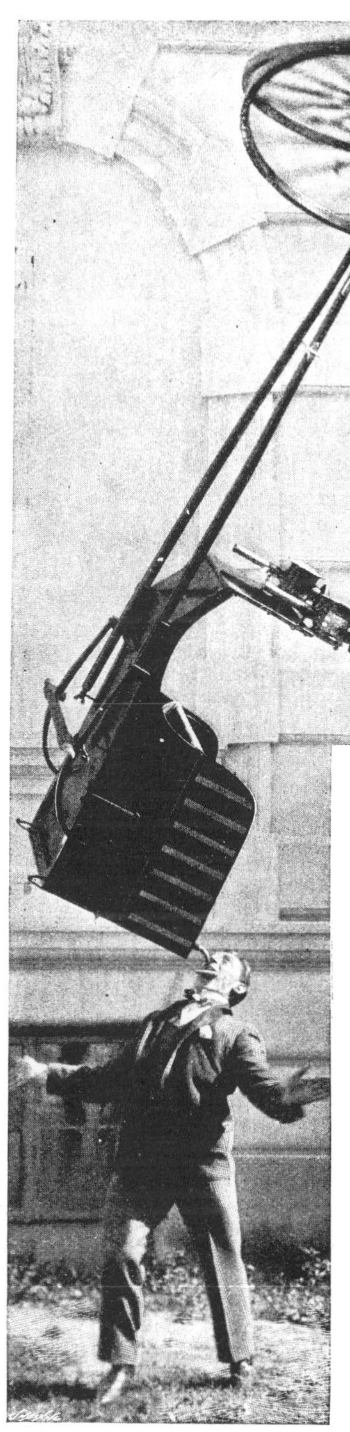

SPADONI CAN BALANCE HIS DOG-CART ON HIS CHIN!

During my peregrinations in quest of the material for this article, I asked a popular amusement caterer how balancing performances suited the tastes of his patrons. "Down to the ground!" was his brief response. In spite of the slight ambiguity of his figure of speech, there was no mistaking what my informant meant. Equipoise of the highest class is undoubtedly a very successful form of entertainment, and it is no strange thing for a capable artist to draw a weekly salary of from £70 to £100!

To Spadoni, the muscular German juggler, the public are indebted for a new form of balancing. He throws enormous weights about as another juggler would glass balls. The greatest heavy-weight balancing act that has ever been accomplished is that performed by this remarkable athlete. He is driven upon the stage in a full-sized dogcart. He dismounts, and the wheels are removed and set spinning on pivots fixed to the points of the shafts. Lifting the dog-cart bodily in his arms, Spadoni proceeds to balance it upon his chin, an act which does not appear to give him any considerable amount of concern.

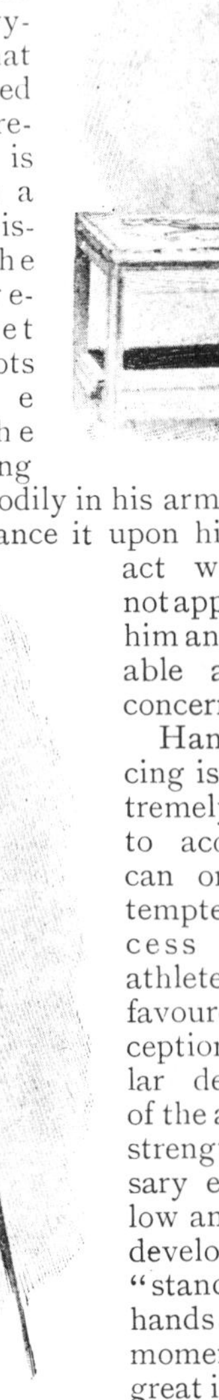

JULES KELLER CAN REST FIVE MINUTES IN THIS POSE.

Hana, Photos

MONS. GERARD BALANCES HIMSELF HEAD DOWNWARDS ON TWO PAIRS OF CUES.

Hand - balancing is an art extremely difficult to acquire, and can only be attempted with success by those athletes who are favoured with exceptional muscular development of the arms. The strength necessary even to allow an ordinarily developed man to "stand" upon his hands for a few moments is very great indeed; yet those whose aim it is to be regarded as first-class hand-balancers not only have t "stand" upon their hands for many minutes but must accomplish as much with thei upper limbs as mos people do with thei proper understandings The whole bod must be supported, unde extraordinary circumstances upon one hand for minute at a stretch. Steep stair must be climbed in an in verted position. Obstacle must be jumped across, an springing from point to poin some feet apart is a *sine qu non* to remunerative engage ments.

Amongst the cleveres class of hand-balancers wh have appeared in Londo and the provinces is Mlle Bertoldi, the charming youn lady wh is know to the Br tish pul lic as th "Quee

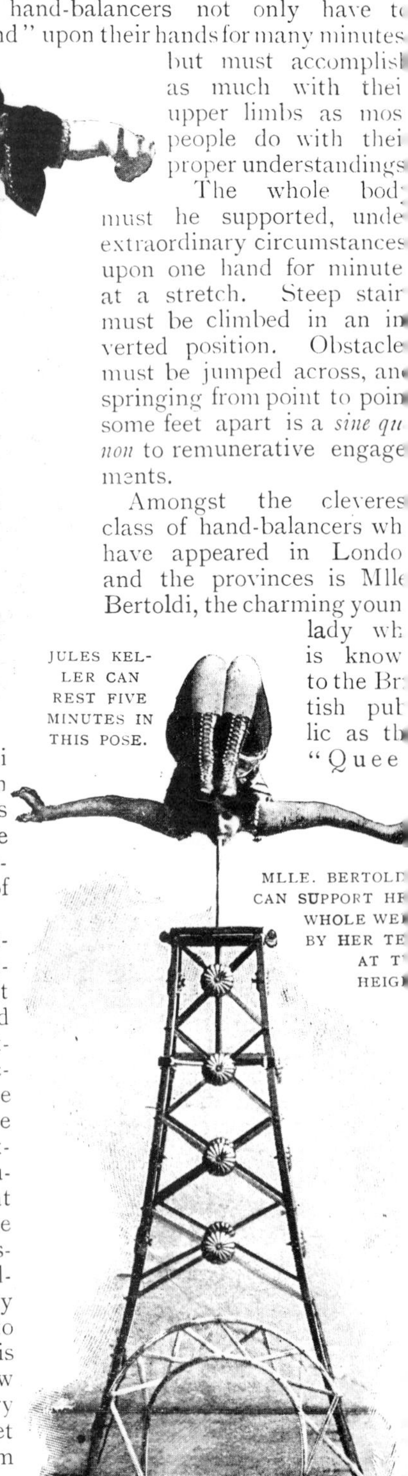

MLLE. BERTOLD CAN SUPPORT HE WHOLE WE BY HER TE AT T HEIG

f Equipoise." What she cannot do with er hands is not worth doing by the ordiary person's feet. From her cradle Mlle. Bertoldi has been a hand-balancer, for, ery early in her career, her nurse dropped er by accident (an unfortunate habit most urses are guilty of) head downwards. The ttle tot succeeded in saving herself from oncussion of the brain by landing upon er outstretched hands.

Since then Mlle. Bertoldi has developed marked tendency to see this world from different point of view to anybody else. At the age of six, one fine morning she stonished her parents by walking downtairs to breakfast upon her hands.

Mlle. Bertoldi informed the writer that he scarcely remembers when she was unble to use her hands as most people use heir feet. She can execute amazing novements in an inverted pose; waltz, valk up and down a flight of stairs, and ump over obstacles. As a hand-balancer doubt if she has an equal in the world; here is certainly no one who can, as she loes, climb a pedestal upon her hands, grip a slender silver bar between her teeth, and, without any other support whatever, balance herself head downward in various poses, finishing by iterally sitting on her own head and spinning apidly around, her only support still beng the small bit of silver bar between her eeth. No more wonderful balancing feat has ever been atempted.

Jules Keller is a hand-balancer of enormous strength of arm. Nature having cheated him of the proper use of his nether limbs, he seems absolutely at home upon his hands. He can rest quite five minutes in the pose shown in the photograph on page 212.

Another wonderful hand-balancer is Mons. Arras, one of the strongest-limbed men in the world. His chair acts are indeed so extraordinary that one would almost fancy that his hands and arms were made of tough steel; for, gripping the upper rail of a chair, he can turn and twist his body into several poses, always maintaining his balance under the most severe conditions.

His most striking acts are, first, to balance himself head downwards between two chairs: then, swinging his body over to an angle of 45 degrees, he raises the left chair in the air and maintains his pose for a considerable space of time.

Another act is the placing of two chairs seats downward, fixing a ladder

T. C Turner, Photo

MR. FREDERICK, THE SMARTEST LADDER BALANCER IN THE WORLD.

between the rungs of each, and lifting himself step by step upwards until the top rung is reached. These remarkable performances are shown on page 215.

Firing off a rifle and hitting a bull's-eye whilst balanced across a rifle standing muzzle downwards is yet another of Arras' smart acts.

T C Turner, Photo

MR. FREDERICK CAN BALANCE HIS LADDER STANDING ON ANY RUNG OF IT.

The billiard-cue balance, illustrated on page 212, is a very difficult feat. The performer lifts himself, head downwards, upon the cues, the points of which rest on the platform. I have seen Gerard, the strong man, accomplish this whilst he held a 112 lb. weight between his teeth!

Judging from the point of the ordinary spectator, perhaps the most wonderful of the various phases of balancing is ladder-climbing. Somehow one cannot grasp the possibility of a long ladder standing erect without any support beyond that given by the movements of someone who is mounting it. It is said that the feat is not so difficult to accomplish as other forms, but the eyes of the onlooker are bound to open pretty widely whilst witnessing this very extraordinary performance.

I have had an opportunity of closely watching a ladder climber and balancer accomplishing the feat, and I know that there is no trickery whatever connected with it. An ordinary ladder is used, and spectators may see for themselves that the whole performance from beginning to end is perfectly *bonâ fide*.

Mr. William Frederick's clever act has been seen by many thousands in London and the provinces, and it is his ladder-climbing ability that I am enabled to illustrate. He is regarded as one of the smartest ladder-climbers in the world. His exhibition is certainly one of the most wonderful I have seen. It can easily be realised, from the photographs reproduced here, how marvellously accurate the balancing must be.

Were the ladder to move an inch beyond the proper elevation, a very emphatic falling off would certainly ensue. Yet Mr. Frederick seems perfectly at home during his act, and not only does he climb to the topmost rung without any appearance of effort, but he actually sits down to play several tunes upon a mandoline which he has carried up with him, afterwards descending as easily as he climbed upwards.

It can easily be conjectured that this type of the balance wonderful demands the most careful and persistent practice. Mr. Frederick informed me that it has taken years of training to enable him to go through his "show" with the confidence which he now exhibits. Rung by rung, the climb upwards and necessary balance had to be acquired by the utmost patience and perseverance; and even now he never fails to practise every day as well as performing nightly.

Cycle-balancing has of late years reached a point which may justly be regarded as wonderful. One of the most striking effects is produced by the collection of a pyramid of riders upon one bicycle which is then propelled at full speed around a limited space, an angle so great sometimes being produced that one wonders how it is that a catastrophe does not happen. Balancing head downwards on the cycle saddle whilst the machine is moving fast is another act capable of making an audience "sit up," and when speed approaches the rate of fifteen miles an hour and the number of inverted passengers is increased to two, the audience is dull indeed that does not yield its full appreciation of the "show." Balancing upon the rear wheel and progressing at high speed thereon is another smart bit of work.

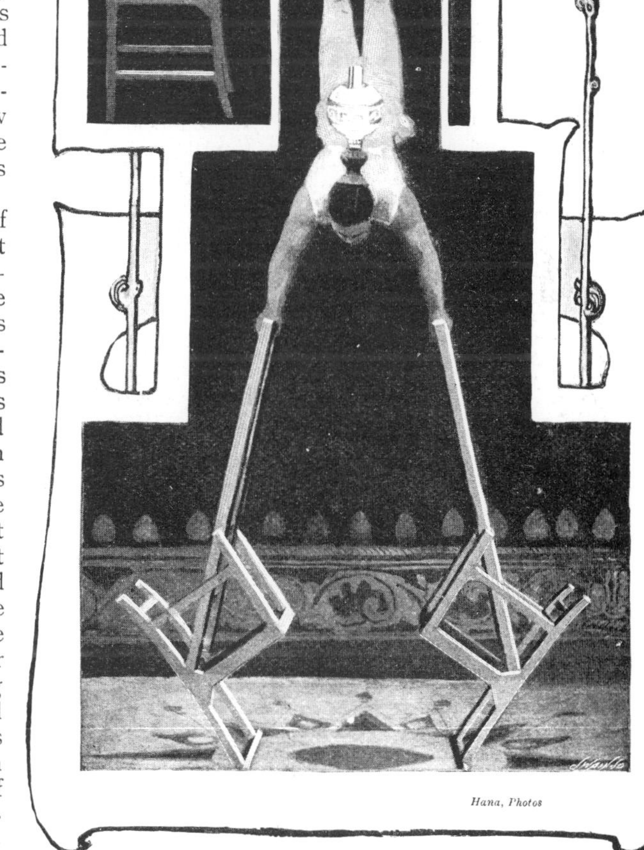

Hana, Photos

TWO REMARKABLE FEATS BY ARRAS, THE STRONGEST-LIMBED MAN IN THE WORLD.

The Kaufman family, the head of whom originally exhibited cycle trick riding in this country, are the most capable exponents of this particular branch of equipoise, and it is part of their remarkably clever performance we are enabled to reproduce from photographs.

Tight-rope walking at great heights is becoming less popular in public favour, to judge from the reduced number of persons who affect this mode of earning a living. I rather think a tight-rope performance is a trifle too sensational for the British public. Few people nowadays care to look at a tight rope walker who goes through various evolutions upon a wire stretched across a space 65 feet above the level of the floor or ground. One of the most daring artists in this direction is Mlle. Ella Zuila, who last year gave a series of performances at the Crystal Palace. Her 'show' was certainly sensational, but was a graceful illustration of the art. Walking on a wire stretched across the central nave of London's mighty glass-house, 65 feet from the flooring, Mlle. Zuila caused many a heart to jump. With her feet in baskets she was as daring on the rope as if on *terra firma*. Made up as an elephant, she guided an assistant across the long journey without a tremor.

EXTRA-ORDINARY BICYCLE BALANCING BY YOUNG KAUFMAN.

NEW METHOD OF BICYCLE RIDING BY THE BROTHERS KAUFMAN.

Cinquevalli is more of a juggler than a balancer, but some of his performances are really wonderful examples of equipoise, such as when he balances two billiard balls on the top of a cue, a feat which only requires a trial by the lay hand to prove its difficulty.

Head-balancing has recently made its appearance in London, and several exponents of the art are able to do some very wonderful things. In these acts the performers assume a head-to-head position, in which they walk upstairs, juggle, sing, and sometimes dance. The Meers Brothers are very smart at this work performed on a telephone wire, the eldest Meers' act of racing on a travelling wire being a sight worth seeing.

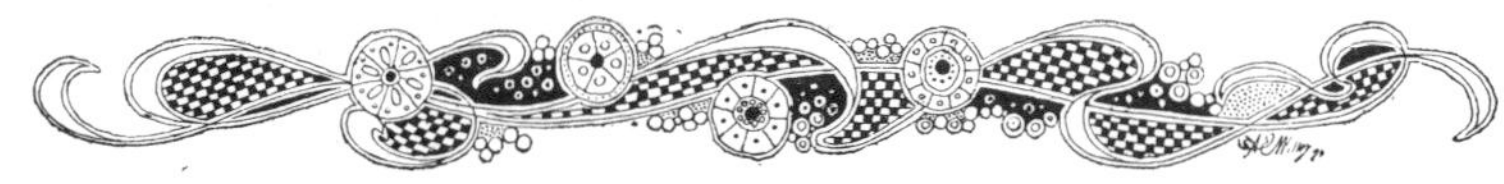

A HUMAN ALPHABET

By William G. FitzGerald.

E think we may fairly lay claim to the title of "Novelty" for this article. The idea of building up each letter of the alphabet and each figure from 1 to 0 out of the bodies of human beings is an absolutely unique "notion." All kinds of difficulties stood in the way of the successful accomplishment of the idea; and even when the very last figure was built up and photographed by our artist, there came the fear that, after all, the letters might not stand the test of contiguity—would not spell words when used as type. Now, we do not know whether printers would refer collectively to these letters as the "fount of life," but that the fears indicated above were groundless will be evident from the very title of the article itself, which is formed from our living letters.

We were extremely fortunate in our choice of "material." We selected the most intelligent and original trio to be found on the variety stage. These gentlemen are known as the "Three Delevines," and in the ordinary way they go through a quaint entertainment, which they call "Satanic Gambols." It will be seen that, throughout the whole of the alphabet and figures, the Delevines retain their diabolical uniform. We found them ideal men for the purpose—splendidly formed, highly intelligent, and full of helpful hints. Now, as to the method of obtaining the photographs. The letters and figures were built up separately and photographed in a special studio in the beautiful town of Plymouth. We will first give a few specimen letters reproduced on a large scale, and then the entire alphabet and numerical figures "in smaller type."

The A is remarkably simple. It would form an excellent design for a Christmas card, with seasonable greetings printed below. The men merely form an isosceles triangle, with the floor for a base and their heads for the apex. The crosspiece is simply formed by the men shaking hands and, as it were, whispering Christmas greeting. It is Messrs. Harry and Sam Delevine who form this letter.

The E, which is the next to be reproduced large as a specimen letter, is elaborate and strenuous. Few will doubt its claim to ingenuity. Mr. Percy Delevine may be called the backbone of the letter; he is the tallest of the three, and therefore will frequently he found doing duty in a similar capacity. Sam is creeping between his legs; and Sam's own shapely members form the

lower out-stroke of the letter. When this was done, Harry climbed upon Percy's shoulders and extended himself down his back; then stretching out his own legs and

arms in the way shown, the letter was triumphantly completed. It is rather a pity that Mr. Harry Delevine's body is so prominent, thereby making the upper part of the letter unduly thick. But what would you? It was quite unavoidable. Remember, the "bricks" out of which we built our letters are human beings, and occasionally a troublesome body or limb was very difficult indeed, if not impossible, to get rid of.

The letter K, which is next seen, is beautifully sharp and clear-cut. Mr. Percy Delevine is again the shank, while Sam is kneeling behind him in an attitude of touching devotion. Harry is kneeling on Sam's shoulders, and inclining himself back at a perilous angle. Poor Sam is looking towards our artist and protesting in a choked voice that "he can only stand it a moment or two longer."

The letter M, which is next shown, is a particularly fine specimen. This time we want the tall man in the middle. It was rather an onerous position, but Percy said he could do it on his head; and he did. On the left-hand side Harry Delevine is seen, wearing a quizzical expression. The right-hand support is his brother Sam. Notice how the feet of the outer men add to the appearance of the letter—a capital one in two senses. The unfortunate Percy was obliged to remain upside down for at least some twelve seconds. Almost simultaneous with the snap of the camera a groan burst from the interior anatomy of our M, and Mr. Percy Delevine righted himself, looking perfectly purple in the face. You should turn the M upside down and study his expression. He tried to smile, poor fellow.

The next letter reproduced large is P, which is at once simple and effective. Percy is again the long stroke, and he is holding Harry at his back in order to form the loop of the letter. It was perfectly marvellous, by the way, how still these gallant fellows kept, even under the most trying circumstances. Like a pair of Greek wrestlers, Sam and Harry form the greater part of the letter Q, which is next seen. In order to complete the circle with human material, Percy has extended himself from one pair of legs to another; and to form the tail of the letter he thrust his own leg out of the circle in a perfectly delightful manner.

We now give the whole human alphabet, from A to Z, together with numerals from I to cipher. We would venture to say that each and every one of these letters and figures will well repay careful individual study. Each one had first of all to be thought out and designed, then built up in a way which satisfied the author, and finally "snapped" by our artist, for the slightest movement of a head or limb altered the physiognomy of a letter in a surprising way.

A MERRY XMAS AND A HAPPY NEW YEAR TO THE READERS OF THE STRAND MAGAZINE

When the human components had so grouped themselves that the result really looked, even "in the flesh," like the letter it was supposed to represent, then the author gave the word "Go," and immediately afterwards, with a sigh of relief, the Three Delevines "stood at ease," wondering how on earth the next on the list was going to be formed. Neither time nor trouble was spared in the preparation of this most unique of alphabets. Observe that, while we *might* have inverted the M to form a W, we did *not* do so; and we think everyone will agree that the last-named letter was well worthy of being designed separately. Fortunately, these trained athletes could not only support heavy burdens, but could also remain perfectly still beneath them—a circumstance which contributed much to the success of the photos. *quâ* photos. In the case of the T, the posturing was particularly arduous, as Mr. Sam Delevine had to balance himself crosswise on the nape of Percy's neck, whilst both had to remain perfectly still and rigid for at least seven seconds.

Will it be believed that some of the letters and figures—notably O, S, Z, 3, and 5—we were almost on the point of abandoning in sheer despair? It was only by dint of trying one combination after another, and exercising a vast deal of patience, that we were enabled at length to get results which are, we venture to say, as satisfactory as could possibly be obtained, without the use of adventitious "properties." We would draw the reader's attention to the fact that the figure 9 is *not* an inverted 6. Every letter and figure received its full share of attention, and however much we were tempted to resort to makeshifts, we persevered until an independent satisfactory design was found and worked out.

After showing the whole of our human alphabet and figures, let us now turn to the building-up of words. The greeting which appears on the preceding page is one of the most extraordinary ever placed before the public. Here will be seen the splendid perfectness of finish which characterizes each letter and figure. We need not weary you by recounting the very technical details of the way in which we obtained duplicates. Only one set of originals was necessary. The greeting speaks for itself. We wish the merriest of merry Christmases to the readers of THE STRAND MAGAZINE all over the habitable globe, and we would gently impress upon them that the very letters which form our greeting are built up of sentient beings, each one glancing anxiously or merrily (according to the position he holds in the letter) towards the camera of our artist.

We next spell out in our human letters the name of a visitor whom every child in England is expecting with exceeding interest—good old "Santa Claus."

SANTA

CLAUS

The next experiment we tried with our living letters was to photograph them down very small and make them into a rhyming couplet—one which should have a seasonable lilt and swing. So successful is the result, that a sub-title or "translation" would be a work of utter supererogation. It will be seen that altogether our artist must have taken at least thirty-five separate photographs—twenty-six letters and nine figures. The letter O does duty for the cipher, by the way.

The next thing was to prepare sets of both alphabet and figures in various sizes. We were by no means sure that the letters would bear reducing, whereas it is a curious fact that the smaller they are brought down, the more perfect they become as letters. Observe the extraordinary human type in which each letter of the Christmas couplet is printed. Who shall say that our living letters must be kept large in order to be recognised? We marvel that no one has thought of a human

CHRISTMAS COMES BUT ONCE A YEAR
AND
WHEN IT COMES IT BRINGS GOOD CHEER

alphabet before—say, for advertising purposes. Eminent artists have been called upon to design posters, and authors of some standing have prepared commercial "puffs." We, too, have engaged "men of letters," but only to advertise the warm feelings which we entertain, more particularly at this festive season, towards our readers in all parts of the English-speaking world.

Our human alphabet may also suggest to hard-worked teachers of infants a novel way of imparting to little ones their letters; or, perhaps, a complete set might be reproduced upon a sheet and pointed out to the children. To others, however, we leave the potentialities of the thing. Perhaps some enterprising publisher would like to publish a whole novel in "living" type. Such a work might, or might not, command a huge sale; but, at least, there can be no two opinions about the human interest of the work.

The last greeting is appropriately enough "God Save the Queen," reproduced in the letters of our human alphabet. Now, our beloved Sovereign, in the course of her long and illustrious reign, has received an enormous number of addresses of congratulation and welcome; but we are under the impression that there is a killing sameness about these costly documents. The phraseology is usually bald and stilted, and the donors are often self-seeking bores. Would not the following be a highly original notion? Suppose the inhabitants of a certain place were about to present an address to the Queen, and that they wanted to strike out a new line for themselves. Very well. Why could not the leading men of the town form themselves into living letters of this kind, and so make up the wording of the address? They would at least be certain that their address possessed original points which Her Majesty could not overlook; and furthermore, they would bring themselves directly under the notice of the Queen, which, we take it, is an important consideration. However, we offer our own humble tribute, and we conclude our article with the sentiment that should animate every loyal Briton at the close of this year of Jubilee.

Foolhardy Feats.

I.—THE NIAGARA FOOLS.

BY GEORGE DOLLAR.

[*Photos. from Underwood & Underwood, Stereoscopic View Sellers.*]

THE ball started rolling in 1829, when Sam Patch erected a ladder on the footpath under Goat Island, and announced that he would jump into the Niagara River. The hotel-keepers patted him on the back, and left no stone unturned to draw the biggest crowd of the season. Patch rested the bottom of the ladder on the edge of the river, with the top inclining over it and staying it with ropes to the trees on the bank. At the top was a small platform, and from this Patch dived 97ft. He jumped again, and proved that the first feat was not a fluke. Then, having established a "record," he left Niagara, went to another place, jumped again—and got killed.

It is easy to brand such men fools. Any man, I take it, who puts his life in jeopardy, unless for heroic reasons, is a fool. Blondin was one, although he died in his bed at Ealing, and left behind him a reputation as the greatest tight-rope walker of his time. It was in 1859 that he first proposed to stretch a wire across Niagara River, and there was a unanimous howl of derision at the idea. At that time, people had no hesitation in ranking Blondin amongst the idiots, but they could not resist the temptation to see him throw his life away, and the crowd that gathered was the largest ever seen at the Falls.

BLONDIN COOKING AN OMELET OVER NIAGARA.

What Blondin did is now stale history. He got out on the rope with a 40lb. pole, crossed the river, and then came back again. He lowered a cord to the old *Maid of the Mist*, and drew up a bottle, from which he took a drink. Then, after some feats of balancing, he came ashore amid the huzzas of the crowd, and the whole country rang with the news of the exploit. A couple of months later he carried his manager, Harry Calcourt, across on his back. It is said, and it has also been denied, that on this occasion Blondin had a quarrel with Calcourt. The latter had previously been trained to balance himself in order that he might be let down on the rope in the middle of the river, while Blondin took a breath. The wind was strong, the manager's coat-tails began to flutter, and the rope swayed in a sickly manner. Then, according to the story, Blondin threatened to leave his manager on the rope, at the mercy of the waters underneath, unless he kept himself under control. Needless to say, the threat was successful, and the trip across was safely made.

A few days later the fearless Blondin again crossed the river, chained hand and foot. On his return, he carried a cooking stove, and made an omelet, which he lowered to the deck of the *Maid of the Mist* for consumption. At another time he crossed with a bushel-basket on each foot, and at another carried a lady on his back. In 1860 he performed before the Prince of Wales, the rope being stretched 230ft. above the rapids, between two of the steepest cliffs on the river. He turned somersaults before His Royal Highness and went through his whole repertory. He even managed to cross on a pair of stilts. But more wonderful than this special feat is the fact that for nearly seventy years he walked the tight-rope without accident. He had several narrow "squeaks," to be sure, but his record was clean.

After Blondin, the Deluge. The last thirty years has witnessed an unending procession of fools to Niagara, some of them to rival Blondin's feats, others to jump, and still others, with various *bizarre* ideas, to risk their lives in the attempt for mushroom glory. A man named Bellini jumped three times into the river in 1873, and in 1886 he climbed to the iron railing on the Upper Suspension Bridge, knocked the ice from

There has hardly been a year in which some tight-rope exhibition has not taken place at Niagara Falls. Some years ago a young fellow named Stephen Peere stretched a cable across and made several passages. In 1878 he gave variety to his career by jumping from one of the bridges, and in 1887 he finished it by leaping to his death. He left behind a reputation and a wire cable. The latter has been used by other gymnasts to save the expense of putting up a new rope. A man named De Leon went out to the middle of it shortly after, and getting frightened, came back to the bosom of his family. McDonell made several very creditable attempts, and proved himself an excellent walker. He went across with baskets on his feet, and frightened the gaping crowd by hanging with his legs from the wire, head downwards. Another freak named Jenkins, with an eye for effect, made the trip on a bicycle. The machine, however, was turned upside down, and had an ingeniously contrived balancing apparatus, in lieu of a pole, attached by a metal framework to the wheels. So the feat was not remarkable, after all.

MCDONELL CROSSING NIAGARA GORGE IN BASKETS.

under his feet to secure a footing, and at the signal of a pistol shot jumped into the air. He struck the water in four seconds, broke a rib, lost his senses, and came to the surface some 60ft. from where he entered. This was the same man who jumped from Hungerford Bridge in 1888 and was drowned.

JENKINS CROSSING ON A BICYCLE.

MCDONELL HANGING FROM THE TIGHT-ROPE.

On the same wire, Samuel J. Dixon,

DIXON CROSSING THE RAPIDS ON A ¾IN. CABLE.

a Toronto photographer, on September 6th, 1890, crossed the gorge, and gave an excellent equilibrist exhibition. One of his crack feats is shown in our illustration, which represents him as lying with his back on the wire. This was a ¾in. cable, and measured 923ft. in length. Dixon has made several other passages, always with great *éclat*.

It is marvellous how few accidents there are on the tight-rope at Niagara. The performers, with one accord and delightful *sang froid*, turn you away with a wave of the hand when you suggest fear.

"Tut, tut! my boy, it's nothing," they say, and look down upon you with contempt. Then, in a fraternal moment, they add, "You can't help getting across. You get out to the middle of the rope, and there you are! If you turn back you lose your money, and if you go on, you get it." That's all.

DIXON LYING ON HIS BACK.

One of the most remarkable feats was the trip of the *Maid of the Mist* through the rapids in 1861. This boat was built to make excursions at the foot of the Falls, but the business did not pay, and it was decided to sell her at Lewiston, some miles down the river. Now, be it known that the Niagara River, below the Falls, runs for some distance between two cliffs of solid rock. This part is called the Whirlpool Rapids, and at the end of the rapids, where the swift and surging current impinges suddenly against the left bank, is the noted whirlpool. It was through this that the *Maid* had to go. She was commanded by Joel Robinson, and she got through; but Robinson never tried the trip again. It is reported that he aged twenty years in appearance in passing through the mighty eddy, and he died a few years later, the first man to get through the whirlpool with a boat and his life.

The biggest of all the Niagara idiots are those who throw dummy men into the water above the Falls, just for the fun of the thing. Of course, the sight of a human figure going to his death is enough to stir a lump of steel to activity—and the number of soft-hearted people who have stood near the rapids throwing out ropes and hopes to a lump of stuffing can be counted by the dozens. It is bad enough to gaze at a live man risking his life for a handful of silver, but it is worse to make a jest of death.

The latest tight-rope exhibitions have been those of Charles S. Calverley, who is styled "The World's Champion." Calverley must have forgotten Blondin, for many of his feats are those which made the Frenchman famous nearly forty years ago. The wheelbarrow business, shown in our illustration, is certainly middle-aged, although it still remains as difficult to perform as it was in Blondin's day. But people never tire of it, and our illustration supports the statement that these same people will even do gymnastics themselves on the framework of a bridge in order to see other fools risk their lives.

CALVERLEY AND HIS WHEELBARROW.

A glance now at Signorina Maria Spelterini, and we have done with the tight-rope. Here she is with baskets on her feet—a dainty figure gradually forging her way to the middle of the rope. The performance brought out a tremendous crowd some years ago, probably because she was the first woman daring enough to try conclusions with Blondin and his many imitators. She got across safely with her baskets and her name, and for ever established the fact that a woman is as level-headed as a man.

SPELTERINI OVER THE RAPIDS.

On September 7th, 1889, Steve Brodie, who had achieved great notoriety by jumping from Brooklyn Bridge, created a greater sensation by going over the Falls. He wore an india-rubber suit, surrounded by thick steel bands. The suit was very thickly padded, yet Brodie was brought ashore bruised and insensible. His victories won, he now rests in New York City, the proprietor of a Bowery bar-room, and the pride of the neighbourhood.

The whirlpool boom was at its height when Captain Webb was killed, but the power of the waters in that deadly hole was first tested as far back as 1811. In that year, a dare-devil British soldier, who was logging near the whirlpool, got afloat on a log and was carried about in the pool for hours. He was finally saved, a wiser and a better man. Then came a long period of quiet, until the *Maid of the Mist* performed her record trip. In 1877 a man named Charles A. Percy got through in a life-boat. Not an ordinary life-boat, to be sure, for it had been especially constructed, and contained two air chambers, in one of which Percy hid himself. Elated by his success, Percy now made a wager with Robert W. Flack, of Syracuse, "for a race through the Whirlpool Rapids in their respective lifeboats for five hundred dollars a side." Flack's boat had no air cushions, and was

GRAHAM AND HIS BARREL.

partly constructed of cork. The race was set for August 1st, 1888, but on July 4th, Flack made a trial trip in the presence of an immense concourse of spectators. At first he went along gaily, but in three minutes his boat was upset and carried into the whirlpool bottom upwards. An hour later it was secured, and Flack's body, a mass of bruised flesh, was found strapped to the seat of the boat.

No lifeboat has since been tried, but several other attempts have been made to get through the whirlpool. Some of these have been successful. A burly Boston policeman, named Kendall, went through in a life-preserver, and several men have done it in barrels. At one time there was a perfect fever in the United States for shooting the rapids and whirlpool in a barrel, though what special honour is due to a man who shuts himself up in a specially-made barrel and goes through seething water, no one seems to know. At all events, Graham did it, and he got a "reputation" from it. His first trip was on July 11th, 1886. On August 19th of the same year he went again with two coopers of Buffalo, named Potts and Hazlitt. Then Mr. Potts and Miss Sadie Allen got into a barrel and performed the trip. The barrels are enormous affairs made of oak, and the voyage lasts about twenty minutes.

The bravest man of all, and yet a fool, was Captain Matthew Webb. He wore no life-preserver, and scorned a barrel, depending on his own strength and no accoutrements to put him through. The disastrous attempt took place on July 24th, 1883. He quickly disappeared from the view of the crowd, came up again, and then went down, sucked and tossed by the raging water. How far he went alive is not known, and several places are now pointed out by the guides where he was last seen. The body was recovered in four days.

The fools are gathered in below the whirlpool. It is an even chance that your body will not be found, but the ferrymen who ply between Queenston and Lewiston may be relied upon to pick you up if you are around. They are always on the look-out for "finds," particularly when it is known that some "crank" has jumped from one of the bridges or swum the whirlpool—and disappeared. Sometimes it is months before the body is found.

THE LAST MOMENT OF CAPTAIN WEBB.

Photo by London Stereoscopic Company, Regent Street.

MR. J. N. MASKELYNE.

THE GREAT WIZARD OF THE WEST

AND MORE MARVELLOUS MANIPULATORS

A building in the style of an ancient Egyptian temple was erected in Piccadilly in 1812, with the gods Isis and Osiris flanking the entrance. Originally built to house a collection of curiosities, the Egyptian Hall continued to display curiosities over the next 93 years, including Barnum's presentation of Tom Thumb in London, until it was demolished in 1905. Throughout the 64 years of Queen Victoria's reign it housed mystics and magicians, one of whom was to be resident for thirty years. His name was J. N. Maskelyne. The article that follows was written in 1894, 21 years after he moved into the hall. It shows the extent of his abilities, ranging from the exposure of bogus mediums to plate spinning; levitation to automata. 'Psycho', his most famous automaton, was a 22-inch-high, cross-legged, turbaned Indian figure, which could solve arithmetical problems, identify playing cards and even play whist. It is now in the Museum of London, while one of Maskelyne's less mystical inventions, a typewriter, is in the Science Museum.

Around the time of this article a magician called David Devant started to perform at the hall. Later to become Maskelyne's partner, he combined a passion for technical perfection with a natural manner of performing that made him a favourite with audiences and one of the greatest magical performers of all time. As can be seen in the articles included here, his skills were not confined just to magic.

Today Maskelyne and Devant are all but forgotten, certainly in comparison to another performer of the era, Houdini, the 'King of Handcuffs', who started performing in America aged 17 and first appeared in London, aged 26, in 1900.

THE GREAT WIZARD OF THE WEST.

MR. J. N. MASKELYNE AT THE EGYPTIAN HALL.

WITH the choice of three rendezvous, I deliberated whether I should pay my morning call at Nevil House—a pleasantly situated and commodious residence overlooking Battersea Park, which Mr. Maskelyne has built for himself, and where he is to be seen before 10 a.m.—whether I should accept his invitation to spend a Sunday at Spring Cottage, Bucklebury Common, in the bracing atmosphere of a lovely plateau between Reading and Newbury, and standing 500 ft. above the sea-level, at which spot Mr. Maskelyne seeks his Sabbath rest and recuperation; or whether I should call upon the subject of this interview during his working hours at the Egyptian Hall, where Mr. Maskelyne spends his mornings, in company with his son, either in the workshop or inventing scientific and mechanical problems and machines to supply commercial requirements.

For various reasons, I elected to pay my visit to the Egyptian Hall, where I was courteously received by Mr. Maskelyne in his cosy office, and where for upwards of an hour I enjoyed a most interesting and instructive conversation.

The man who holds the trickery of Conjuring, Card-sharping, Spiritualism, and Theosophy in the palm of his hand is of a genial nature. He is full of humour, apt of speech, and replete with quotation when occasion arises. Yet, in his quiet manner, you would scarcely suspect his possession of the lightning speed of sleight-of-hand, his quickness of eye in the detection of imposture, and his genius in all mechanical avocations. Perhaps his very demeanour is part of the art by which he conceals his art. His discoveries of imposture are all the more wonderful because, especially of late years, he has been handicapped by his public appearances. He has laboured constantly under the disadvantage of his personality being so well known that chicanery can never be brought to face him—impostors naturally refusing to meet him on any terms whatever. The laurels of his victories have sprung from his *modus operandi* of fighting trickery with weapons forged at the same smithy. The homœopathic principle "*Similia similibus curantur*," apparently, has been Mr. Maskelyne's prescription, although his cures have not been administered in at all minute doses. In effect he says: "The same phenomena you profess to produce by supernatural agency I can produce by the ordinary laws regulating Nature." Indeed, a knowledge of science makes an open book of so-called occultism, while it also explains its existence.

"You are an Englishman, Mr. Maskelyne, I believe, in spite of the fact that your name has a foreign ring about it?" I said, commencing our conversation.

"Oh, yes," he replied, "I am English to the backbone. I was born at Cheltenham in 1839, consequently I am fifty-five years of age. I am a member of an old Wiltshire family which can be traced back to the Conqueror—not that that is anything to be proud of. I suppose all our ancestors were robbers at some time or another; but, as somebody has said: 'It is as well to know that the robbers were so many generations back.' One member of my family, Dr. Nevil Maskelyne, held the post of Astronomer Royal for forty-five years, and was the first compiler of the 'Nautical Almanack.'"

"It would be interesting to learn who first instructed you in the art of conjuring?"

"Well, then, I never had a lesson in my life; to which fact I attribute the originality of my mysteries. For, instead of working in the old grooves and performing old tricks which I should have been taught, I set to work inventing tricks for myself. There were no Hoffmann's books of magic when I was a boy. The conjuring books at that time were frauds. They either explained nothing worth knowing or gave false explanations. I remember, as a boy, saving up my pence to buy a book which professed to explain the production of bowls of water containing goldfish from a shawl, and was disgusted to find it stated that the fish and water were carried in a belt round the waist, that the empty glass bowls were taken from the pockets under cover of the shawl and filled by means of a tap concealed under the waistcoat. At the age of sixteen I could give an hour's performance of sleight-of-hand and optical and mechanical illusions, using apparatus invented and constructed entirely by myself."

"You must have had a previous knowledge of mechanics to construct the apparatus?"

"Oh, yes, I had. You see at that time I was apprenticed to a watchmaker and jeweller. I believe I can trace my first desire to become a conjuror to watching Blitz—a popular entertainer in the forties and fifties—who was a friend of my father's, and he would frequently amuse us with tricks of sleight-of-hand. I have a vivid recollection, although my chin was not so high as the table at the time, of being taken in to see Blitz spin dessert-plates after dinner. I watched him with breathless astonishment, and when he had finished he patted me on the head, saying, 'What do you think of it, my little man?' I replied, 'I will do it too, when my fingers grow big.' And you see I have kept my word."

"It must be an exceedingly difficult feat. How long did it take you to become proficient?"

"I must have spent several years upon it altogether. I have practised it for eight hours a day months in succession. In fact, there is no feat of jugglery half so difficult, certainly none so elegant, and very few have had the patience to master it throughly. Like many other feats, the least difficult part appears most wonderful to the public. But I never allow that to influence me; there is more satisfaction to myself in accomplishing what is most difficult. For instance, if I set a large washhand-basin spinning, it creates much more applause than the manipulation of a seven-inch plate; yet the basin requires little or no dexterity — it will keep in motion a long time, and a dozen or more can easily be kept spinning at the same instant. A small plate, on the contrary, requires the most delicate touch, and will spin only ten seconds; consequently, it is impossible to keep more than five or six in motion at one time."

Here Mr. Maskelyne took up a cheese-plate and put it through the most extraordinary gyrations: making it walk, gallop, waltz, play see-saw, and dance a hornpipe.

Photo by W. Child, Leeds.

THE FAMOUS PLATE-SPINNING.

Resuming our conversation, he said: "I have devoted most of my attention to the production of optical and mechanical mysteries; in fact, I have not practised sleight-of-hand for more than thirty years. I observed when a youth that mechanical mysteries always created the most astonishment. For instance, when Houdin apparently threw a coin into the air, and the audience saw and heard it fall into a closed crystal box suspended over their heads, it created much more surprise than the most finished sleight-of-hand of Hermann. I allude, of course, to the original Hermann, who has been dead some years."

PIPE-REFLECTOR *IN SITU.*
From "Sharps and Flats."

At this point I asked Mr. Maskelyne if he did not think some of Houdin's tricks would be interesting if revived at the present day. To this he replied: "Certainly they would be interesting, inasmuch as they would show what was considered marvellous forty years ago, but they would not astonish anyone now. In Houdin's time electricity was in its infancy (indeed, he was the first to utilise it for conjuring), but its capabilities are so well understood nowadays that little effect can be produced by its aid. Houdin would hang a drum over the heads of his audience, and when by means of an electro-magnet and beater, concealed in the drum, it would rap out the names of cards and so on, the most profound astonishment was created. But in these days none but the merest yokel would wonder at such a trick. If I require to play drums by electricity, as I do with my electric orchestra, no attempt at concealment is made. The magnets and beaters are placed outside, and the public can see the sparks given off by the contact-breakers. No; Houdin's tricks would not draw sixpence now. We have gone a long way beyond them, in the natural course of evolution."

"I believe it is a popular idea that all your wonderful illusions are produced by the use of mirrors," I presently remarked. "Is that so?"

"Well, as a matter of fact, I have not employed any kind of mirror upon my stage for several years. It is true I have used them in every conceivable manner, and they are still used frequently in appearing and disappearing illusions at music-halls; but the audiences here are much more critical, being largely composed of persons who take an interest in mysteries. Therefore, mirrors are practically useless to me, for the merest tyro in optics can detect by the 'fit-up' the presence of looking-glasses the moment he glances at the stage, the drapery or decoration of which must necessarily possess a certain uniformity in order that the part reflected shall be the counterpart of that concealed by the mirror."

"Shall you ever introduce your wonderful automata again?"

"Yes. I think that will be the next change I shall make in my programme. I am at work upon 'Psycho' at the present time, making repairs and improvements in the mechanism. I was obliged to withdraw the automaton, not because it had ceased to interest the public, but because after four thousand consecutive performances the delicate mechanism—and it *is* delicate—required overhauling. Besides, I had a number of improvements to add which will make it infinitely more wonderful."

"I have heard it stated that the secret of Psycho has been discovered and published. Is that the case?"

"Indeed it is not! Some years ago an American journal put forward a pneumatic theory as a possible solution of the mystery. I at once offered a reward of £2000 to anyone who could produce an automaton capable of performing the same movements under the same conditions. I also offered a similar reward for a correct imitation of my sketching automaton, 'Zoe.' This challenge I advertised in all the principal newspapers throughout the world, but it has never been accepted, though it is still open. This fact in itself is a more than sufficient refutation of the statements repeatedly made by irresponsible busybodies. The late Richard A. Proctor took a great interest in Psycho. At first he was under the impression that there must be some intelligent midget concealed inside; but I quickly proved that to be impossible. Shortly before he died, Mr. Proctor replied to a correspondent that Psycho was a profound secret, and that none of the theories which had been suggested could account for the movements of the automaton. A great number of tricks and toys have been constructed and called 'Psychos' and 'Zoes.' I remember an amusing circumstance which occurred at the time I was advertising my £4000 challenge. Next to my advertisement in the *Era* appeared the following: 'Psycho for sale, exactly the same as Mr. Maskelyne's now performing at the Egyptian Hall, together with a dress-coat nearly new to fit a stout gentleman, price £8.' Psycho occupied me for upwards of two years in its construction, and I and my son have spent quite eighteen months upon improvements. In fact, Psycho when he next appears will perform miracles, and be the only genuine 'Mahatma' (of the Theosophical order of architecture) ever seen, except in the 'Astral Body.'"

"You appear to have your eye upon the 'Mahatmas' at present, and to be giving spiritualism a rest?" I asked, in reference to the latest "turn," entitled "Modern Witchery, or the Miracle of Lh'asa."

"Yes, I think spiritualism may now be left to drag on its dreary existence. It is impossible to stamp it out entirely. To this day I frequently receive letters from devotees. For instance, here are two letters I received quite lately. They are not long ones, so you may care to read them. 'You had better call Ruby,' said one. The other correspondent wrote, 'I have been informed by spiritualism that the recent horrifying impending catastrophe to the moon by Sirius, or a planet, was the work of the great poet, William Shakespeare. [Signed] A Lady.'

"You must bear in mind that spiritualism has always existed in one form or another, but as far as the general public is concerned it is as dead as a door-nail. No exposure of its frauds can excite the slightest interest, the majority regarding it as simply exploded humbug. In America, I believe, matters are in much the same condition. Only a few weeks ago the surviving 'Davenport Brother,' Ira, and Mr. Fay, attempted to revive the rope tricks in Washington. Mr. Fay, you must know, was an understudy who travelled with the brothers, and took the place of either of them who happened to be indisposed. After thoroughly advertising the revival, and obtaining a number of preliminary puffs in the Press, the receipts at the first performance amounted to only 11 dollars 50 cents. They were advertised for six nights, but they closed after the first performance, and their 'cabinet' was distrained on for rent. The famous 'Dr. Slade,' who created such excitement in London in 1876, and made so much money with his slate-writing, was recently taken to a workhouse in America, penniless, friendless, and a lunatic. Contrast this state of things with the palmy days of spiritualism, when Home and the Davenports hob-nobbed with princes and emperors, and received costly gifts from the hands of princesses and empresses. Surely it is a vain hope for Mr. Stead to attempt to revive this exploded imposture. In adopting spiritualism for business purposes, I think he has made a very grave mistake. Certainly, he does not confine his business to spiritualism alone, but appeals for support to Theosophists, hypnotists, clairvoyants, crystal-gazers, thought readers, faith-healers, astrologers, and a host of other impostors and their eccentric followers, who are blindly wandering on the borderland of insanity."

"I suppose you have met Mr. Stead?"

"Oh yes, more than once. When Mr. Stead first commenced his investigations in spiritualism, he appealed to me, through a mutual friend, to assist him, which I willingly consented to do. He was then holding *séances* with Mr. Eglinton, who was formerly a 'materialising medium'; but having been frequently detected in fraud, had turned his attention to the less risky business of slate-writing. Mr. Stead had been successful in witnessing, alone with Eglinton, such startling manifestations that he suggested a *séance* should be arranged to which I and a mutual friend should be invited; but Eglinton flatly refused to meet me under any conditions whatever. The next best thing for me to do, then, was to suggest certain safeguards against imposture, which Mr. Stead adopted, but although he sat with Eglinton for hours, not a ghost of a letter was written under those conditions. I will show you one of the tests I arranged," said Mr. Maskelyne, as he turned to a cupboard, and took down from an upper shelf what

THE DISCOVERY OF KEPPLINGER'S TRICK.
From "Sharps and Flats."

appeared to be a flat tin box. Continuing, he said—

"One of the things which slate-writing mediums profess to accomplish is to write answers to questions upon slates securely locked up in a case, with a fragment of slate pencil inclosed. Therefore, I procured two small slates, upon one of which I wrote a question. The slates were then screwed together, with a morsel of slate-pencil between them, and then put into this tin case, which I soldered up as roughly as possible, leaving marks from the soldering-bolt which it would be impossible to reproduce, and which were photographed. I sent this case to Mr. Stead, desiring him not to let Eglinton know that it came from me, but to tell him that if he could get an answer written inside, it would be of the greatest possible advantage to spiritualism, and would make a convert of a great antagonist who had promised to proclaim the result to the world. Eglinton was to be allowed to take the slates home with him and keep them as long as he pleased. He promised to do so, but he ultimately refused to have anything to do with the test. I have suggested dozens of similar tests for other people, but always with the same result. Subsequently, Mr. Stead arranged with my son to photograph a spirit under conditions which would preclude the possibility of trickery. To this end, Mr. Stead endeavoured to find a medium of unimpeachable character, but was informed by the spiritualists that they only knew of one—a lady who had left for Australia, and therefore was not available. Some months afterwards, I received a letter from Mr. Stead saying that he

Photo by London Stereoscopic Co., Regent Street.

MR. NEVIL MASKELYNE.

had met with a wonderful materialising medium, and desired that we should attend to photograph a spirit at a *séance* to be held the next day; but, as usual, the next post brought the information that the medium had been taken ill, and the *séance* was postponed. Since then the camera and accessories have been constantly in readiness, but we are still waiting."

"It would be interesting to know how you first began to suspect the *bonâ fides* of spiritualism?"

"Well, I will readily tell you that. The first awakening of my interest in the exposure of spiritualistic frauds arose in

APPARATUS FOR TABLE-RAPPING.

this way. It was during my apprenticeship. Adjacent to our place of business there resided a man and woman who professed to effect cures by mesmerism. About that time table-turning became a fashionable amusement, and the Fox family had startled America by a second edition of the 'Cock Lane Ghost.' Well, these mesmerists commenced to hold spiritualistic *séances*, and one day the woman brought to our shop what she called a surgical appliance to be repaired. It consisted of two levers, a long one and a short one, each mounted upon a pivot attached to a strap, and connected by a piece of catgut. I will make you a sketch of it. As you may suppose, I entirely failed to see what kind of surgical appliance this thing could be, and was curious to discover its real use. Having repaired it, I devoted a few minutes to experimenting with it, and found that by buckling the strap of the short lever round the left ankle, and that of the long lever round the leg just below the knee, by pressing the right heel upon a projection at the side of the short lever the long one could be jerked up and made to strike the under side of a table. Accordingly, I booked it as a table-rapping apparatus, and the bill was sent in: 'Repairs to table-rapping apparatus, 1s. 6d.' This I considered very sharp on my part at the time, but it was about the worst thing I could have done, as it prevented a complete exposure of these impostors being made. Although several persons, at my suggestion, attended the *séances* afterwards, with the object of catching the lady red-handed, no table-rapping was ever attempted. This was a lesson by which I profited greated in my subsequent investigations."

"Of course you have no belief in apparitions, Mr. Maskelyne?"

"None whatever. I am certain that, apart from mere ordinary objective illusion, they exist only in the imagination. The great proof of this is the question of clothes. If spirits appeared, like some of the 'living pictures,' apparently in the nude, one might be inclined to believe in their reality. I believe I was the first to suggest this objection, about thirty years ago. I was having a discussion with Mr. Benjamin Coleman, surnamed 'The Father of English Spiritualists," a very nice, amiable, and credulous old gentleman. He was describing a *séance* he had attended and where a lady saw the spirit of her grandfather. She had never seen him in earth-life, but recognised him from a painting. The spirit appeared in periwig, knee-breeches, and a green coat with gilt buttons. 'Then,' said I, 'this lady not only saw the spirit of her grandfather, but also the spirit of his green coat and gilt buttons!' Mr. Coleman looked at me with rather a puzzled expression. I continued: 'Do you really believe that there is such a thing as the spirit of a coat?' 'No,' said he, 'I can't think that, and I can't account for the appearance of the clothes, but I will ask the spirits.' The old gentleman told me afterwards that he had consulted 'Katey King' upon the subject. Katey King, as you may remember, was a very popular spirit at that time, so much so that she was frequently known to have appeared at several *séances* at the same moment. She was also the spirit who was said to have carried Mrs. Guppy from Balls Pond to Lamb's Conduit Street, and it was the exposure of this spirit which sent poor Robert Dale Owen to a lunatic asylum. Well, Katey King shirked Mr. Coleman's question for some time, but he persisted in having an answer, and at last she replied, 'Why, of course, we materialise the clothes out of particles in the atmosphere.' This was a perfectly satisfactory explanation to the spiritualists, but even the most credulous members of the Society for Psychical Research cannot at present believe in the ghost of a pair of breeches. If they could, they would at once accept every nightmare story as a spiritual visitation. That cunning old impostor, Madame Blavatsky, tried to bridge over this difficulty by inventing the theory that there is an 'astral body' or counterpart to everything in existence and everything that has existed. So there must be an astral sea-serpent, an astral big gooseberry—in fact, an astral world and an astral universe."

"By the way, speaking of Madame Blavatsky, are there really any such persons as Mahatmas?"

"Certainly there are—but not of the Theosophical or occult type. A Mahatma is any person of superior attainments, nothing more. How we should smile if we heard of a Thibetan asserting that our professors of Oxford and Cambridge possessed occult powers! Yet that is precisely the position of the Theosophists with reference to the 'Mahatmas' of Thibet."

Leaving the subject of occultism, we then conversed upon the revelations

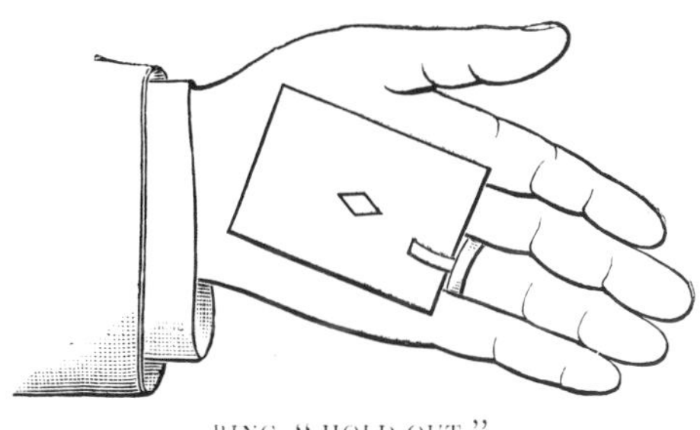

RING "HOLD-OUT."
From "Sharps and Flats."

contained in Mr. Maskelyne's book, "Sharps and Flats." This is unquestionably a work of absorbing interest, and I expressed some curiosity with regard to the appliances for cheating described therein. One of the most exciting incidents detailed in "Sharps and Flats" (Longmans) by Mr. Maskelyne is the discovery of the Kepplinger "hold-out." The *dénouement* is illustrated by a picture which is reproduced herewith, but the story must be read in its entirety to be fully appreciated. Turning to his cupboard, Mr. Maskelyne produced a variety of most

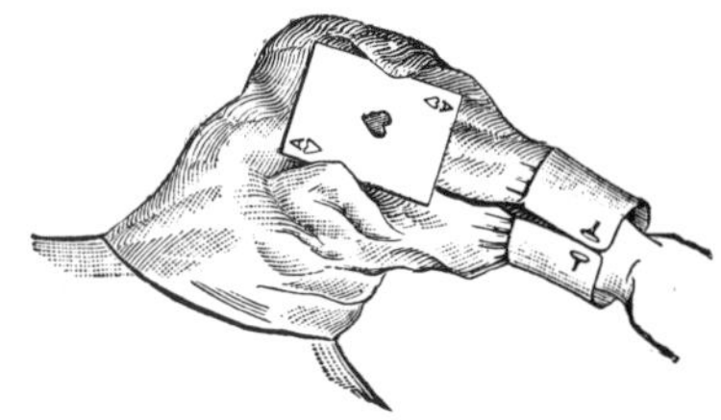

SHOWING CARD HELD UNDER THE ARM.
From "Sharps and Flats."

beautifully finished instruments, every one of which had been bought in the open market, and had been manufactured expressly for the purposes of cheating. There were "hold-outs," whose mission is to secrete any required cards until they can be advantageously employed in the game; there were minute reflectors constructed for the purpose of being concealed below the table, in pipes, snuff-boxes, and toothpicks, and thus enabling the dealer to obtain a surreptitious knowledge of the cards dealt; there were recipes for card-stains, and instruments for marking cards either before or during play; there were marked cards of every description, which told to the initiated the value and suit of every card in the pack—in fact, there were appliances of every kind that the "sharp" could desire. Loaded dice of the most finished construction were put into my hands, and I examined with interest the internal arrangements of the "Electric" variety. Mr. Maskelyne also explained to me so many sleight-of-hand dodges for cheating with a pack of cards that I felt quite convinced that the opportunities for cheating are far more numerous than anyone—including the "fly flat"—has any idea of. It would seem almost impossible that such mechanical contrivances should exist in our midst, did one not know that these things are extensively sold in America and are used—well, pretty nearly in every big city in the world. We give a few illustrations of some of these fraudulent devices, and can only remark, with Mr. Maskelyne, "Suspect your best friend if he is a gambler."

Pointing to an elegant machine which stood upon the table, I asked if that was the famous Maskelyne Typewriter.

"Yes," said Mr. Maskelyne; "that is the joint invention of myself and my son. Indeed, my son is responsible for the major portion of the invention. I arranged the differential spacing device which so many mechanicians have tried to accomplish, but this is the first successful machine with varied spacing."

At my request, Mr. Maskelyne gave me a demonstration of the working of the machine, which proved most interesting. The type-bars are on the top of the machine, and when the keys are operated they look like so many grasshoppers jumping with lightning rapidity from the ink-pad upon which they rest to the paper, and producing most beautiful work resembling letterpress. There are no crowded "M's" or "W's," or straggling "I's" or "L's" like rows of dilapidated railings stretching across the landscape, but each letter has its proper space, and the work is in full view of the operator, every character being seen the moment it is printed.

From his rich storehouse of facts, Mr. Maskelyne evidently could have prolonged this interview indefinitely, but the sound of rushing footsteps up the stairs announced the fact that it was half-past two, and that a crowd of people was fast filling the cosy little "Home of Mystery," anxious to witness one of the most attractive programmes Mr. Maskelyne has ever arranged for his patrons—the playlet "Modern Witchery," evidently founded upon the conversion of Mrs. Besant to Theosophy, and smartly written by Mr. Nevil Maskelyne, being the *pièce de résistance*. It is bristling with sarcasm, and not only exposes the frauds, but also holds up to ridicule the weak points and gross follies of this new cult. At the same time, it is made the vehicle for the introduction of two of the most inexplicable wonders ever seen in this or any other age. One is called "The Miracle of Lh'asa." An Indian attendant is bound upon a plank which rests on the backs of two chairs, and is covered over with a shawl, a flaming goblet being placed beneath. In the full light of the stage the plank, with its living burden, is seen to rise into the air, the chairs are removed, and a sword is passed completely round and about, thus proving the absence of any tangible support.

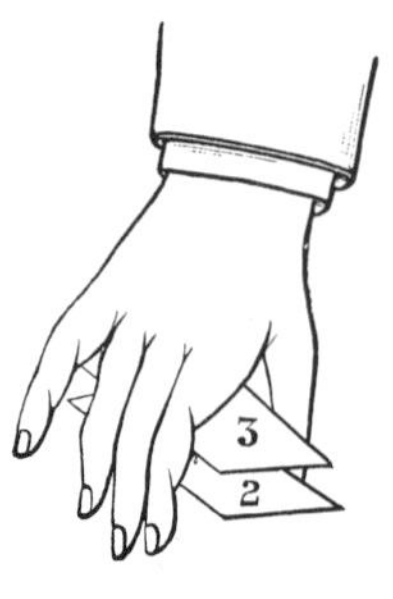

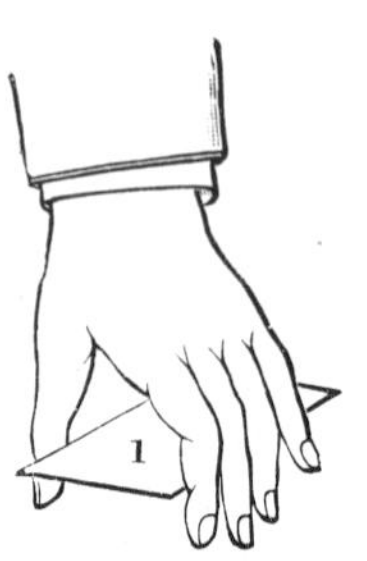

1 2 3

THE THREE-CARD TRICK.
From "Sharps and Flats."

I also went into the Hall with the hope of finding out how the illusion—which Mr. Maskelyne admits is a mechanical one—is effected, but the performance seems to me to increase in marvel the more often one witnesses it.

T. HANSON LEWIS.

Hand Shadows.

By Bernard Miller.

T is not too much to say that this pastime is as universal as light itself. The Chinese practised it thousands of years ago; and it flourishes at the Egyptian Hall to-day. That there is money in shadows, as well as in more substantial commodities, will be testified by Mr. David Devant, the eminent *ombromaneur*, who is depicted at work in the first photograph reproduced here (Fig. 1). The apparatus is not elaborate—merely a powerful arc light of 2,000 candle-power, whose beam passes through a small circular opening on to a sheet of ticket-writer's holland. Occasionally some little property—a pipe, a piece of cardboard, or what-not — is used for adventitious effect; but for the most part the "artist" uses his hands simply and solely. What is more, the arc lamp can be dispensed with, and almost equally amusing results produced by the aid of a clothes-horse, a sheet, and a candle. If an oil lamp is used, care must be taken to turn it so that the edge of the flame is towards the sheet; otherwise the shadows will be blurred and hazy.

Mr. Devant on one occasion actually gave his shadowgraphic entertainment in the dazzling glare of a noon-day sun, the figures being produced on a sheet spread on the lawn at a fashionable garden-party; much manœuvring was necessary, however. Also, he has done without a sheet altogether, projecting the shadows direct on to a wall.

No one who has not actually seen a professional entertainment of this kind can form an idea of the amusement that may be derived from these hand shadows. Of course, the pictures largely depend for their effect upon incessant movement; yet so cleverly are the figures rendered, that even this series of "still" photographs bears powerful testimony to the skill of the artist.

FIG. 1.—BEHIND THE SCREEN: MR. DEVANT AT WORK.

The "British bulldog" (Fig. 2) is a capital example of unaided hand-work. His ferocity on the screen is extraordinary. He advances threateningly, albeit with the unsteady gait of his kind; and his terrible eye rolls in fear-some style by a truly ingenious finger-tip movement on the part of the shadowgraphist. As Mr. Devant's hands enter the illuminated disc they are quite separate, all the fingers being extended. The operator then proceeds dexterously to "mould" his subject, but in such a manner that all may behold the clever

FIG. 2.—"THE BRITISH BULLDOG."

evolution of the figure. The placing of the hands and the disposition of each finger are swiftly seen by an intelligent audience, who appreciate this method far more than they would the instantaneous appearance of perfect figures.

Before preparing this article, we approached the two great shadowgraphists in this country—Mr. David Devant, of the Egyptian Hall, Piccadilly, and M. Trewey, who, at the moment of writing, is conducting an entertainment at the ever-popular Crystal Palace. M. Trewey is a veteran entertainer, who has travelled the world over, and he was the first to produce elaborate hand-shadow *séances* in England. Both these gentlemen assure us that the illustrations reproduced in these pages are the very first *photographs* of shadow pictures that have ever been really successful. Obviously, the entertainment is one that does not favour the camera.

But to proceed. In Fig. 3 we have a singularly ingenious representation of a swan, no "property" of any kind being used — unless one so describes Mr. Devant's own head. Of course, that same head *is* a valuable property — quite a gold mine, in fact, by reason of the paying notions that have their origin therein. The photograph scarcely requires explanation. The stately bird, here shown, well maintains its ancient and familiar traditions. The long, graceful neck comes back in sinuous curves that the plumage (Mr. Devant's hair) may be preened and pecked; and the stiff little tail waggles in pleasurable anticipation as the swan dives beneath the surface of the supposed lake. Finally, the bird sails out of the disc by the simple process of Mr. Devant inclining himself gradually forward. He tells us, by the way, that he has spent many hours feeding the swans in Kensington Gardens and elsewhere, not so much out of benevolence as from a desire to take mental notes of the attitude and general demeanour of the swan in her native element.

From this it will be seen that in these shadowy figures, as well as in more ambitious pictures, extraordinary attention is given to detail. Indeed, the thing is an art; the faintest movement of a finger altering an expression, and the imparted motion giving an amazing amount of appropriate realism to each subject. Figs. 4 and 5 admirably illustrate this — although, of course, the ceaseless motion is absent. The first of these is supposed to represent the working-man of the demagogic, or tub-thumping, order. Plainly, he is not an amiable person; ignorance, obstinacy, and truculence are writ

FIG. 3.—HOW THE SWAN IS FORMED.

large in his silhouetted profile. Nevertheless, with his pipe he is fairly content — still grumbling and "viewy," of course; but, on the whole, comparatively good-tempered. Now observe that suspicious angle in the pipe where the stem meets the bowl; it is a "trick" pipe, and our friend's soothing smoke is about to be interrupted. In Fig. 5 the accident has happened—the bowl has fallen off. Surely this is a shadowgraphic triumph, which can in some measure, at least, be appreciated, even in the photos. Look at the swift change of expression from comparative placidity to fierce disgust and (probably) blasphemous imprecation. Interesting to relate, Mr. Devant had a typical sitter for this admirable incident.

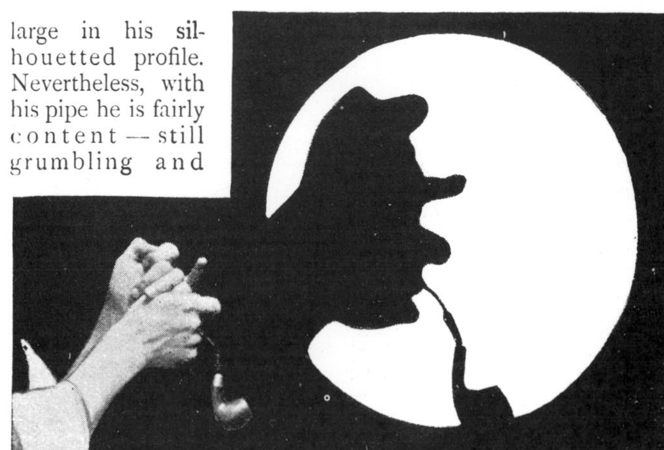

FIG. 4.—"COMPLACENCY."

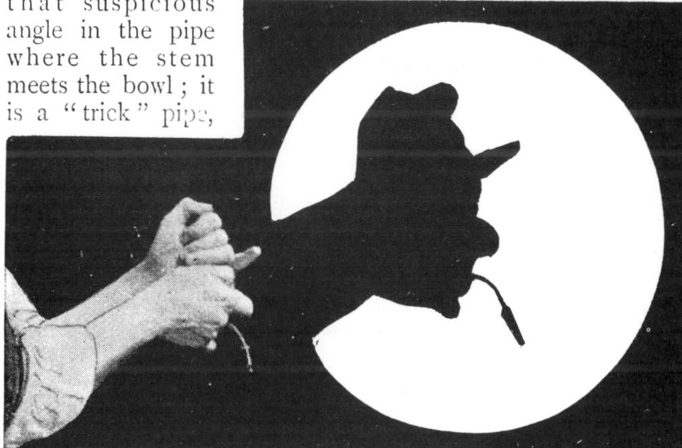

FIG. 5.—"MALEDICTION."

Turn we now for a moment to M. Trewey, whose capital bull is shown in Fig. 6; this, as you may see, is a wholly unassisted hand shadow. When about to produce a new figure, M. Trewey takes a seat between his light and the screen, and then commences to practise patiently and persistently, introducing tentatively delicate little lines here and there, and trying various motions that he has previously noted mentally while studying the living prototype. Sitters, it should be said, are not always complaisant towards the shadowgraphic artist. Take the figure just shown, for example. The original of that bull was an aggressive customer, who spent most of his time in browsing on the uplands of the Haute Savoie. M. Trewey was one day observing the handsome animal, unaware that the latter was also observing *him*. The story is not long. The bull resented the whole business and charged. He charged far more heavily than an ordinary human model would, so that what with damaged clothes and person and shattered camera, M. Trewey found the bull a costly sitter.

These shadowgraphists have pupils. Fathers of large families pay Mr. Devant eight guineas for a course of ten lessons in the art, that they may amuse their wives and offspring during the long winter evenings. Mamma cuts out and

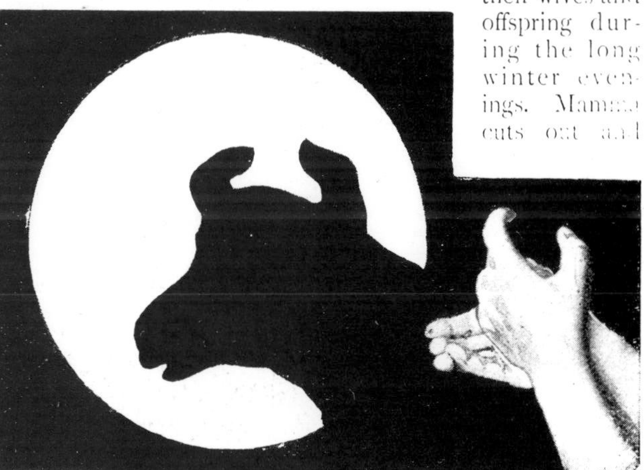

FIG. 6.—THE BULL.

FIG. 7.—A SHADOW PORTRAIT OF THE QUEEN.

hems the sheet, while daddy gesticulates strangely in the endeavour to portray new figures of his own invention. M. Trewey's most interesting pupil was an enterprising dentist, who wanted to learn shadowgraphy in order to beguile timid children whilst he removed their offending molars. Then clergymen take a few lessons that they may not be outshadowed, as it were, at parochial tea-parties by the efforts of amateur entertainers. Even lunatic asylum officials have been among Mr. Devant's pupils.

Trewey is a wonderful old veteran, as full of fun as his own entertainments; which is saying much. Amazing as the statement sounds, he can make anything with his hands, from a monarch to a mill-wheel. With becoming gravity and reverence we here reproduce M. Trewey's shadow portrait of our own venerable Queen (Fig. 7). Her Most Gracious Majesty's nose will, we fear, cause some regret among loyal subjects; evidently the artist's knuckle protruded a little too much. It must be admitted, however, that portraits of eminent personages produced in this way are absolutely unique. What is more, many of these portraits are transformation portraits, one changing into another in sight of the audience, but yet not so quickly that the various motions are indistinct, or untraceable by the keen-eyed. As a rule, M. Trewey uses a cloak with which to cover his wrists and forearms when producing portraits; this does away with undue slenderness of neck in the figures. Figs. 8 and 9 represent respectively (and respectably too, considering) Mr. Gladstone and Lord Salisbury. The Conservative leader looks somewhat cynical, while the immortal Hermit of Hawarden has a firm, purposeful appearance. As a matter of fact, M. Trewey made his notes and sketches for this portrait during Gladstone's last speech in the House—the impassioned attack on the House of Lords.

Talking of these transforming "finger photos.," there is a certain appropriateness in the G.O.M. swiftly giving place to Lord Salisbury. Only, in this case, one can see at a glance how it is all done; there is no diplomatic concealment, every movement being visible. Occasionally, some little article or "property" is required to complete a portrait. In the case of the Queen, the artist's fingers are so taxed to form the head and face, that there are none left for the necessary crown;

FIG. 8.—THE G.O.M.

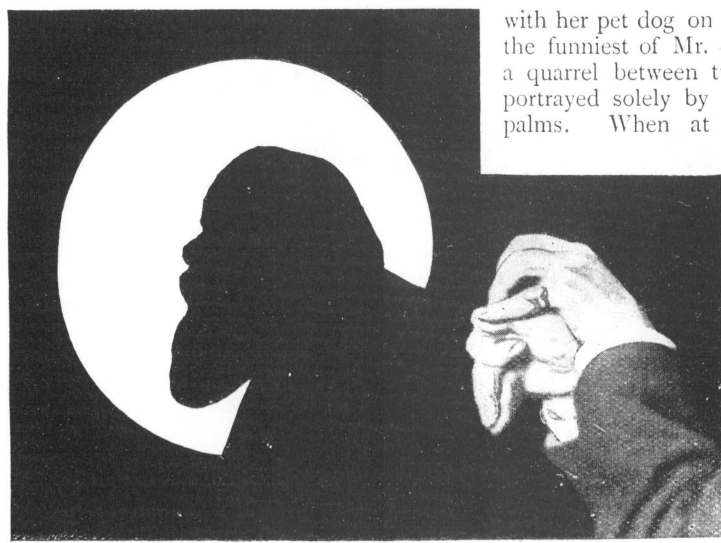

FIG. 9.—LORD SALISBURY ON THE ALERT.

therefore the regal emblem has to be portrayed by means of a piece of cut cardboard. In the Gladstone portrait, the only "property" necessary is something which will indicate the peak of the familiar collar. Strange as it may sound, Lord Salisbury figures without "property" of any sort, the well-known beard being produced in a remarkably ingenious fashion by the fingers of one hand extended downwards.

One of the most effective of these shadow portraits is that of our premier actor, Sir Henry Irving (Fig. 10). The long hair is very cleverly indicated, while a slightly protruding finger-tip produces on the sheet the effect of the *pince-nez*. Of course, as we have remarked before, hand-shadow pictures cannot be judged when stationary. For each and every one of them is designed a certain marvellously appropriate movement: and even the great personages whose portraits appear on the disc are made to exhibit some mannerism or characteristic whereby they are known.

Mr. Devant was on one occasion giving his shadowgraphic performance in the famous subterranean saloons at Welbeck Abbey; and the Duchess of Portland was present with her pet dog on her knee. Now, one of the funniest of Mr. Devant's scenes depicts a quarrel between two big dogs, which are portrayed solely by the operator's own two palms. When at length these shadowy animals were depicted at it tooth and nail on the sheet, Her Grace's pet could no longer resist joining in the excitement.

"That little dog," remarked Mr. Devant, "howled and barked with all the vigour it could muster. Evidently it was backing one or other of the combatants, or perhaps it wanted to have a hand—or rather a tooth—in the fight. At any rate," added the popular entertainer, "I considered the incident one of the sincerest and most unique compliments I ever received."

Talking about pupils, the first exercise given to the aspiring amateur is working the fingers in various directions. When the fingers are completely independent of one another (and it is no easy matter to make them so), the hands are considered sufficiently supple to commence upon the simpler figures, such as a rabbit, an elephant, and so on. Thereafter, Mr. Devant considers that it takes an hour's lesson to render the pupil proficient in each "advanced" picture.

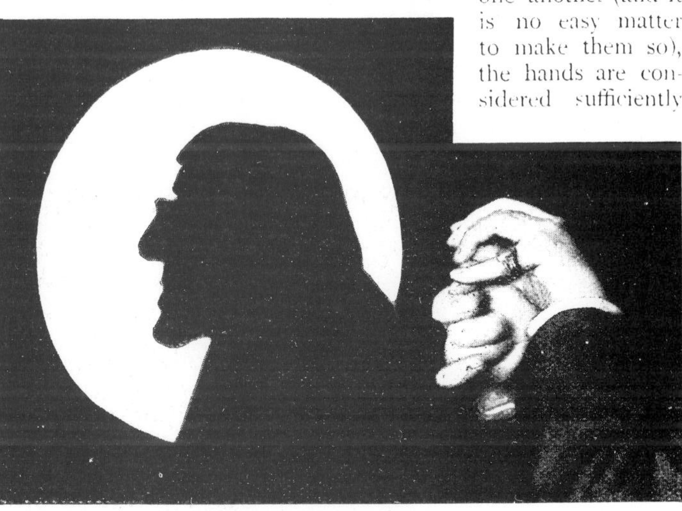

FIG. 10.—SIR HENRY IN A SMALL PART.

The goat (Fig. 11) is a very successful shadow, which on the screen exhibits a praiseworthy degree of contrariness and cussedness. You recognise the goat who will walk into your front garden and devour all the geraniums as a kind of *hors d'œuvre*, taking the open door as an *entrée* to daintier things out the back. Notice the uncompromising horns and the contemplative beard, which nods comically to and fro on the screen.

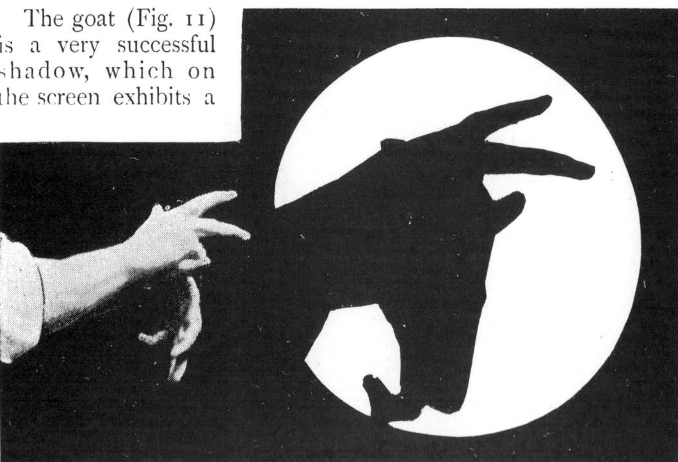

FIG. 11.—THE GOAT.

The close finish of a hotly-contested Derby is shown in Fig. 12. Of course, these photographs tell their own tale of cleverness and ingenuity, but we cannot help drawing attention to this shadow picture. The noble steed, though obviously handicapped by a big head (M. Trewey's extensive palm), is evidently straining every nerve to respond to its jockey's imperative demand. Observe the set purpose in the intelligent face, the erect ears, and the slender neck which speaks of proud pedigree. And that jockey! Why, he seems actually sobbing with ill-suppressed excitement. He is leaning forward to exhort his gallant horse to another spurt, and the whip is conspicuous by its absence. Truly a thrilling moment!

Turning to Fig. 13, a holy calm settles upon us. We are transported from the vitiated atmosphere of the race-course to the sacred precints of the church. The reverend gentleman is in the middle of an earnest discourse; you can

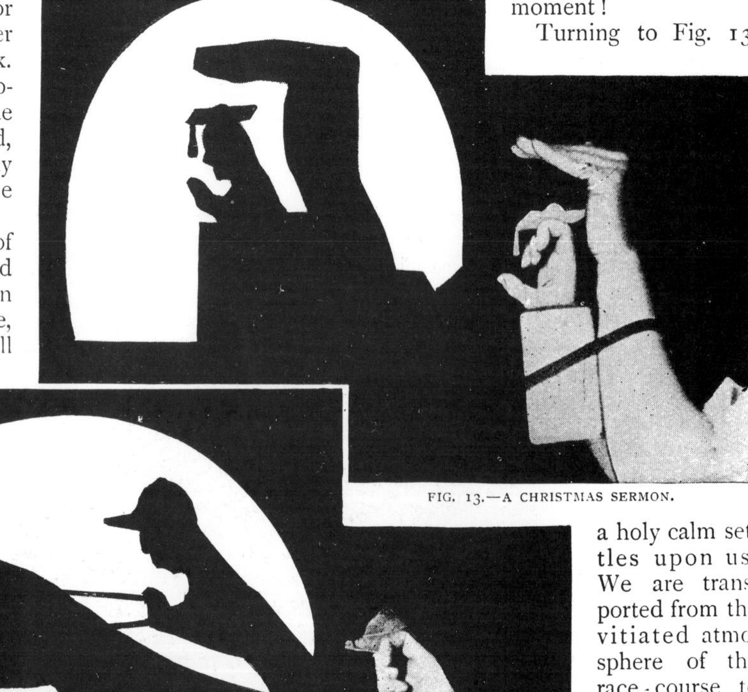

FIG. 13.—A CHRISTMAS SERMON.

FIG. 12.—A DERBY FINISH.

FIG. 14.—DRESSING FOR A PARTY.

see that he is advising his flock to have nothing to do with book-makers—that he is warning his people to mend their ways and turn their gaze heavenward. At the same time we may point out that if he obeyed this last injunction himself, his benignant eyes would encounter M. Trewey's monstrous fist, which not only does duty as sounding-board, but also forms the back of the pulpit. The body of the pulpit, by the way, is formed by a piece of wood or cardboard fastened to the operator's wrist.

But the world is full of change, and another turn of the artist's hand carries us away to femininity and vanity. Consider for a moment Fig. 14, which depicts a young person of little refinement immersed in the mysteries of the toilet. The properties here used are: (1) a piece of cut cardboard on which coarse wool has been fastened; (2) a few hairpins; (3) a pair of curling-tongs; and (4) another piece of cardboard which casts the shadow of the mirror of a dressing-table. The lady's face and somewhat spare neck are formed by the hands of the shadowgraphist. The pantomime gone through is amazingly effective. The lady is very much in earnest; evidently it is a toilet with a purpose. The hair is gradually curled, the hairpins placed in position one by one, so as to support an artificial dab of wool, which represents, we believe, a "bun" unknown to confectioners. All this, with many delicate, inimitable touches; a look in the glass now and then; expressions of alternate disappointment and delight, and final movements of triumph that are simply irresistible.

If anxiety and grim determination are manifested in Fig. 14, the next photo. (Fig. 15) shows unmistakably a complacent survey through a pair of "property" lorgnettes. Now and again during this wonderfully funny dumb pantomime the lady's enormous hand is seen busily at work placing the hairpins. Finally the exit of the "belle" causes roars of laughter, her mincing gait and languishing mien being reproduced with overwhelming comicality.

Some of these shadow pictures are very much advanced—positively life-like in movement and expression. Remember, there is no dialogue to help out and emphasize the

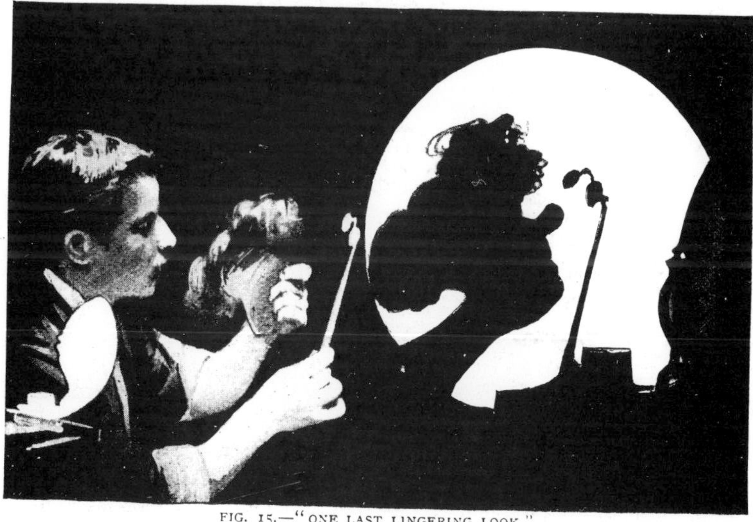

FIG. 15.—"ONE LAST LINGERING LOOK."

FIG. 16.—REMONSTRATION.

in a manner beyond all praise; at the same time his instrument is not far from his lips, so as to be ready to renew hostilities when the parley is ended.

He refuses to go. Probably he says, doggedly, "*J'y suis, J'y reste*"; but he is far more likely to say "nasty, noisy, offensive" things. The householder retires—not to bed, but to his washhand-stand. Seizing a big jug full of water, he goes to the window once more. The musician has recommenced tootling-tootling (Fig. 17), that is, with a kind of exaggerated, defiant vigour, simply because he has been told to go away; he little dreams of the Damocletian jug above. As the water (sand, really) teems down, amid shouts of laughter from the audience, the musician collapses, sadder and perhaps wiser, while the triumphant householder shuts down the window with a self-satisfied bang. A moment later Mr. Devant's flexible hands loom large upon the illuminated disc, and the performance is at an end.

action. But the wonderful artistry brought to bear on these hand shadows is nowhere better exemplified than in the little pantomime comprised in Figs. 16 and 17.

It is here necessary to explain that shadowy incidents must be, above all things, simple and obvious. Take Fig. 16. In order to produce this "scenery," a cut-out square of cardboard was placed between the arc lamp and the operator's hands. Then the itinerant musician comes along looking a little mournful; his hat is another little piece of card held between Mr. Devant's fingers. He stops beneath the window and plays a simple, touching air—or, rather, the band does it for him, while he sways rythmically his aggravating person. The householder is aroused, and goes to the window in his night-cap and a towering rage. "Go away, nasty, noisy, offensive fellow," says he. The "fellow" looks up with an injured air that is reproduced by finger movements

FIG. 17.—RETRIBUTION.

Paper-Folding.

By L. S. Lewis.

PERHAPS no more entertaining form of indoor pastime has ever been devised than the rapid folding of a sheet of pleated paper into various shapes, such as those reproduced in the following pages. First of all, however, let us acknowledge our indebtedness to Mr. David Devant, the well-known prestidigitateur (horrible word !) and popular entertainer, of the Egyptian Hall, who very kindly gave a complete "lightning paper-folding" *séance* to our own artist at these offices.

The only "apparatus" required is a sheet of paper; wherefore will this entertainment find favour in the sight of all. You are not tied to size; indeed, it may be advisable to commence with a sheet of note-paper and then work up gradually to a great square of stout cartridge or water-colour paper, such as Mr. Devant himself uses and supplies to his pupils. With just such a sheet as this, the various figures in this article were fashioned, and it measures rather more than 4ft. by 3ft.

Dexterity will come with practice. Mr. Devant evolves from his paper no fewer than forty different figures in five minutes; his record is ten in thirty seconds. The proper folding of the paper in the first instance is an absolute condition *sine quâ non.* It is necessary to bear in mind that you don't fashion your figures direct from the plain sheet, but from the cunningly pleated folds of the paper.

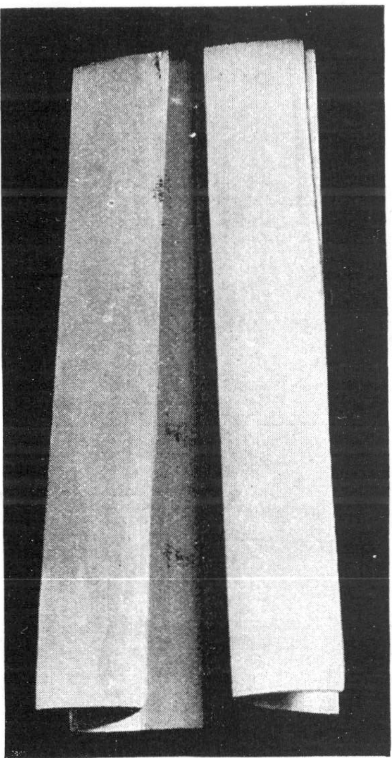

FIG. 1.—THE FIRST FOLDS.

FIG. 2.—COMMENCING TO PLEAT.

Fig. 1 shows us how to commence folding better than pages of description would do. The central space between these first folds, however, is a little exaggerated, solely in order to emphasize the necessity for that space. In the big sheet we are considering the folds should only be about half an inch apart, the *raison d'être* of the margin being to leave room for corners and angles to work round.

One can't dwell too forcibly on the necessity for care in the primary folding. The cartridge paper is stout and stiff, so that one wrong fold is all but irreparable. However, supposing that Fig. 1. has been correctly negotiated, the next illustration (Fig. 2) plainly indicates the manner of pleating. In this, correctness of spacing is everything. You may rule out beforehand the spaces for your pleats if you like, only don't think that

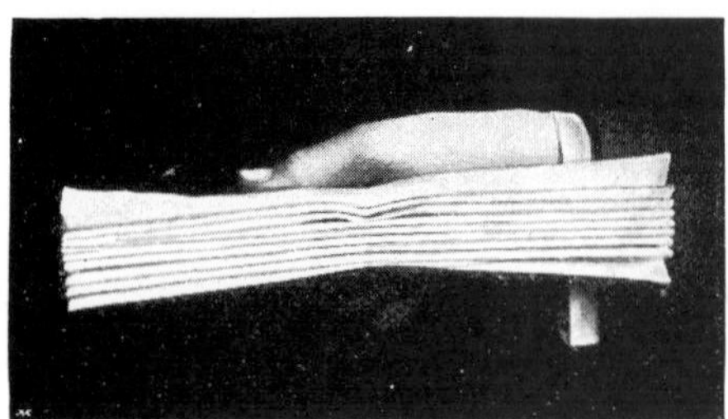

FIG. 3.—READY TO BEGIN.

they can be manipulated as easily as a concertina on Boxing Night. You may console yourself, though, with the thought that after your paper *is* completely pleated, you can with a little practice confidently set up as a society entertainer. Here I may mention that the paper, too, has to get used to its own pleats. What I mean to say is, that a little manipulation is necessary before the folds work easily. Practically, then, the older the pleated paper is, the better it is for the operator.

Fig. 3 shows the paper completely folded and ready for use. It also indicates the method of folding for what is the very first figure—the Venetian blind. This is produced

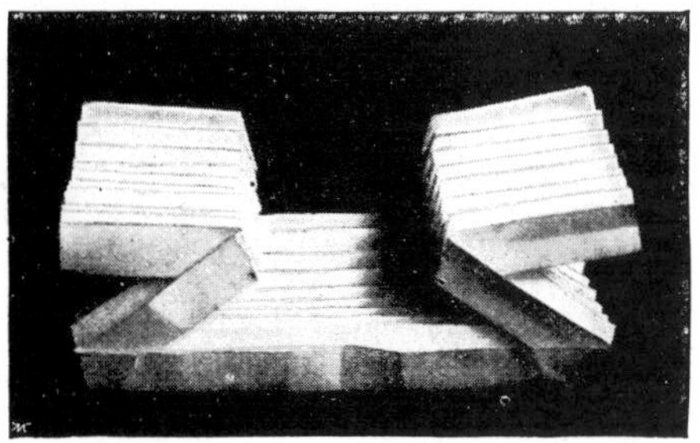

FIG. 4.—SHOWING THE FOUR "SECRET FOLDS."

by simply letting go the bottom and holding up to the audience the *front* of the pleated paper. Here may be interpolated an important piece of advice: Never, by any chance, let the audience see the *back* of your paper—I mean that side on which the narrow space runs up between the folds. The fact is, the spectators are led to believe that it is a plain piece of pleated paper; which it is not. Whether you are aware of it or not, it contains four secret folds, all of which are shown pulled out in Fig. 4. Now, a certain number of figures can be produced with the pleated paper just as it is; others—more showy subjects—with one secret fold out; and still more intricate articles with two, three, and four folds called into play. The onlookers, knowing nothing of these secret folds, marvel greatly at every item in the performance; which is as it should be. Like many other simple yet genuinely entertaining things, paper-folding is not new. A century or so

FIG. 5.—THE ROSETTE.

ago the pastime was known as "Trouble-wit," and much earlier even than this we hear of a French priest—Père Mathieu—introducing the pastime into France.

Fig. 5 illustrates one of the first figures that can be made with the pleated paper. It is a big rosette, and is formed by bringing together each end in a semi-circle. Needless to remark, all the movements should be executed with tremendous *élan*. While there are no definite rules governing the manipulator's dress, the unwritten law of professional demeanour compels him to wear at least a worried look. He should bound hither and thither, wave the paper up and down, round

FIG. 6.—THE TABLE-MAT.

Fig. 3. This, however, scarcely applies closely to the more elaborate subjects. It goes without saying that the ambitious operator must "act the part" — particularly if he aspires to be a "lightning" paper-folder. He must help to accentuate the impression his creation makes on the audience by striking a suitable posture. All of us cannot hope to look our best when assuming an aspect of "flirtatious archness," yet this is more or less indispensable to the success of Fig. 7. In the case of this fan, the "secret-fold" side of the pleated paper is turned towards the entertained; but this is exceptional. The fact is, the space or margin which runs between the folds greatly assists this figure—as you may judge for yourself by inspecting and comparing the reverse side of your own fan when formed. Moreover, it is only held in position for a second or two, so that the audience haven't time to grasp the meaning of the double folds. The fan is made simply

and round, and generally convey the impression that the whole business is a severe strain upon him, physically as well as mentally.

Look at Fig. 5, and then at Fig. 6. When, after apparently superhuman endeavour, the rosette has been formed, and triumphantly presented for applause, the operator "goes off" again to his arduous pantomime. After a certain number of fantastic gyrations he blows upon the rosette, and, lo! it instantly becomes—a table-mat (Fig. 6). So prosaic an article as a table-mat may (considering the gyrations) be considered something of an anti-climax; but, at any rate, the manner of its evolution is sufficiently obvious. One simply extends, by a swift simultaneous movement of both hands, the semi-circles that form the rosette.

Held vertically, by the way, and with one end flat, a Norman church window is formed. But, above all things, go through your list with *verve* and energy, barely giving your audience time to admire your creation. Also, don't forget the "as you were"; that is to say, after the formation of each figure, bring your paper back to the formation shown in

FIG. 7.—THE FAN.

FIG. 8.—TWO FOLDS OUT.

forming the upper part of that article. One extends the pleats horizontally in a semi-circle, and then places the epaulette on one's own shoulder with a smart military salute. Fig. 8 shows a movement preliminary to the formation of some of the most striking subjects. It will be seen that there are two folds

FIG. 10.—AN EASTERN WATER-POT.

by bunching together the pleats at one end and extending them at the other. Of course, there is the expression to be assumed. It seems that the most correct way of producing the fan is to throw the paper into the air and catch it as it falls, presenting the figure instantaneously. This, in the language of the local reporter describing a melodrama, "electrifies the audience"—whatever that means.

In Fig. 8 we see the secret folds coming into play; but there are some figures omitted through want of space. The "epaulette," for example, is made from the fan, by pulling out the set of folds out. Turn your paper up the other way and spread it out, when you will have a capital representation of a drawing-room settee (Fig. 9). This settee, whose surface is mainly composed of acute angles, is not one on which lovers (or others) would care to linger long, but all the same, there is no denying the effectiveness of the thing, an article of "paper sculpture." Now close up the settee and reverse the paper, as in Fig. 8. Then bring the whole round in a fine sweep for the Eastern water-pot (Fig. 10)—

FIG. 9.—THE SETTEE.

FIG. 11.—A LAMP-SHADE.

perhaps the most successful of all the paper shapes. Here, again, you have to act the part by placing the jar on your shoulder and posing as though it were full of water instead of the lighter element.

Another very remarkable figure is the "lamp-shade" (Fig. 11). No one would think, at the first glance, that this is formed by turning the Oriental water-pot upside down, and giving it a very wide spread. Yet so it is; but as a rule the elegant little flower-holder (Fig. 12) comes between the two, in order that their connection may not be too obvious.

When taking out a fold to form further articles, much mystery is thrown about the business. As I have remarked elsewhere, the plain pleated side is always turned towards the audience; and when the required fold is pulled out all the way down, the pleats are gathered up ladder-wise with nimble fingers, and to the accompaniment of a rustling noise that is not a little puzzling to those who know nothing of the secret folds.

FIG. 12.—FLOWER-HOLDER.

FIG. 13.—THREE FOLDS OUT.

So elegant are many of these folded paper figures that one might almost think some of them worthy of remaining in permanent form. Take Fig. 11 for example. If that lamp-shade were in green or red paper, and made quite circular, it is obvious that it would serve a useful as well as ornamental purpose; it would, in fact, be "just the thing" for a table-lamp or a big drawing-room floor-lamp. In Fig. 13 we see that three folds

FIG. 14.—HOW THE SAUCEPAN IS MADE.

have been taken out, forming a saucepan in embryo. Fig. 14 shows the manner of actually fashioning that homely utensil, and the next illustration (Fig. 15) depicts it complete, though in highly ornamental and "fluted" guise. Of course, these comparatively intricate shapes and figures are exhibited rather longer than the more simple ones. Also, appropriate gestures and movements are devised for each.

But supposing that the saucepan has palled upon you and your audience—and too much saucepan is apt to pall—there are many other capital subjects left in the paper-folder's repertoire. "As you were," then, in Fig. 13. Now, by an elaborate (and exaggerated) movement you bring round the pleats to form the "cosy corner" represented in Fig. 16. The magician is not nearly done yet, however, and as roars of applause (more or less) greet the results of his wonderful art, he contrives yet another restful abode—one for rather a different season, though — namely, a garden-seat (Fig. 17). That is rather a nice garden-seat, with a sheltered mushroom top. In a way it reminds us of those arranged round big trees in the London parks. I refer, of course, to those seats which seem to be intended solely for the amusement of muddy-booted children playing at circus, and for the benefit of the great family of unprofessional wood-carvers, whose deplorable efforts to attain immortality are

FIG. 15.—THE SAUCEPAN COMPLETE.

writ (or carved) large on the monuments and places of the world.

But we have digressed, as the novelist says when he or she (especially she) is conscious of having worked in a fine slice of irrelevant

FIG. 16.—A COSY CORNER.

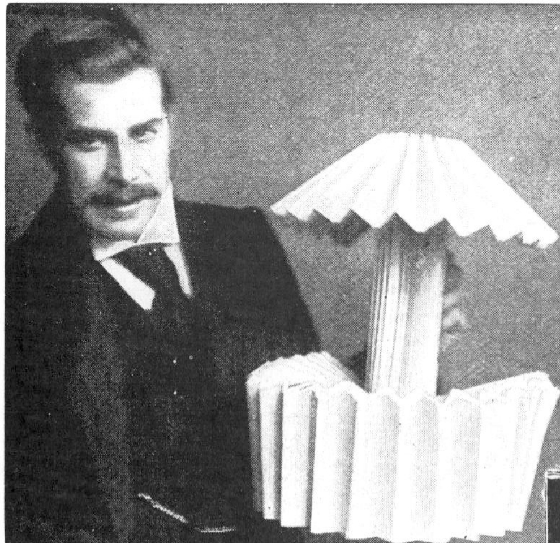

FIG. 17.—THE GARDEN-SEAT.

padding. Evidently the range of subjects in paper-folding is extremely large. Articles of clothing, of comfort, of utility, of ornament—all these can be shown; in short, no phase of life is neglected. Even that which is reputed next to godliness is represented in Fig. 18, which shows what purports to be a portable and collapsible foot-bath.

The connection between the different figures will be noted by those who closely follow this subject. Thus, the handle of the saucepan is the frill of the lamp-shade and the seat of the settee. Comparing the garden-seat (Fig. 17) with the saucepan, we find that the seat of the one is the handle of the other. By taking that part of the paper which forms the lower vertical section of the garden-seat, and inserting it in the corresponding fold (thus making the two one double fold), the lower part

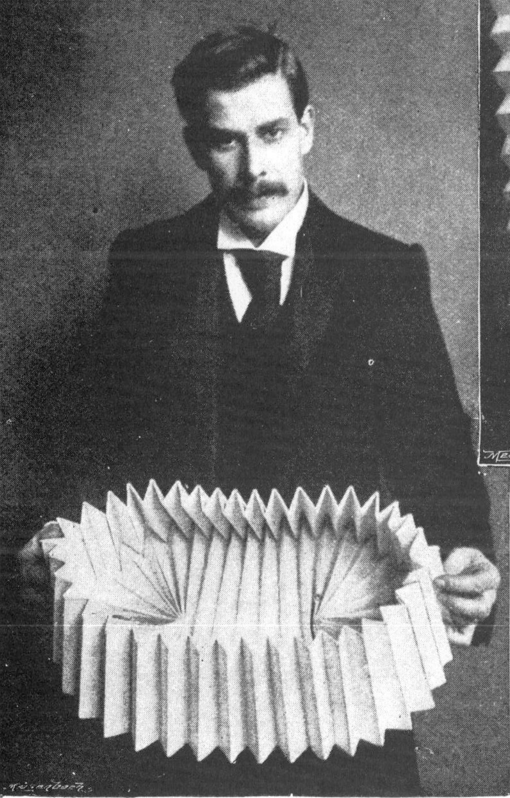

FIG. 18.—A FOOT-BATH.

FIG. 19.—THE SENTRY-BOX.

of the figure will be found to resemble the top—only reversed, of course. Now close up the whole and then make the ends meet, until you have the saucepan without the handle. So far, good. Take hold of the ends now, and pull out until the foot-bath (Fig. 18) is produced.

Next comes one of the "lightning changes" before described in regard to the rosette and table-mat. Let go one end of the foot-bath and pull out until you are able to announce the "sentry-box" (Fig. 19).

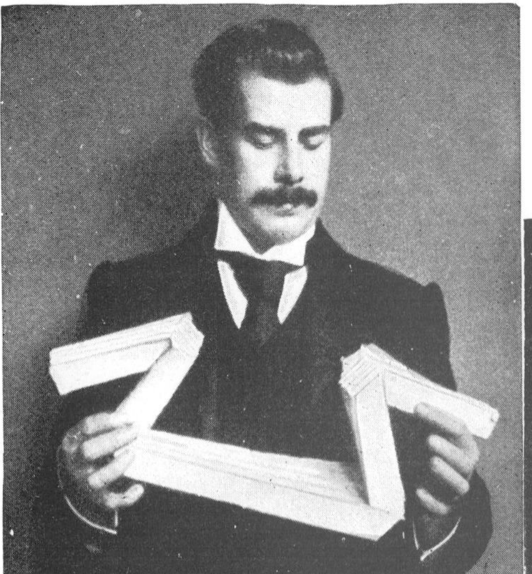
FIG. 20.--FOUR FOLDS OUT—FOR BON-BON.

This evolution is much appreciated—only don't forget the mystery and gyrations. Once you have your paper correctly folded in the first instance, the rest is easy enough, but your audience are not to know that. Of course, practice is required to go through the "show" with credit to one's self and amusement to others.

We now take all four folds out, as in Fig. 20, which illustrates the preparations necessary for making the gigantic bon-bon. The next illustration (Fig. 21) shows the completion of this always-popular subject. Indeed, Fig. 21 is considered by some the very best of these paper shapes. To make the bon-bon from Fig. 20 you simply take hold of the centre, and describe with the pleats a circle round the folds themselves.

FIG. 22.—A DUMB-BELL.

FIG. 21.—THE BIG BON-BON.

You may then, if you wish, partly close the figure, turn your paper round the other way, and evolve from this the great dumb-bell seen in Fig. 22. Not even Sandow, in all his glory, ever saw such a dumb-bell as this, for, by a little judicious manipulation on the part of the operator, it can be made to do duty as the paddle-wheel of a Thames steamer.

The evolution of the Beefeater's hat from Fig. 20 is very well shown in Fig. 23—a photograph which speaks for itself. After having presented the dumb-bell, close your figure and draw two ends together until they meet, as in the accompanying illustration (Fig. 23). If you do the same with two ends on the other side, you will then find that the Beefeater's hat is ready to be placed *in situ*, as in Fig. 24; which, it will be admitted, is quite an elegant and creditable form of head-gear, that might very well be copied by the Bond Street shop-keepers.

FIG. 23.—SHOWING HOW TO MAKE A BEEFEATER'S HAT.

I have omitted such elementary forms as the candlestick, which when inverted masquerades as a mushroom. Doubtless, many other shapes will be designed and fashioned by the ingenious. At the same time, it is well to point out that figures which are made by reversing other subjects should never be given in consecutive order. The

FIG. 25.—DUTCH GIRL'S BONNET.

audience must have time to forget, say, the Oriental water-jar, before the lamp-shade is presented for their approbation. And in order to assist this convenient obliviousness, other figures must be presented in between.

Now, returning for a moment to Fig. 24. Catch hold of the brim of the hat where the ends meet, stretch out the pleats a little to fit the head, and then the Dutch girl's bonnet is complete (Fig. 25). Here, again, the effect may be heightened by a well-simulated simper—expression is everything; but beware of over-stepping the mark in this direction. Take heed, we say, lest in straining after adventitious effect you excite perversely the risibility of your audience.

FIG. 24.—THE BEEFEATER'S HAT COMPLETE.

A Lightning Modeller.

By Frank Holmfield.

Illustrations from Photographs.

THERE are tremendous possibilities in a lump of modelling clay—when manipulated by a skilled artist.

Such will be the conclusion that must be arrived at by anyone who has witnessed, at the London Pavilion, the remarkable performance of Mr. De Bessell, before whose lissom fingers an unshapely mass of brown mud-mixture assumes, in an almost incredibly short space of time, forms and features as true to life as may be.

There is a slap-dash and "go-ahead" style about Mr. De Bessell's work which adds to his artistic performance a drollness irresistible to most people. Whilst he is always thoroughly in earnest, he manages—I will not say unconsciously—to make the most hardened cynic chuckle with mirth.

His is a truly unique entertainment. With an oblong slab of wood fitted upon an ordinary easel, and supplemented by a big lump of the necessary material and ten deftly artistic fingers, he can produce effects simply marvellous in detail, considering the wonderfully short time occupied.

The smart variety theatre "turn" known as "lightning modelling" originated with Mr. De Bessell. And he may be said to have retained a monopoly of the interesting and amusing entertainment. Of course, there are the usual crop of imitation "acts." The writer has seen some of these. But in skill, artistic effect, and humour they are simply not in the running with the original. To produce a first-class caricature in clay of, say, Mr. Kruger within a space of 100sec. is a feat not to be tackled by any save the smartest modellers. And certainly Mr. De Bessell is smart, ahead of all others.

One can't become a successful lightning modeller at a moment's notice—nor at a year's, for the matter of that! It has taken the subject of this article the greater portion of his lifetime to reach the standard of smartness and artistic completeness.

"From my very earliest schooldays," said Mr. De Bessell to me, "I always had a liking for such work. They told me, too, that my mud pies and sand castles were always eminently superior to the efforts of my most enthusiastic playfellows! I have even been complimented," went on the clay king humorously, "by one of my school teachers on the excellence of what I'm afraid was a rather rude caricature model of his own face!

"With such encouragement there was only one profession open to me!

HURLING THE CLAY AT THE MODELLING SLAB.

I went on the stage! Yes; after a great deal of study under some of the best masters in the States"—Mr. De Bessell hails therefrom—"I saw that there was an opening for such an original 'turn.' There was absolutely nothing like it. It was quite new. And you know what managers want. They are always crying out for novelty—and not often with success, so scarce has become the material to be drawn upon.

KRUGER BEFORE GETTING HIS HAT AND WHISKERS.

"It was not long before I found myself in England — by the way, what an extraordinary theatre-going nation England is! The enormous patronage given to the 'halls' particularly astonishes us Americans, even accustomed as we have been to big audiences."

Clay modelling on the stage would be rather slow under ordinary methods of manipulation. In fact, it would not "go" were there not plenty of life and dash introduced.

Mr. De Bessell's methods "fill the bill." As soon as he has made his bow to the audience he catches up a great chunk of clay in his hands. Standing a yard or two away from the modelling slab he hurls lump after lump, with unerring aim and wonderful rapidity, at its centre, to the sound of lively orchestral tunes.

THE HAT AND WHISKERS ARE ADDED.

Every lump is thrown with a particular purpose, and even before the artist's fingers touch it the outline of a face is plainly discernible. As soon as he has hurled the last lump at the slab, with a rush he has crossed to the easel and with extraordinary swiftness his fingers are darting hither and thither. A dab here, a pinch there, a rub yonder, a punch below—those deft fingers get in their work. Not a tool is used from beginning to end, only the fingers. In and out, out and in, they twist and twirl in a truly bewildering fashion.

"DE WET'S SLIPPED THROUGH!"

In something like fifteen seconds that mass of brown clay has been pinched, punched, rubbed, and shoved into features which the spectator begins to recognise as having come within his vision somewhere at some time—he can't exactly say. Fingers and thumbs raise both eyebrows in a certain peculiar twist only known to be characteristic of one man—"the whole discovery is now found out," as they say in the melodramas. Those eyebrows have given the necessary expression to the incomplete features. It is our old friend Kruger! But where are his famous whiskers? Wait a moment.

"DE WET'S CAUGHT!"

A few little lumps of clay are flung from the lightning modeller's hands. They form a fringe to the face—and are Kruger's whiskers in embryo. A few quick dashes of the artist's fingers, and the hirsute ornamentation is complete!

Kruger's hat has played as big a part in caricature as did the collar of a famous statesman. Without his hat Kruger would be a mere nonentity. Shall this particular Kruger remain hatless? Never! Grabbing up one more lump of the pliable clay, Mr. De Bessell's fingers soon model it into the typical old "topper" of renown. Another second and it is reposing, somewhat jauntily perhaps, on the well-worn cranium. Kruger is all there. The entire operation has taken up 1min. 43 2-5sec. by Benson's chronograph.

MODELLING AN OLD WOMAN.

Who has ever seen a picture of Kruger otherwise than depicting a very worried state of mind? Well, Mr. De Bessell shows us what Oom Paul would look like if he were ever persuaded to smile. The effect, however, is not particularly complimentary. Even though adorned with a smile, Kruger refuses to be beautiful. The model is now supposed to represent Kruger on hearing for the tenth time that De Wet has "slipped through."

SHE LAUGHS.

Another movement or two of the artist's deft hands, and lo! we see Kruger as he will be when the sad but inevitable news arrives at last that "De Wet is captured."

The next operation of the clay shows that the venerable Boer is to be made good use of. His whiskers are whisked away; his hat decapitated and turned into an old woman's bonnet. The features are still Kruger's, but the change in accessories has transmogrified him into an old woman in a state of intense grief. This presently changes to a different frame of mind, until a punch below the chin from the modeller's clenched fist produces a lugubrious effect on the old lady's features.

Next we are treated to another lightning production of a present-day celebrity. This is no less a personage than Li Hung Chang, who, with pig-tail, peacock's feathers and all, turns from a mass of clay to an excellent model of the wily Chinese statesman in the course of 1min. $25\frac{3}{5}$sec. A truly wonderful feat.

A PUNCH UNDER THE CHIN AND SHE WEEPS.

"John Bull and Jonathan," a tribute to the excellent feeling existing between the

LI HUNG CHANG.

two nations, is tackled and finished in 2min. 45sec. It is a revelation to see Mr. De Bessell with both hands at work, each on a different face, at the same time!

Such an entertainment does not run for any length of time without meeting with some odd little experiences. I have referred to the hurling of the clay from Mr. De Bessell's hands on to the modelling slab. This has led to more than one little humorous episode, as the following anecdote proves—the victim might differ as to the point of the humour.

In Vienna last year the lightning modeller had begun as usual to hurl the clay upon the slab preparatory to forming a caricature. He stood about two yards away. He had barely begun to throw when the electric light throughout the theatre was accidentally turned off. Thinking that it would be a good hit if, during the temporary darkness, he could get the caricature partly done, the modeller continued hurling the clay. Suddenly he heard an awful howl of agony. At the same moment the electric light was switched on discovering the stage manager (who had rushed across the dark stage to see what had happened to the lights) endeavouring to remove from his features a huge lump of the clay, which, coming with full force from the modeller's hand, had struck him across the eyes, which were black for days afterwards.

LI HUNG CHANG IS THROWN AWAY.

JOHN BULL AND JONATHAN—MODELLED SIMULTANEOUSLY, ONE WITH EACH HAND.

[The writer desires to acknowledge the courtesy of Mr. Frank Glenister, the manager of the Pavilion, in enabling the accompanying photographs to be secured under difficult circumstances.—F. H.]

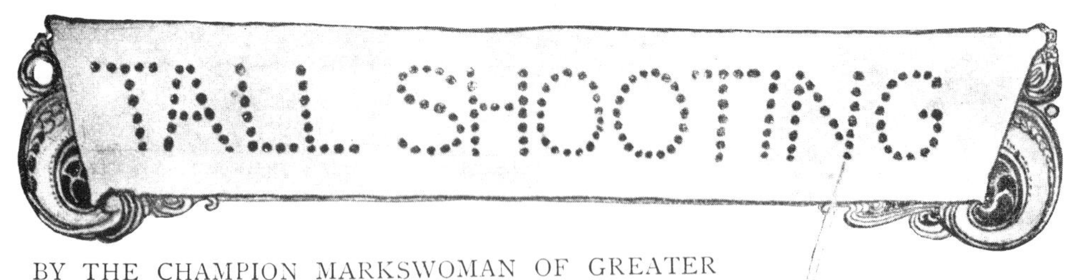

TALL SHOOTING

BY THE CHAMPION MARKSWOMAN OF GREATER BRITAIN.

BY STEPHEN VINCENT.

FOR some months past visitors to the Royal Aquarium, Westminster, have twice a day witnessed a remarkable exhibition of expert rifle shooting by a lady whose performance never fails to evoke loud applause from the audience.

This lady is known in private life as Mrs. Swallow, though she prefers to be known professionally as "Nell, the champion rifle shot." She and her brother "Joe, the living target," make up the company now known as the Lynch Rifle Experts.

Mrs. Swallow's claim to be the champion lady rifle shot seems to be well founded, and her challenge to any man or woman in the world to fire a hundred shots with her at any range with any ordinary rifle has not, so far as we are aware, been accepted up to the present time.

This lady may almost be said to have been born with a rifle in her hand, for she was only seven years old when she first used one. At that time her parents were living in Canada, though at the time Nell was born they were residing at North Shields. The new home on the North-West frontier was well suited to develop skilful shooting, for there was not only plenty of hunting, but at that time the new settlers were in constant danger from the ill-concealed hostility of the native Indian tribes.

A FLYING SHOT BY MRS. NELL SWALLOW—THIS LADY AT THE AGE OF ELEVEN YEARS ASSISTED IN DEFENDING HER HOME FROM A RAID BY RED INDIANS.

At last this volcano of hostility, which had long been smouldering, broke out into violent eruption. When Nell was but eleven years old a determined attack was made upon her home, and, in company with her brother Joe, who was but slightly older than herself, she used her marksmanship to good purpose.

The boy and girl defended the homestead, and by their rapid and accurate shooting were successful in driving off the band of Indians, and thus saved the lives of their parents and brothers and sisters.

Soon afterwards the family went to India, and Nell had considerable experience of jungle life and hunting. She had many narrow escapes, but the extraordinary quickness and accuracy of her shooting always brought her through. On one occasion, however, a bear got her down, and she would have undoubtedly met her end but for the appearance of her brother on the scene, a shot from whose rifle terminated the career of the bear.

A STRANGELY DIRECTED BULLET FINDS—

After this they returned to England. The boy Joe joined Her Majesty's forces, and Nell soon afterwards started on her career as a professional rifle shot. That was between thirteen and fourteen years ago.

....

In the course of her professional career Mrs. Swallow has visited many parts of the world, and has experienced many strange adventures. For a long time she was associated with Colonel Cody, the well-known "Buffalo Bill," and astonished everybody by her shooting from horseback.

ITS BILLET, A CLAY PIPE BOWL HELD THUS BY MRS. SWALLOW'S BROTHER.

To appreciate the accuracy of this lady's shooting, it is necessary to remember that she uses bullets only, and never resorts to the not uncommon trick of using a large charge of small shot. This last is the usual device of a certain type of so-called rifle experts.

By the use of a large charge of shot, fired from a sufficient distance, it is almost impossible to miss the mark, so great is the spread of the shot.

Another device is to use a large hollowed metal target, so constructed that if struck in any part the vibration is so great that the fragile mark is destroyed as certainly as if it had been struck by the bullet.

Now it is pleasant to be able to testify, from personal knowledge, that Mrs. Swal-

A PARTING SHOT AND A REMARKABLE POSE.

low's shooting is entirely *bona fide* and above board. We have been present at several of her performances; we have examined the rifle and the bullets whenever we pleased; we have stood beside the target and seen difficult marks hit by the bullet within a few inches of us; and we are able to say that no spread shot is used, there is no trickery about the target, and the whole performance is one of honest skill. The rifle used is a Colt repeater of ·22 calibre.

BY THE REFLECTION IN HER SIGNET RING SHE CREATES—

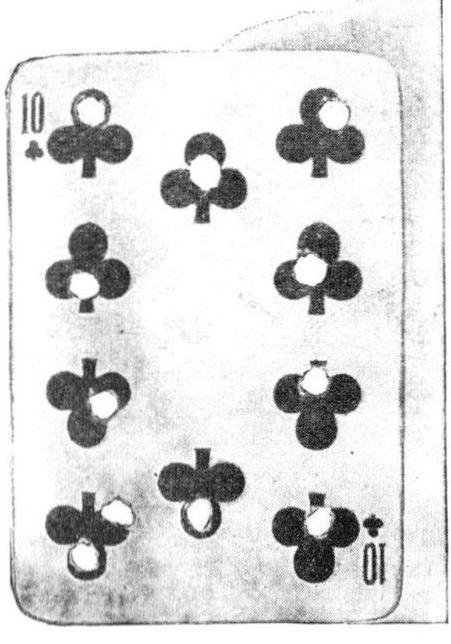

THIS QUEER CARD.

The impossibility of using spread shot will be obvious when it is remembered that most of the marks aimed at are either held in the hand or placed on the head of Nell's brother. Even in long-distance shooting at a mark on an iron target, the human target sits with his head only about a foot below the mark.

Many of the shots are fired under circumstances that would puzzle many a Bisley prize winner. In addition to most of the ordinary postures of standing, sitting, kneeling, and lying, Nell has a few peculiar to herself. She can sight just as readily with the rifle held upside down and pointed directly above her head.

Hanging head downwards over the back of a chair is not a position that most of us would choose for shooting purposes, but Mrs. Swallow's aim is equally sure, however awkward the posture.

One of her special feats is that of firing over her shoulder at a mark placed directly behind her. In this case she aims by means of the reflection in her finger ring, which is an ordinary one of the signet type, but containing a tiny scrap of looking-glass instead of the customary stone.

Perhaps the most sensational of her feats is that of firing backwards over her shoulder when blindfolded. This is a most mystifying business to the spectator, but we can say from personal knowledge that a true aim is taken and the mark is hit *bona fide*, but how the feat is done it would be unfair to disclose. We can only suggest that our readers should witness the performance and try to find out.

THIS SEVEN OF HEARTS WAS SPLIT EDGEWAYS BY—

The quickness as well as the accuracy of Mrs. Swallow's shooting generally impresses the spectator greatly. In our presence she undertook to hit some twenty-four marks, each about the size of a penny, in thirty seconds. We timed her, and found that the feat was successfully accomplished in a little more than twenty seconds.

This lady rifle-shot's skill is only equalled by her retiring modesty.

A BLINDFOLD SHOT.

DIVING HORSES AND OTHER ANIMALS

Many people today do not care to see wild animals in performance, arguing not only that they may be ill-treated or trained to do undignified tricks, but also that natural history programmes on television allow the animals to be seen and heard (if not yet smelt) in their proper habitat. Alternatively you may choose to take a quick, safe and comfortable flight to watch exotic animals in the wild. Obviously, these options did not exist at the end of the 19th century and audiences were thrilled by the sight of elephants, tigers and the like.

When W.C. Fields appeared at London's Hippodrome in 1903 the bill included Busch's Plunging Elephants diving into the flooded arena. The audience was protected from splashes by a 20 foot high glass screen. The year before at the Hippodrome, he had to compete with a baboon that cycled down a slope, round the curves of a loop, and onto the stage.

Exoticism was one attraction, sheer numbers another. In 1886 the combined Barnum and Forepaugh circuses at Madison Square Garden in New York boasted sixty elephants, and a production at the Hippodrome in 1908 featured no fewer than seventy polar bears.

Unlike today, the general public was in daily contact with large animals, since buses, trams and carriages were horse-drawn. People understood and were appreciative of the skill involved in training and handling horses. In 1904 Oswald Stoll opened the magnificent new Coliseum and, as part of the opening production which was presented four times a day, a capacity 2,000 audience sat enthralled as the Derby horse race was re-run with horses and jockeys on a vast revolving stage, which could reach 20 miles an hour.

For all the popularity of animal acts, concerns about animal welfare were already being expressed, as the article on diving horses makes clear with its reference to the Society for the Prevention of Cruelty to Animals.

Diving Horses.

By Albert H. Broadwell. Photographs by A. J. Johnson.

FLYING GIRAFFES, crawling elephants, or grass-eating tigers are merely possibilities, but diving horses are an accomplished fact. The horses whose doings we propose to describe dive for the very fun of it—there is no prodding or pushing; they require a great deal of holding when they scent water in the distance or suspect it to be anywhere within a hundred-mile radius.

They will not run in harness, neither will they be ridden like common horses; they have been accustomed, from their very earliest years, to a life of freedom, of wild rushes and plunges, in the Everglade Swamps of Florida.

Not very long ago London was startled by huge hoardings showing a milk-white steed diving head-foremost into a rushing torrent some thirty feet below. London shrugged its shoulders, said it was all bunkum, and then went—as London always does and ever will do—to see the fun.

London flocked to the Crystal Palace in its tens of thousands, and when London got there its amazement knew no bounds when the horses' clever diving feats actually took place amid thunders of applause.

Mr. H. Gillman, the popular manager of the Crystal Palace, had, with characteristic energy, secured the diving-horse show as his very own and "exclusive." Moreover, he very kindly extended his usual courtesy to the writer, inasmuch as he offered every facility for the taking of the extraordinary pictures which serve to illustrate this article.

WAITING AT THE FOOT OF THE INCLINED PLANE.

In order to get some interesting particulars about those two beautiful milk-white diving steeds we secured an interview with Captain Boynton, the great showman who owns the immense pleasure grounds and water-chutes in Coney Island and Woodside Park, Philadelphia. In the course of our chat we learned that as soon as Captain Boynton heard of the diving horses and their marvellous performances he communicated with their owner and trainer, Professor Geo. F. Holloway, of Bancroft, Iowa, and secured their performances for his chutes at Coney Island.

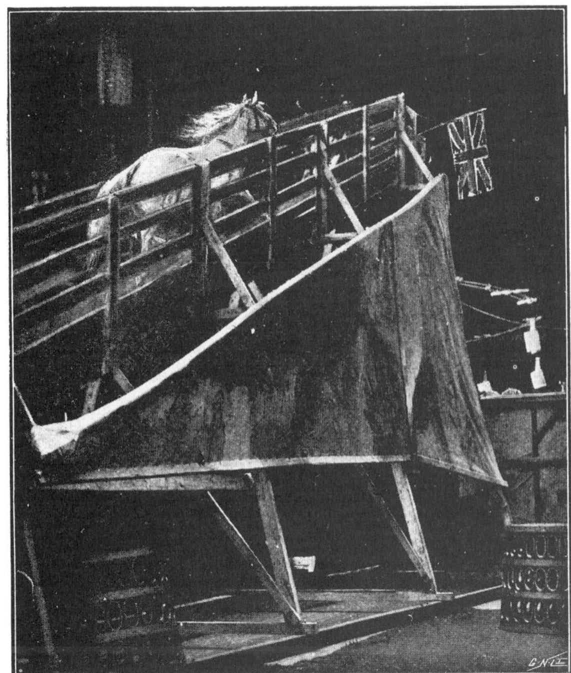

VIEW OF INCLINED PLANE FROM BEHIND—HORSE RUNNING UP.

of them on the prairies, has never been successful in training another pair to perform the same diving feats. He selected eighty-five of the most likely animals from his stock, but met with failure every time. None of these were of the same breed as King and Queen. Curiously enough, *all* the horses under trial dived with their heads held high, while King and Queen always dive head-foremost, as will be seen in our illustrations entitled "leaping" and "nearing the water."

At Coney Island Captain Boynton possesses an extensive lake, wherein the horses dive from an elevated platform. Lakes are not made to order, however, so that in their travels the horses are accompanied by a tank, which is fitted into an excavation made for the purpose; the water in winter and autumn is always kept at an almost uniform temperature, somewhere between 65deg. and 85deg., the water being warmed by means of steam-pipes — a precaution which is, of course, unnecessary in the summer months. The elevated platform also accompanies the horses wherever they go.

Captain Boynton had much of interest to communicate, inasmuch as he has the horses under his management to "do" the Continent, and especially the Paris Exhibition, under the care of Professor Holloway's nephew, Mr. John Whalen, whose thoughtfulness for the animals' welfare is charming to witness.

It appears that King and Queen, as these equine beauties are justly called, are actually descendants of the wild horses that in times gone by disported themselves on the Everglades in Florida. Water, it seems, is partly their natural element, inasmuch as swamps of vast extent are to be found in the Everglades, and part of the distances in their wanderings, which these animals had to cover, had to be done by swimming.

This interesting fact goes a long way to prove that no compulsion has ever been necessary in their training. When they were colts, Professor Holloway's sons used to ride these pets when going for their morning dip, and strangely enough the horses would dive after their masters and follow their gambols in the water.

Another curious and significant fact is that Professor Holloway, who is a great breeder of horses, and owns thousands

ARRIVED AT TOP, KING HAS A GOOD LOOK AT HIS AUDIENCE.

PREPARING TO LEAP.

stable are kept to a uniform standard. Their blankets, of which they possess a seemingly unlimited supply, are frequently changed, washed, and aired with as much care as the personal linen of a Vanderbilt!

Upon their arrival in London the performance seemed so exceedingly novel and daring that it was openly asserted that cruelty had to be used to make the animals go through the dives in which, as a matter of fact, they take great delight. Such assertions were speedily squashed by a thorough inspection of the show by specially deputed members of the S.P.C.A., who, in the exercise of their commendable duties, investigated charges which were found to be utterly groundless. It may be mentioned, also, that while these horses were performing in Philadelphia an agent of the S.P.C.A. was, by the special request of Professor Holloway, appointed to live with the horses during the whole time of their stay there; he remained with the

Mr. Whalen, who has charge of these pets, has given the writer some interesting particulars as to the way in which these beautiful creatures are cared for. It appears that during their trip across the Atlantic his charges had never been ill, or did they even seem to feel uncomfortable. They had extra large padded stalls, each having as much room to himself as would fall to the lot of six less illustrious creatures. Cleverly enough, they made a point of lying down whenever the weather was rough, and the captain, with the majority of the passengers, used to visit them and feed them with dainties every day.

Their food is always examined before it is given to them, and consists of the very best grain sorted by hand, also hay of the very finest quality. In addition they get potatoes, carrots, and apples every day; their food is always kept under lock and key, and they are never, under any pretext whatsoever, left without an attendant to look after their every wish.

The horses' temperature is taken daily, and the degrees of heat in the

LEAPING.

animals day and night, and it is pleasing to record that he expressed himself as entirely satisfied as to the genuineness of the horses' desire to dive of their own free will.

Immediately after their dives King and Queen expect a lump or two of sugar each, and that is a time-honoured custom with both, as Mrs. Holloway always made it a practice to reward them in that way when they had dived well in the course of regular tuition. This also explains their particular fondness for ladies.

King and Queen are passionately fond of each other and have never been separated. They have never been shod, and have also never been in harness for any length of time. In fact, they don't like harness, and they hate buggies, of which they have smashed one or two, which seems to prove once more that they are essentially children of Nature and of a breed as yet so wild as to be likened to the zebra of untamable reputation. King and Queen are pink-skinned and have black eyes, a very pretty combination, coupled with almost milk-white coats that shimmer in the sunlight like the *moiré* silk of a bridal dress.

NEARING THE WATER—NOTE THE PERFECT DIVING ATTITUDE.

THE SPLASH.

Twenty thousand dollars have been offered for them, and yet their owner would not part with what may be reckoned to be the most unique pair of horses on earth; no fewer than two millions of people have flocked to see them in their wanderings, and small wonder, for they are assuredly as pretty a pair of steeds as ever trod the green.

There is happily only a single dramatic incident to record in the career of these equine pets, and it occurred at Captain Boynton's show on Coney Island. Captain Boynton keeps any number of pets in his

SWIMMING TO SHORE.

waters, and among those are numbered some huge turtles. It happened that after one of the horses had dived a hard-shelled monster was discovered within less than a yard from the place where the horse had first struck the water. Had the diving animal collided with the turtle it is terrible to think what the consequences might have been. A halt was therefore called, before the second horse was allowed to go through its performance, and every endeavour was made to induce the turtle to seek more convenient quarters, but instead of doing so the obstructionist calmly sank to the bottom of the lake, at the very spot where the horse was expected to dive.

Strong measures were used: a dynamite cartridge was lowered directly over the spot where the turtle had sunk, and was fired in order to dislodge it from its awkward place of concealment. Strange to say, the animal, while duly blown out of bounds, sustained no injury beyond a thorough shaking, from which it recovered in less than a week!

BEING SCRAPED DOWN AFTER DIVING.

Bears at School.

By Albert H. Broadwell. Photographs by A. J. Johnson.

“BRUISES, did you say? Look at my arms!” We looked and wondered. Big patches of blue stood out, witnesses of Mr. Permane's encounters with his pupils. Some twelve years ago this famous trainer took a particular fancy to bears, and he confidentially asserts (and no one will doubt him) that not one of the many bears he has handled during that time has ever taken any particular fancy to him. We have had occasion to assist at a private performance, during which the accompanying photos. were taken. Mr. Permane, whose nightly performance with his bears used to form one of the principal draws at the Alhambra, Leicester Square, need have no fear of our ever starting in the bear-training line after that experience. Bears at school are very amusing to look at from a distance, but our photographer absolutely refuses to focus bears again at any price.

OUT SHOPPING.

“They catch them in Russia, and we train them in England,” said Mr. Permane. “Curiously enough, every tenth house in St. Petersburg owns at least one pet bear cub during the season. The Russians are fond of pets, and the bear cubs are bought as they are brought in by the peasants. They are only kept for a short time, however. When about three months old they exhibit certain signs of familiarity which to the average man in the street seem rather uncalled for; they are then generously presented to the nation, and find a home in the bear-pits at the Zoological Gardens, where as many as sixty cubs are to be found at a time.

“Familiarity breeds contempt,” says Mr. Permane, and familiarity has led him into some tight places.

Though he and the lady bear shown in the first photo. seem on very good terms, there are moments when such familiarity is undesirable.

“It was a hot summer in Madrid,” said the trainer, “and the weather seemed to affect my pets rather more than usual. After feeding time I went to caress one of the bears, who was chained to an ordinary manger. Not seeming in a mood to accept my overtures, however, the brute seized me by the arm just above the shoulder, and shook me as a terrier would a rat, and then threw me in a heap into the furthermost corner of the stable. This being the second time she had attacked me in a determined manner that week, I thought it high time that the good people of Madrid were enjoying some bear's meat for supper—and so they did!”

Bear's meat for supper seems a strange dish, but curiously enough there are many people on the Continent who delight in bear-steak.

This statement seemed so extraordinary that we determined to sound Mr. Permane thoroughly on that point. We will let him tell how it is that bear-steak is offered to the public for consumption, though they little guess how the transaction comes about.

“You must understand,” he said, “that after a certain age, which after all depends much upon the temperament of the animal, a bear will become unmanageable. There is no coaxing him into good behaviour, either by threats or kindness. He simply will have his own way, and then the best thing to do is to get rid of him at an early date.

THE SERPENTINE DANCE.

"The last two bears which I had to destroy under such circumstances became unmanageable whilst I was performing in Paris. It was in the middle of winter, and though I unsuccessfully tried to reform their unruly ways, I had to decide to do away with them.

"Now, I love my bears greatly—they dance for the very love of me, as you see in the Serpentine Dance photo.; so you will understand that I never could take it into my head to shoot them myself. I have always had to secure the good offices of another to give the *coup de grâce* to my unruly ones. The two bears in question were accordingly shot and sold to a butcher in the Place de la République for £30, dead meat. The run on those bears was tremendous—the meat was sold at two francs a pound, and the skins fetched nearly £10 each! A Commissaire de Police had to be called in to stop the rush on the remains of my pets, and I felt sad indeed at the sight of such a pitiful end to their theatrical life.

"When I buy a 'guaranteed' bear from the Zoo at St. Petersburg I can bet my bottom dollar that he has never been tampered with before. These bears come straight from their native wilds, and that is how I like them best. I am always on the look-out for a bear that has never been handled before. I like him young. You can educate him like you would a child; but, mind you, you must be very firm, otherwise he will take the upper hand, and then it is all over.

"The best time to start the bear in the training business is when he is about eighteen months old. The Swinging Feat shown here took me quite six months to teach. Curiously enough, the bear enjoys the swinging immensely now, though the first few lessons were not quite so pleasant.

"How long it takes to thoroughly train a bear is difficult to say. It depends entirely upon the bear's disposition. Some bears are slow, others are quick to understand what you want, and the rest are too quick altogether, and those I drop like hot dishes.

"The cost, you say? Well, I pay from £7 to £10 each delivered in London. But I do not think that a bear could be obtained as a pet under £15.

IN FULL SWING.

THE SEE-SAW.

feat consists in rolling a huge ball up one half of a see-saw, rocking freely, and down the other half. He is shown here anxiously awaiting the dreaded moment when the ascent quickly changes into an abrupt descent with a bang.

"There is one thing about which the public at large seem to be under a wrong impression, and this I should like to correct," added Mr. Permane. "Bears are herbivorous, not carnivorous. They will attack either animal or man only after a somewhat protracted fast. There is, therefore, no necessity for giving bears any meat whatsoever.

"Wherever I go," says Mr. Permane, "I am always besieged by the local butcher offering to provide me with the necessary meat and bones for my bears, and when I send him away, telling him that I only give them carrots and bread, he departs with a knowing wink, and probably imagines that I am utterly mistaken as to the food I ought to provide for my four-footed friends."

From the evident enjoyment shown by one of the pets in "Do let me have some," we

"This reminds me of an amusing incident. I expected a consignment of eight bears, which arrived at a certain London terminus rather late in the evening. I was sent for rather urgently, and though I resented that somewhat unwarranted intrusion upon my evening pipe, I went, and I now think it is as well that I did so. The whole station staff had assembled around the cage containing my 'goods.' The passengers were adding materially to the crush, and I had to exercise the utmost patience and goodwill to overcome the confusion that unhappily arose over my 'wild dogs,' for, let me add, they were, curiously enough, registered as such. They had been in their cage a week, and, of course, they tried their level best to get out of it at the earliest possible moment. I inwardly thanked the Russians for their common sense in providing iron bars of great strength."

One of this unruly party is shown at work a year after his arrival on English soil. His

"DO LET ME HAVE SOME."

have evidence enough that carrots are considered quite a dainty.

"My large bears," Mr. Permane adds, in explanation, "will eat 4lb. of bread and 10lb. of carrots per diem, and I do not believe in limiting their green food on any account. It is a splendid thing for their coats, and I can remember my four bears eating nearly two sacks full of freshly cut grass in one day.

THE PICKPOCKET.

"Food, however, is not the only thing to be considered. Bears, as a rule, drink water; that is, of course, in their native country. But, will you believe it, my bears were once confirmed bibbers. Do you see that little bear? His name is Fatty, and that name has been given him on account of his rotundity. He used to have beer for luncheon and beer for dinner, and so did the others. I had to put a stop to that, however. He is a clever little chap, and has learnt to be a pickpocket of no mean merit. Look at the knowing way in which he steals the bottle in The Pickpocket, and the joyful look when he finds himself the sole possessor of his plunder.

"In days gone by I used to give my bears what is commonly called 'four ale' beer; one day, however, while performing at Kidgrove, I was unable to obtain any of their every-day liquid. In the hurry of the moment I accordingly had to purchase some bottled Bass. That settled the bears. Some days later I had to move to another place, and I used 'four ale' again, but, alas, the bears would not drink it—they knew what they were about. One of them, on tasting the contents of his bottle, showed his indignation by throwing it right across the stage, smashing some half-dozen footlights, and growling in a way that caused some trepidation among the audience. Upon my explaining the reason, however, I met with a tremendous ovation. This incident ended the beer business altogether. I cast about for ways and means, and decided to give my bears sugar water. They took to it in the kindest fashion, and their bibbings are now exclusively confined to temperance drinks, a course which they have adopted with much wisdom, and to the benefit of my balance at the bank."

We ventured to ask Mr. Permane how his bears happened to acquire their former vicious habit in preference to temperance drinks, especially before large audiences, when it might have been thought that they, in the ordinary course of modesty, would have chosen the ample opportunities offered by elaborate stage scenery to hide their blushes.

"It was quite by accident," said the trainer. "One day one of my bears got loose in a stable, and seeing a bottle containing the remainder of some beer, he very ingeniously started to empty the contents thereof. I saw at once that there would be a good stage trick in this, and so I went ahead and taught them the use of the sugar-water bottle."

HIS PLUNDER.

The Dog Orchestra.

By John West.

[*From Photographs by Marceau, San Francisco.*]

THE DOG ORCHESTRA—A DRESS REHEARSAL.

THE "Dog Orchestra" is the property of Mr. Louis Lavater, and a very respectable property it is. Anyone with a head for figures can calculate the profits on the investment. Mr. Lavater pays from eighteenpence to five shillings (never more) for a dog, and the orchestra brings him in £50 or £60 a week.

The orchestra consists of six dogs, gorgeously dressed, and provided with specially made instruments. They are not remarkable for pedigree, but they *are* remarkable for intelligence. Let us introduce these canine instrumentalists. Commencing on the left-hand side of the photograph above we have Jack, the trombone player. Next comes Tim, the bass; followed by Patsey, the first violin; Prince, the big drum; Peter, the cymbals; and Bob, the small drum. The bows, drum-sticks, etc., are fixed to the dogs' paws by means of little bracelets.

Mr. Lavater has been a public entertainer (and a lover of dogs) all his life. Many years ago, whilst performing with a circus at Copenhagen, he resolved to set about getting his dog orchestra together—for it had long been his pet idea. He therefore went to the Dogs' Home in the Danish capital and paid five kroner for a nondescript cur. He took that cur home, fastened a stick on his paw, and persuaded him to beat a tea-tray. This same mongrel's musical education was in a fair way to be completed, when his master had to get rid of him on account of his pugnacious disposition.

"A LITTLE QUIET PRACTICE."

Here is Jack, the trombone player. Now, it is a comparatively easy matter to get a dog to stand upon his hind legs, but give him a relatively heavy instrument to hold in his front paws the while, and see if he does not overbalance himself and relapse into his natural position. Jack had to be taught to stand on his hind legs for half an hour at a time; next, to balance himself, holding the trombone in position; then to work the instrument properly; and, finally, to act in conjunction with his colleagues. And this with six different dogs, having six different instru-

A MUSICIAN OF IMPORTANCE.

ments, to say nothing of the "funny" dog, who makes blunders purposely, and is betrayed by his neighbour, who leaves his instrument and "informs" in his master's ear! The thing seems impossible, but was not so to Mr. Lavater, to whose skill and patience and humour and fertility of imagination the dog orchestra is a living monument.

But look at Jack, the trombone player. Long association with that doleful instrument has made Jack a mournful dog. It took him three months to learn to keep his balance. Mr. Lavater was almost in despair at the end of the first, and bought Jack a pair of cymbals, each weighing 8oz. "This," thought Jack, "is *not* beyond me," and he pounded away at the "sounding brasses" with no regard for tune. This dog has had an adventurous career. He was once locked up in Basle for wandering at large without a muzzle. He swam across Niagara rapids, and has been "held up" by robbers in America.

It is Mrs. Lavater who makes the dresses for members of the orchestra. Tim, the bass viol player, next depicted, wears an almost painfully sumptuous suit of bright green satin. He is a Maltese, is Tim, and this is probably why he wears at all times an air of dignified alertness, as who should say, "I'm doing my very best, but don't trifle with me." Tim's immediate predecessor had a rooted objection to all forms of work. He was as obstinate as he was lazy, and so he had to go.

Mr. Lavater was years getting together his orchestra and rehearsing before he ventured to appear in public. The *début* took place in a theatre near Amsterdam, and the trainer won't forget it this side of his grave. "They came out reluctantly," he said, "dazed by the glare of the footlights When they *were* out, they sat there looking helplessly at each other as if to say: 'What on earth are we doing here?' Then they did wrong things at wrong moments. Prince fell over his big drum. The others got up and tore aimlessly about the stage, scared by the trailing of their instruments behind them; and to crown all Jack, the trombone 'man,' fell into the (human) orchestra. My Dutch audience were hysterical with merriment, and even my wife, who stood in the wings, couldn't help laughing, in spite of her vexation and dismay."

The first violin is next represented—a quiet, sober dog, of evident culture and re-

PATSEY—THE FIRST VIOLIN.

AN ENERGETIC PLAYER.

finement. Not even the highly inappropriate clown cap, stuck rakishly on one side of his head, can detract from this animal's musicianly appearance. Patsey—a hideous name for a canine Sarasate—is clothed in a dress of green and mauve-striped silk. We fear his real character belies his appearance, however. He is always in trouble, being—like Esau—a mighty hunter, mainly of cats and people's pets generally.

Prince, who plays the big drum and whose portrait is next given, has but one fault—he is too excitable, too strenuous. Look at him in the photo. reproduced on the front page of this article. He is panting with excitement; his sharp little teeth are showing; he is pounding away for dear life. And yet he occupies the position of deputy-conductor under Mr. Lavater himself! However, although Prince may lack the composure of a Mottl, a Richter, or a Seidl, yet he makes up for it in feverish zeal. He is a Yorkshire, and affects a suit of pink and white satin.

"The first big drummer I had," remarked Mr. Lavater, "I bought at Frankfort. He was a half-bred terrier. I took him away and tied him up, but he broke loose time after time and ran back to his master, who was a stableman. He was a queer dog. At rehearsals, and even on the stage during public performances, he would wait until I wasn't looking, and then he'd give his nearest neighbour a sharp nip. For a long time I could never make out what caused those frightful yowls now and again, because, after biting his fellow, Prince would thump his drum anxiously, as though his soul was in his work and he wanted to get along with the show."

This dog (the predecessor, that is, of the "Prince" shown in our photo.—the same name is handed down, so to speak, from dog to dog) went mad on board a steamer going from Rotterdam to Antwerp. It was the funniest sight imaginable. The dog had the deck to himself in less than ten seconds. The captain wanted to have Prince thrown overboard, but Mr. Lavater wouldn't hear of his property being disposed of in that way. The trainer threw some water over the dog, and that brought him round—for a time. Not long afterwards he went mad again, and finally ran himself to death in the streets of Antwerp. Another member of the orchestra was torn to pieces by pariah dogs in the streets of Constantinople. The present big drummer, Prince, was bought from a butcher in Hamburg, so they are a cosmopolitan lot, these performers.

"WARBLING A LITTLE THING OF HIS OWN."

It took one or two of the dogs some time to forget their former owners after passing into Mr. Lavater's possession. Bob, the small drum, belonged to a widow who kept a perfumery shop, and for years that dog would run after ladies with black dresses.

Next comes Peter, the cymbal player. Many vicissitudes has Peter seen. Originally he belonged to a Paris *chiffonier*, or rag-picker. He used to go out o' nights with his master and mind the little cart, whilst unconsidered trifles were being gathered in. Peter is an Irish terrier, and he is a little sentimental, as may perhaps be judged from the portrait, in which Peter seems to be crooning a simple love song, accompanying himself on the cymbals. This is the manner of the whole performance, as told by Mr. Lavater:—

"The dogs follow me on to the stage and take their seats—the small drum first, then the big drum, the bass, the first violin, the cymbals, and last of all, the serious trombone. I stand up in the middle and commence by playing 'The Girl I Left Behind Me.' A waltz comes next, and then the dogs follow with 'The Last Rose of Summer'—played, I should explain, by means of bells on their paws, and not by their several instruments. It was an awful job to get them to play the bells properly. Either they would all play together or not at all. Later on in the performance, I call upon the dogs to sound a preliminary chord. They do so, and I say, 'That is a false chord.' Prince, the big drum, then hops up officiously and whispers something in my ear, whereupon I say, aloud, 'Oh, is he, indeed? Tim, I hear it is you who are out of tune.'"

THE SMALL DRUM.

Mr. Lavater tells us that each dog knows his own dress, so that the moment it is held up he runs forward to push his little head into it. The dogs are fed well—their ordinary diet consisting of biscuit, soup, bread, rice, and occasionally boiled cabbage. Each acting member has an understudy, so as to avoid hitches when the unforeseen happens. A former "big drum" came to a bad end on board an Atlantic liner by swallowing a lot of tow or jute, with which the engineers had been cleaning the machinery.

The last member of the orchestra to be introduced is Bob, the little drum. Bob is a water-spaniel, whose lines are cast in pleasant places. He is a painstaking dog, devoted to his profession. He is apt to thieve a little, but he is very lovable with it. "He forgot himself one night," remarked Mr. Lavater, sternly, "and made away with a pound of steak. I didn't beat him; I never do. I ignored him. He became penitent at once, and tried to attract my attention, but I would not look up from my paper. At last he was struck with an idea. He knew that whenever he did a smart thing he was applauded, so patting my knee eagerly with his paw to attract my attention for a moment, he began to parade across the hearth-rug on his hind legs!

Asked as to whether the dogs and their instruments were interchangeable, so to speak, Mr. Lavater sadly replied that they were not. "One night I tried it," he said. "I put the first violin on the big drum, and *vice-versâ*. The result was comic in the extreme. The big drum began to bang his fiddle as though he would knock a hole through it, whilst the first violin seized his stick and began to draw it slowly across his drum."

At the same time, the dogs have a keen sense of duty. Mr. Lavater was one evening taking them in his brougham to the theatre, when suddenly a Volunteer band struck up outside. The effect was extraordinary. The dogs leaped up in their baskets. One commenced to saw the air, another to clap his paws together, and so on. They thought they had received their cue, and they hastened to respond according to their lights, notwithstanding the trying circumstances.

A MISCELLANEA OF SWORD SWALLOWERS, HUMAN ARROWS AND STRONGMEN

If one thing has an enduring appeal to humans it must be novelty. The appeal of the new has inspired show producers to find, and performers to create, innovative and extraordinary attractions. For such attractions to be successful they must also appeal to the sensibilities of the public; sensibilities which change over time. It is doubtful that all the acts that follow would attract an audience today.

In the absence of the new, the fall-back is to be the greatest in some other way, whether as the largest, smallest, fastest or whatever. Tom Burrows made his first long club-swing in Aldershot, England, setting a record of six hours and establishing himself as the Champion Club-Swinger of the World in 1893. Over the next 14 years he improved on his record around the world, in Cairo, Montreal, Buenos Aires, Auckland, and other major cities. In 1907 the record was set at 66 hours and 15 minutes without a pause, this feat being achieved at the Empire Palace Theatre of Varieties in Johannesburg by Burrows and his rival Lloyd. Burrows was judged the winner on points, having displayed every possible club-swinging combination. Although the display, lasting nearly three successive days and nights, opened and ended on the stage the two men moved around the theatre to allow other acts to break the monotony.

Clearly not all claims made by performers, promoters or journalists are to be trusted. Here you will read about Cliquot's feat of swallowing 14 sabres. Before anyone attempts to emulate him, I should point out that an earlier article gave the number he swallowed as a mere four.

Some Peculiar Entertainments.

I.

By Framley Steelcroft.

YOU will often hear a man say, with smug, smiling wonder: "It's amazing what people will do for a living"; and, really, it is. Now, while I don't claim to have brought together —"right here" as the Americans say—all the peculiar items of "business" that are at this moment amusing, thrilling, or horrifying the paying public of both hemispheres, yet I have secured a representative lot, each one of whom I have at one time or another interviewed personally.

First of all, then, let me introduce to your notice (I feel something of a showman myself, now) Professor James Finney and his sister playing nap beneath the water in their big tank, which holds 300 gallons and cost a £100 note. And I should mention that it would be utterly impossible for these well-known swimming experts to simulate interest in the game, were it not that the water is heated to a temperature of 80deg. The porcelain cards are specially made at the Staffordshire potteries.

PROFESSOR FINNEY AND HIS SISTER PLAYING NAP UNDER WATER.

Another feat performed by Finney under water is the picking up of seventy or eighty gold-plated halfpennies with his mouth, his hands being tied securely behind his back. Just consider what this means. The expert assures me he finds the picking up and stowing away of the coins one by one in his mouth a most arduous and even painful task. He has, however, remained nearly four and a half minutes beneath the water, and is the possessor of a whole museum of cups and medals, whose mere intrinsic value is about £1,000.

Miss Marie Finney is, perhaps, our premier lady swimmer; and among her remarkable feats may be mentioned a header from London Bridge. It is not known what useful end this served, but it is duly recorded in the printed matter relating to the lady herself. This peculiar pair perform a variety of antics beneath the water, including eating cakes, drinking milk, and smoking. "Professor" Finney (this is the generic title of these specialists) makes some interesting calculations as to the quantity of comestibles consumed by him under water every year; and without prolixity I may say that this is enough to stock one of the Aerated Bread Company's well-known establishments.

I believe that in certain unexalted circles the expression "Go and eat coke!" is sometimes used as an opprobrious admonition. Into the derivation of this I will not go, but I have seen the thing done by an artiste (save the mark!) yclept "the Human Ostrich." He was this and much more; for not only did the man swallow every day sufficient carboniferous fuel to cook a respectable dinner for an ordinary Christian, but he also "chawed" and ate at each meal a stout glass tumbler and a lot of wood shavings. The "dessert" (note the ghoulish humour of the printed *menu*) consisted of a couple of lengthy tallow candles, and the whole was washed down by copious draughts of water, while the pianist played a suitably fantastic fantasia.

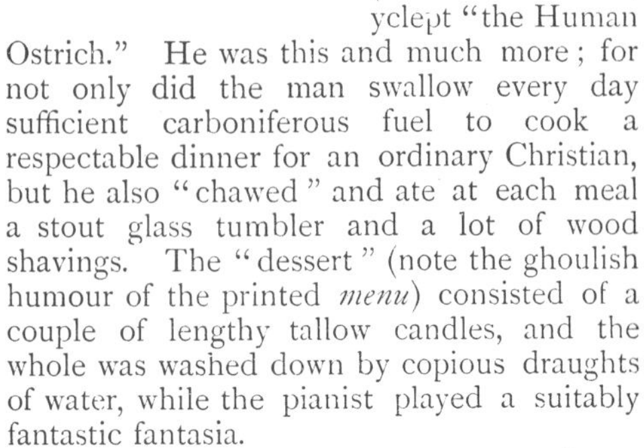

But some people will swallow anything—especially at £40 a week. We next see the Chevalier Cliquot (these fellows *must* have titles) in the act of swallowing the major part of a cavalry sabre, 22in. long. Cliquot,

CLIQUOT SWALLOWING A 22-INCH CAVALRY SABRE.

whose name suggests the swallowing of something far more grateful and comforting than steel swords, is a French Canadian by birth, and has been the admitted chief in his dangerous profession for more than eighteen years. He ran away from his home in Quebec at an early age, and joined a travelling circus bound for South America. On seeing an arrant old humbug swallow a small *machete* in Buenos Ayres, the boy took a fancy to the performance, and approached the old humbug aforesaid with the view of being taught the business. Not having any money, however, wherewith to pay the necessary premium, the overtures of the would-be apprentice were repulsed, whereupon he set to work experimenting on his own æsophagus with a piece of silver wire.

To say that the preliminary training for this sort of thing is painful, is to state the fact most moderately; and even when stern purpose has triumphed over the laws of anatomy, terrible danger still remains. On one occasion, having swallowed a sword and then bent his body in various directions as an adventitious sensation, Cliquot found that the weapon also had bent to a sharp angle; and quick as thought, realizing his own position as well as that of the sword, he whipped it out, lacerating his throat in a dreadful manner. Plainly, had the upper part of the weapon become quite detached, the sword-swallower's career must infallibly have come to an untimely end. Again, in New York, when swallowing *fourteen* 19in. bayonet-swords at once, Cliquot had the misfortune to have a too sceptical audience, one of whom, a medical man who ought to have known better, rushed forward and impulsively dragged out the whole bunch, inflicting such injuries upon this peculiar entertainer as to endanger his life and incapacitate him for months.

CLIQUOT SWALLOWING A WEIGHTED BAYONET-SWORD.

In the second photograph, on page 329, Cliquot is seen swallowing a very real bayonet-sword, weighted with a cross-bar and two 18lb. dumb-bells. In order to vary this performance, the sword-swallower sometimes allows only part of the weapon to pass into his body, the remainder being "kicked" down by the recoil of a rifle, which is fixed to the spike in the centre of the bar and fired by the performer's sister.

The last act in this extraordinary performance is the swallowing of a gold watch. As a rule, Cliquot borrows one, but as no time-piece was forthcoming at the private exhibition where I saw him, he proceeded to lower his own big chronometer into his æsophagus by a slender gold chain. Many of the most eminent physicians and surgeons in this country immediately rushed forward with various instruments, and the privileged few took turns in listening for the ticking of the watch inside the sword-swallower's body. "Poor, outraged Nature is biding her time," remarked one physician of courtly mien and shabby attire; "but, mark me, she will have a terrible revenge sooner or later."

The circumstances under which the next photograph was taken are not likely to fade easily from my mind; indeed, the task proved one of frightful suspense and anxiety to everyone concerned, including the artist of THE STRAND MAGAZINE. For in this very cage was a so-called "lion tamer" fearfully mauled by a majestic brute on Christmas Eve last; and this very man—Ricardo—dragged his dying colleague literally from the lion's jaws.

The fact is, we did not know what effect the magnesium flash would have on these four formidable beasts. Would it irritate them, and cause them to vent their leonine spleen upon the daring man in their cage? Nor do I use the word "daring" for cheap effect. The convenience of the lions—so to speak—was materially interfered with. They were not accustomed to do this sort of thing in the early morning; and, besides, the set performance was commenced in the middle. Frankly, the lions were fearfully excited, and at times they were only restrained from flying at Ricardo by men outside the cage who were armed with spiky poles like boat-hooks. At the moment of taking the photograph, the two lions in the middle of the cage remained perfectly still, their horrid jaws open, their great, lustrous eyes blazing, and the hot steam of their breath playing directly on their "tamer's" face.

RICARDO IN THE LIONS' DEN.

This man has practised his calling for seven years. He is not troubled with nerves; his constitution is of iron and his philosophy equally sound. "Of course, it *is* dangerous," he said to me, quietly; "but, then, might you not meet with a far less dramatic and more unexpected death beneath an omnibus in Piccadilly Circus, or the Clapham Road?

"At first I was a stableman in a travelling circus," he continued. "I always watched the old lion tamer's performance (he has now retired after more than twenty years of it); and I gradually got on fairly good terms with his beasts. The first cage I entered contained a mixed breed of Alpine and Siberian wolves. Yes, they were very 'ugly' and made for my throat."

One day Ricardo unceremoniously slipped into a den of three newly-purchased lions, who were more than equal to the occasion, since they nearly killed him forthwith. After three months' private intercourse with the huge animals, he was permitted to remain in their cage under protest. And this protest is quite permanent. Ricardo has known what it is to have a monstrous black African lion on his chest, his left knee well in the fearful brute's capacious mouth.

But you know the kind of thing. Let us pass to the "Singing Strong Lady," whose business is as funny as it is original. Really, I don't think the picture needs any explanation at all. This lady, by name (professionally) Miss Darnett, extends herself upon her hands and legs, face uppermost, while a stout platform with a semicircular groove for the neck is fixed upon her by means of a waist-belt, which passes through brass receivers on the underside of the board. An ordinary cottage piano is then placed by four men on the platform, and presently the lady's callous spouse appears, bowing, and calmly mounts upon the platform also, presumably in order that his execution may carry greater weight with the audience—and with his wife. First of all the pianist plays a dreamy, soothing Strauss waltz; and then the lady warbles a simple love-song—under difficulties and half a ton. But upon the burden of her song we need not dwell; she has enough to bear already.

THE SINGING STRONG LADY.

Although the foregoing performance appeals directly to any chivalry that may be in a man's nature, I doubt greatly whether it would make much impression on Rannin, the thick-skinned Cingalese, whose unique business is next depicted.

I saw this man last year at Ronacher's in Vienna; and of course there was the customary crowd of doctors and professors—real professors, this time—from the great hospitals in the Austrian capital.

Neither Occultism nor Theosophy have anything to do with this individual. Although, however, everything in the nature of the supernatural is wanting, the performances of the "man with the iron skin" are extraordinarily interesting; and in spite of their thrilling details they are given with decided grace. On the platform were the requisites with which Rannin conducts his show. Among them were a double ladder, the steps of which were formed of sabres ground to the sharpness of razors; also a kind of bed, thickly sewn with sharp-edged nails whose "business" ends were uppermost; and finally a barrel-shaped utensil, the inside of which was bristling with sharply-pointed nails. Rannin appeared with his shoulders, arms, and feet

"THE MAN WITH THE IRON SKIN"—(RANNIN, THE CINGALESE).

uncovered, and advanced lightly to the front of the platform. After showing how the sabres shred pieces of thick paper into atoms, he ran with bandaged eyes up one side of the sharp sabre-ladder and down the other, at the same time balancing a lamp on his forehead. He next lay down in the barrel, curled himself up closely, and allowed himself to be rolled up and down the platform. Extricating himself with some difficulty from the barrel, he offered himself to those present for their inspection. The impressions of the nails were certainly there, but not the slightest suggestion of a wound. Afterwards he placed himself on the spiked bed, and a man in thick boots mounted on his chest. This individual then placed an iron bar on his own shoulders, and from this two other men hung on the right and on the left. After several other marvellous performances, concluding, as here shown, with a jump from a high spiky platform through a hoop of razor-sharp sword-blades on to the nail-covered bed, Rannin ended his exhibition amid the plaudits of his audience. The medical authorities who had attended the séance of this veritable "man with the iron skin" asserted that it had nothing to do with the supernatural, but was the effect of a kind of anæsthesia, which is the insensibility of certain nerves to exterior impressions, occurring sometimes in peculiar natures. You have probably met such—though perhaps in different degrees.

My next performer is a man of retiring disposition—so retiring, in fact, that his professional *habitat*, so to speak, is a box measuring barely 23in. in length, its depth being 29in. and its width 16in. Nor is this all. When inside, six dozen wooden bottles, of the same size and shape as those which contain soda-water, are carefully stowed in with him, and then the lid is slammed down, leaving the audience, and especially disappointed farmers, to marvel that it should be possible for a man to make such a handsome living out of so infinitesimal a portion of the earth's surface. This man, Mr. Walter Wentworth, whom I met at Moore's Circus in Toronto, is the oldest contortionist living, being now about seventy years of age. He bestows upon his act the quaint name, "Packanatomicalization." In the second photograph he is seen asserting

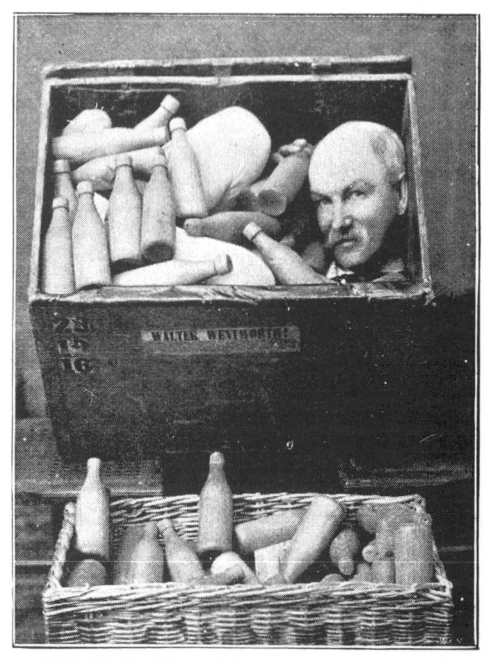

WENTWORTH, THE CONTORTIONIST, PACKED WITH SIX DOZEN BOTTLES.

his presence in the box in a very comic manner.

Wentworth married the lady whose portrait is next reproduced; this is Miss Grantly, the Albino Princess, who is believed to be a descendant of an albino tribe formerly found in America. The lady's appearance, *per se*, is supposed to constitute an entertainment. She has the usual characteristics of her kind — pure white complexion, pink eyes, white lashes and eyebrows.

As is well known, these "freaks" are well paid in the United States (Miss Grantly received 200 dollars a week); but this showman has a code of rigorous compulsory modesty for them—instituted, of course, in the interests of the paying public. For, clearly, if the dog-faced man or the bearded lady is foolish enough to go for a walk in park or street, followed by an ever-increasing crowd of unprofitable sight-seers, is not he or she doing a serious, wicked thing by spoiling potential patrons? Most certainly; if these well-paid "entertainers" *must* go out, they are compelled to take proper precautions. The Albino Princess, for example, invariably makes an elaborate toilet before venturing abroad, using cosmetics galore, and wearing an artful wig over her own snow-white hair.

WENTWORTH ASSERTING HIS PRESENCE IN THE BOX.

The reproduction on the next page depicts that curious mode of progression known as "ceiling-walking," as performed by the Vol Beck children. They were trained by their father, who has had thirty-two years' experience as a professional gymnast, and, therefore, plenty of time in which to invent new "business." On retiring, Mr. Vol Beck thought he could not do better than put his enthusiastic boys in the way of climbing the ladder of fame; or, at any rate, teach them to make inverted progress along a horizontal ladder—an equally arduous task.

This "property" ladder is of steel and brass, elaborately and beautifully made in thirty-three pieces, each fitting into the other. The apparatus weighs about 4cwt., and cost considerably more than £300; it is 34ft. in length, fitted with rings for the boys' feet, and is 3ft. 6in. wide.

"Seven long months of careful, anxious training took place," remarked Mr. Vol Beck to me, "before I could trust my children to walk upside down as you see them now, eighty or ninety feet from the ground. They can walk or run backwards and forwards at the rate of four miles an hour if necessary," he went on; "and they can cover 200ft. of 'ground' — or, perhaps, I should say air — without stopping for a moment."

And, certainly, the boys seem very much at ease during this novel act. On the occasion of the private performance they gave before THE STRAND MAGAZINE artist and myself, they

WENTWORTH'S WIFE, "MISS GRANTLY," THE ALBINO PRINCESS.

CEILING WALKING.

skipped alternately backwards and forwards with surprising celerity, considering the position and altitude; and the rapidity and confidence with which they hooked their feet in the rings, chatting as they went, was nothing short of marvellous.

Here is a lady with much dependent upon her, yet she bears up wonderfully well. Across her shoulders is a 700lb. bar-bell, on each end of which is a hanger-on whose attentions are frequently almost beyond endurance. This is Madame Elise, a professional strong lady, who is, on occasion, the sole support of a young elephant weighing half a ton, or perhaps ten able-bodied men. She was born at Neuilly, near Paris, and performs with her husband, who is in the same respect-compelling line. Her greatest feat was the lifting of eight men weighing altogether 1,700lb.; the lightest individual on this occasion weighed fourteen stone, and two among them turned the scale at twenty-one stone each. Truly a moving spectacle, this raising of gross, material men by a true, strong woman to her own exalted ethereal level.

And Madame tells funny stories. Travelling with a circus some years ago, the caravan in which she sat with five other "artistes"—trapezists, *haute école*, and "bareback" ladies—came to a standstill in the middle of a very steep hill in Cornwall. What with passengers and circus accessories, the horse was quite overcome, so he just stopped and, while awaiting further developments, commenced to browse peacefully at

MADAME ELISE, THE STRONG LADY, AND HER HANGERS-ON.

the wayside. Persuasion with a boat-hook was tried, but in vain, so Madame Elise, seizing a bit of rope, hastily alighted, harnessed herself to the heavily-laden van, and dragged it in triumph to the brow of the hill, where her place was taken by the ungallant brute.

Next is seen a party of Poona snake-charmers—a terribly dangerous performance, this, in spite of fallacies prevailing to the contrary. I interviewed the man who is playing the "tumri" while the cobra dances—Syad Jamal, of Sholapur. Strangely enough, this, he have seen many bite, then die and get black face," remarked Syad Jamal's interpreter; and no wonder, since either the double-spectacled cobra-de-capello of the town, or the nâgsarap of the thicket can, when fresh and angry, lay a strong man dead within two hours.

The newly caught snakes, some only as big as a lead pencil, and others 10ft. long, are taken home and placed in blanket-lined baskets. For days they eat nothing; but after a week or so the charmer takes his

INDIAN SNAKE-CHARMERS.

his philosophy was practically identical with that of Ricardo, the lion tamer. "He says," remarked my interpreter, in guttural tones, "that in Chapter 17 of the Koran is written: 'The scroll of every man's fate is tied on his neck at birth.'"

I learn that this profession remains in one family for centuries. Water-snakes, cobras, and pythons are used, and they are caught in the warm month of May, when the reptiles emerge from their holes. The hunting party in the hill districts are armed with forked sticks, with which the snakes are struck down when they erect themselves to bite; and on curling round these sticks they are thrust into a bag carried by a boy. Before this is done, though, the expert catcher seizes the deadly reptile with three fingers—two at the throat and one on the back of the head—and deftly cuts out the two poison fangs with a penknife, the operation lasting from ten to fifteen minutes. "While do

tumri—a villainous instrument, seen in the photograph, and with the squeal of a bagpipe, only more so—and on playing this the cobras begin to lift their horrid heads from the baskets, whereupon each reptile receives one egg and a pint of milk. The water-snakes are fed on whitebait, and the larger reptiles receive a chicken every fortnight. These snake-charmers, who are also jugglers, occasionally buy their snakes from the fakirs, paying from 1s. 2d. to £1 each for them.

"Tell him," said Syad Jamal, anxiously, "that we are beggars by birth and education, depending on the merchants for food and shelter; thus all our earnings are clear profit, or nearly so. And, also, that I have received as much as £20 for a performance from the Nizam of Hyderabad, besides gold and silver bracelets, and turbans of cloth of gold." Here the sâmp-wallah, or snake-charmer, fixed his mysterious eyes on me, probably to see if I was properly impressed by these details.

I desire to gratefully acknowledge here the very courteous assistance rendered me in preparing these articles by the following well-known caterers for public entertainment: Mr. Ben Nathan; Mr. Josiah Ritchie, of the Royal Aquarium; Mr. Read, of the Agricultural Hall; and Mr. Maurice De Freece, Manager to Messrs. Warner & Co., of Wellington Street.

Some Peculiar Entertainments.

II.

BY FRAMLEY STEELCROFT.

IT was, I suppose, the apocryphal feat of William Tell that suggested this item of sensational "business" to the crack rifle-shot, Mlle. Diana, who appears in this picture, and recently fulfilled a London engagement. But the analogy is not complete. It is no loving, fearful father that takes aim at the "apple" (in this case an evil-smelling, hollow globe of resin), but just a Winchester rifle of uncertain habits, and addicted to the vagaries and cussednesses common to all firearms.

In the first place, the resinous ball is suspended in mid-air by a string, and then the stand is rigged up with its rifle. The latter is then sighted by the expert with scrupulous care, so as to cover the pendant globe. After this has been done, Mlle. Diana takes up her position, rifle in hand, exactly beneath the "apple," and blazes away at the trigger of the other gun. Simple, isn't it? The discharges are practically simultaneous, and the lady's dark hair is in most cases instantly powdered with particles of the shattered ball of resin. I say "in most cases" advisedly, because it sometimes happens that the bullet passes over or at the side of the "apple," and on one occasion the rifle-ball actually passed between the globe and Mlle. Diana's scalp, the weapon having been aimed a shade too low.

"I must say," remarked the lady rifle-shot, "that it wants a lot of nerve to face and fire at that rifle. You see, the slightest deviation in sighting may be fatal; and then, again, the cartridge may be a poor one, causing the rifle to hang fire. In such cases the first thing to be done, of course, is to get out of the line of fire without a moment's delay, for the rifle may go off immediately on its own account, as, indeed, it has done more than once."

Now, was ever such an opportunity given an experienced angler as that suggested by my next picture? And he *is* an experienced angler—perhaps I ought to say a professional angler—who has played bigger salmon in the Fraser River than ever Scotland produced. And surely this is a novel angling contest—Rod *v.* Woman. I witnessed the interesting event in a specially-arranged swimming-bath, the "fish" being the well-known expert, Miss Annie Luker, whose father trained Captain Webb, and who is herself engaged at this day in imparting the natatory art to a couple of thousand London Board School children. Miss Luker's biggest feat was a swim from Kew to Rotherhithe.

This angling contest is tremendous fun. The salmon-line is hooked in the lady's belt, and she certainly gives fine play. Sometimes the line breaks, sometimes the rod. Occasionally the fair "fish" is too much for her would-be captor, who, *nolens volens*, is drawn into what is emphatically *not* his element. If Miss Luker is landed in the corner within

MLLE. DIANA SHOOTING THE "APPLE" FROM HER OWN HEAD.

A NOVEL ANGLING CONTEST—ROD *v.* WOMAN.

ten minutes, however, the victory is given to the angler, who, it is significant to note, does not stand at the shilling side of the bath. This is, of course, in order that when the "fish" allows herself to be drawn quite close, and then dashes away through the water, splashing frightfully, the sixpenny public only get the benefit of whatever moisture may be going about.

A very different kind of entertainment is provided by the blindfold child pianist, Jennie Gabrielle, a Birmingham girl, who, at the age of seven, could positively play anything that was set before her. A few years ago the child was taken to the Gaiety Theatre to see a burlesque, and next morning she surprised her parents by sitting down to the piano and playing off the whole score—songs and all.

Not only is Miss Gabrielle blindfolded by any member of her audience who may wish to undertake the task, but the keys of the instrument are completely covered with silk ; and yet, under these difficult conditions, you may give her elaborate pieces from such masters as Beethoven, Mendelssohn, Bach, and Schubert, which will be rendered with surprising accuracy and delicacy of touch.

Chimah was born in Ning-po fifty-seven years ago, and, briefly, he may be described as a diminutive man with monstrous ideas. I saw him in Kohl and Middleton's Museum at Chicago. As a rule, the showman gives an exhaustive and sometimes exhausting description of each individual freak in the show. The bearded lady beams benignly, while the

JENNIE GABRIELLE, THE BLINDFOLD CHILD PIANIST.

CHIMAH, THE CHINESE DWARF.

length of her hirsute appendage is measured for an appreciative public; and the armless man paints dexterously with his toes, what time the showman indicates the beauties of the landscape that is growing under his artistic foot. But Chimah needs no one to tell his story. His height is exactly 24½in., and in his best days he received nearly £500 a week; for, to the potent attraction of his diminutive stature, he added the great reputation of a *raconteur* skilled in the lore of many lands. Also, he smoked cigars nearly as big as himself; and his appetite was prodigious. I have seen him eat a great dinner, whereof a pound-and-a-half of steak was but a part. Last summer Chimah bought a farm of 20,000 acres in Ohio, and celebrated his establishment thereon with a big house-party, Cliquot, the sword-swallower, referred to last month, being among the number of invited guests. The tiny Chinaman is very fond of jewellery, owning quite a fortune in diamonds and rubies; and he is extremely religious, after the manner of his kind. He worships his ancestors—as, indeed, he ought, seeing that they did a big thing for him in bringing him into the world so small. At home Chimah's hobby is singing, and he is for ever practising duets with his wife, the midget Princess Josepha, who is seen by the side of her gigantic sister in the next illustration.

Lady Amma, the French giantess, and her two sisters stand next on my programme, and, mind, they *are* her sisters. In this case age—and appetite—is in an inverse ratio to size. The smallest of the three is known as Princess Josepha, and is thirty-two years of age; there are not nearly so many inches in her stature, however. The next sister is shown with the giantess and the dwarf simply to emphasize Nature's strange freak. There is nothing abnormal about her, though—"just an or'nary cuss," as her unfeeling showman remarked.

Lady Amma herself, although only twenty-two years old, is nearly 7ft. 9in. in height; and yet I am assured that she eats less than an ordinary woman. I last saw her in Harry Davis's Museum, in Pittsburg, Pennsylvania, where she had a special conveyance built for her convenience. The curious thing is, that her eldest and smallest sister, Princess Josepha, fell in love with and

LADY AMMA, THE FRENCH GIANTESS, AND HER TWO ELDER SISTERS.

married Chimah, the extraordinary Chinese dwarf whose portrait is seen at the top of the preceding page.

The next illustration depicts the "strong-man" craze *in excelsis*. The individual upon whom all this responsibility rests is one Milo, a young Italian, whose novel turn was first introduced to a British audience on August 24th, 1891. The roundabout which he supports on his chest was made by half-a-dozen different people, and fitted together by Milo himself, who is something of a mechanic. This was to obviate the possibility of the idea being pirated too soon; for I should mention that all innovations in the entertainment world are copied sooner or later by unintelligent performers whose creative power is a minus quantity.

Without passengers, the apparatus weighs 8½cwt.; loaded, more than a ton. Although only seven persons are being carried in the illustration (and notice the gentleman saluting as though he were doing a smart thing) it is possible to accommodate a round dozen on the machine, by means of extra seats placed on the bars. Moreover, on occasion, a barrel organ is placed in the centre and slowly ground by a dismal-looking Italian, who seems utterly unconscious of the fact that he is rendering himself and his music a heavy burden to at least one of his neighbours.

The roundabout is about 12ft. high and 14ft. in diameter across the ornamental top; it cost a trifle over £50.

Next comes Jules Keller, the upside-down man, whose arms are to him what legs are to more ordinary folk. He is a Polish Jew, thirty-three years of age, and is a giant of strength from his waist upwards. Keller has managed to support himself, independently of his lower extremities, with very great success. His legs, although outwardly almost perfect, contain no bone, or next to none; consequently his people very properly apprenticed him to the tailoring business. He developed the extraordinary power of his arms, simply because he had to get about somehow. By degrees he forsook the tailoring platform on which he had squatted for years, and took to another and far more profitable stage.

MILO, THE STRONG MAN, SUPPORTING A LOADED ROUNDABOUT.

Amazing as it may seem, the "upside-down man" can take a clear leap of 4ft. over an obstacle on his hands; and he can in the same way jump down from a platform 9ft. high. I saw him do this, and noticed that his tremendously powerful arms yielded as he struck, letting his chin almost touch the ground in order to break the fall. Keller's elastic "step" cannot be described. In Vienna he walked on his hands for a wager against a young athlete, and beat him; of course he had a little start, and his opponent walked after the manner of men.

JULES KELLER, THE "UPSIDE-DOWN MAN."

In the photograph Keller is seen going up one side of a double ladder at a fine springy pace. He runs, too, in an extraordinary way, his legs dangling carelessly over his head; and he concludes his performance with an American sand-dance or jig—positively the most unique thing you ever saw, since the man's lower limbs are useless—a mere encumbrance thrown on his hands, as you may say.

My next item is not meant to advertise an already notorious patent medicine, although the "spot"—a 6ft. straw target—is in a fair way of being touched. This is the Human Arrow, "a thing the imagination boggles at," as Browning's incomparable parodist once remarked. And yet the lady is actually shot from a monstrous cross-bow, and traverses some 30ft. of hot, vitiated atmosphere before striking the target.

I think it was Dr. Johnson who remarked, speaking of a dog that walked on its hind legs, "the thing is not well done, but the wonder is that 'tis done at all." So with this startling feat. You can't expect the girl to be sent hurtling half a mile against a brick wall. The distance is short, the regulation net is used, and the target, on being touched, retires as gently and gracefully as the "Arrow" herself does shortly afterwards. Then, again, I must confess that powerful springs have more to do with this aërial flight than the string of the bow.

Fleas, like the poor, are always with us; of course, I refer to performing fleas. And I was fortunate enough to light upon the only original discoverer, inventor, trainer—call him what you will—of these interesting creatures. He is a Roumanian (a native of Bucharest), so that you may say, "Here is another irritating Eastern question sprung upon us," more especially since the "Professor" (all he professes is fleas) obtains his stock in the wilds of Bethnal Green.

THE HUMAN ARROW.

He was a jeweller in the dirty but picturesque Roumanian capital, and having caught one of these insects—by no means an isolated specimen—he amused himself by twisting fine gold wire round its body, and watching its struggles. These must have been diverting, for the idle assistant presently fixed his captive flea in a little box beneath one of those peculiar eye-glasses used by watchmakers when inspecting the works of a watch. This was the nucleus of a show which, in its palmy days, brought its lucky owner £40 a day in the European capitals.

When the young jeweller, encouraged by his fellow-assistants and his master's patrons, resolved to give up his calling and go into the trained-flea line, his people very properly objected; and, indeed, finding him obdurate, they shut their doors against him when he chanced to be in their vicinity—"*In propria venit, et sui eum non receperunt*"—if the quotation be not irreverent.

I asked the Professor how he fed his insects. He promptly pulled up his coat-sleeve and bared his arm. "I lives on dem, an' dey lives on me"; and he laughed heartily at what was evidently a stock witticism.

The fleas are shown on a circular, white-topped table. They are "stabled," as the Professor puts it, in a shallow box filled with cotton wool. As the insects themselves could not be photographed in their performance, I reproduce here a facsimile of the showman's "play-bill." The draughtsmanship may not be anatomically correct, but beyond question it is funny. The tiny vehicles are of brass; and for harnessing, fine gold wire is used. Wire is also used for chaining up the odious "house-dog," and it figures likewise in the balancing-pole of the tight-rope performer, the swords of the duellists, and the tackle of the windmill.

Noticing the dejected aspect of the "house-dog," I asked if the fleas lived long at this sort of work. "Ubbowd doo year," was the reply. The only remarkable incident the Professor recalls took place in Berlin, at the time when the insects were kept in a glass bottle. One morning, just as the show was about to commence for the amusement of a crowd of ladies and gentlemen, some awkward individual knocked the jar, "stock" and all, on the ground. "Dat dime," remarked the Professor in tones of reminiscent sadness, "my badrons garried avay de vlees, an I ad to ged zum more."

The dangerous "Monte Christo" diving feat, which forms the subject of the next two illustrations, is performed by Baume, the swimming expert, who has already saved more than twenty lives from drowning. Baume first appears clad in a shabby suit of clothes, which, however, conceals the smart diving costume he wears beneath. He is then hoisted by means of a rope and pulley

"PLAY-BILL" OF THE PERFORMING FLEAS.

to the platform, seventy or eighty feet above the tank and the audience. Here the diver is bound hand and foot, and then enveloped in a sack which is tied over his head.

All that remains for the gratification of an expectant public is a well-judged leap into the tank of water below, and a subsequent re-appearance—unfettered and free from the sack; in short, "without encumbrance of any kind," as the advertisements have it. This is far easier said than done. The leap is one of over 70ft., and that very much in

THE MONTE CHRISTO DIVE—FALLING.

the dark, not to speak of the transformation beneath the water. When all is ready, the shapeless bundle bends over to glance at the bright spot far below; this is the tank, containing 7ft. of water, on which powerful beams of lime-light are flashed. Finally, Baume gives the sack a hitch up, in order that it may not get entangled in his legs or be caught by the rush of wind during the descent, and then he takes a long breath before leaving the platform. On striking the water (the mighty splash very literally damps the ardour of many of his incautious admirers) the diver executes a somersault, during which he unties his bonds, and kicks the sack upwards off his body. A man is in waiting to seize the sack the moment it reaches the surface. The next thing Baume has to do beneath the water is to divest himself of his outer garments—the shabby suit aforesaid—and then he is free to rise to the surface, amid thunderous applause, climb the iron ladder at the side, and finally retire breathless and dripping.

It was at the Soldiers' Club in Cairo that I witnessed the very peculiar entertainment given by the King of Clubs—Tom Burrows, champion club-swinger of the world. Burrows was born at Ballarat, in January, 1867, and came to England in 1891, when he became teacher of boxing and club-swinging at the Royal Military Gymnasium, Aldershot.

On March 20th, 1895, Burrows swung a pair of clubs for twenty-four hours at our famous camp; and it was in order to break this record that he gave an exhibition in Cairo before Lord and Lady Cromer, the Sirdar, Sir Herbert Kitchener, and many other distinguished folk.

The champion made the following conditions for the undertaking: (1) The clubs were to weigh 2lb. each, and to be 24in. long; (2) To swing at least 50 complete circles each minute; (3) No rest or stop allowed during the 25 hours; (4) No artificial aid of any sort allowed; (5) To swing no fewer than 70,000 complete circles in the record; and (6) That there should always be at least two judges present to watch the swinging.

Burrows commenced swinging the clubs at 9.18 on Wednesday evening, every person in the distinguished gathering being filled with admiration at the graceful way in which he manœuvred

THE MONTE CHRISTO DIVE—GETTING OUT OF THE TANK.

SWINGING CLUBS FOR 26¼ HOURS WITHOUT REST.

his clubs—circling, curving, twirling. From thence onward through the evening, and throughout the whole of the night, and all next day, this athlete swung the clubs without stopping for a moment: until a mighty burst of cheering at 9.18, on Thursday night, proclaimed that he had equalled his Aldershot feat. At 10.18 further enthusiastic cheering greeted Burrows, having established a world's record of twenty-five hours' continuous swinging.

Still, the indomitable fellow went on, until he finally stopped at 11.33, on Thursday night, having swung the clubs without one moment's cessation for twenty-six hours and fifteen minutes.

But surely thirty-five years' manipulation of marionette strings is also something of a record; this is claimed by Mr. R. Barnard, who had the old witch and her satellites in hand when this photograph was taken. The smaller figures are, in the first place, secreted in the witch's pockets, so that the operator had to control no fewer than fifty strings at once while putting this one figure through its performance.

These marionettes have quite a charming little portable theatre of their own, besides scenery to the value of £150. Altogether Mr. Barnard possesses seventy figures, which cost, undressed, about £2 each. And although the clever little man knows no more about art than he does about the integral calculus, yet he carves the heads himself out of yellow pine, while his wife dresses the perfect puppets; and the result is creditable in the highest degree to the taste and skill of both. A surprising amount of attention is paid to small details of dress. The satins and silks used in the dresses of the "ladies"

THE OLD WITCH AND HER SATELLITES—A MARIONETTE FIGURE WITH FIFTY STRINGS.

MOUNTING THE LADDER OF SWORDS.

(there are $2\frac{1}{2}$yds. in that of the fairy) cost from 3s. 11d. to 5s. 11d. a yard; and then there are numerous costly items of under-clothing, lace, spangles, bead and bugle trimmings, and innumerable miscellaneous "properties." I was confidentially assured that the columbine wears silk stockings and twelve or fourteen petticoats; and also that the clown has to be repainted once a week, owing to the tremendous lot of knocking about he receives at the hands of impossible policemen.

The string used is bought white at eighteen-pence per ball, and then dyed by a special process. Of course, the strings get entangled sometimes, but the ready wit of the operator, who stands on the narrow platform above the scene, hardly ever fails; and when such awkward incidents do occur, dialogue and business are swiftly changed to meet the emergency. I can only say that Barnard's marionettes constitute a miniature theatre and variety show combined. The figures are infinitely more amusing than many *lions comiques* who drive from hall to hall of an evening, and far less vulgar.

Talk about a sharp climb up the ladder of fame! Just look at this Japanese girl—one of the Chyochis family—who made her *début* in the City of Mexico, as a sword-walker, six years ago. As will be seen in the photograph, the rungs of the step-ladder consist of Japanese scimitars, and there is no mistake about the keenness of their edge. The lady tells me that the secret of the thing lies in gripping the edge of each sword in a fearless way with the toes, and stepping up briskly when the bare foot is properly placed. Of course, the slightest cutting or sawing movement must be avoided. And she needs no apostle to admonish her to "walk circumspectly."

I have now to introduce with becoming gravity the Boneless Wonder—one Ames—a man with an accommodating vertebra. Nor am I jesting when I assert that this contortionist has quite a bump—one of those hard, permanent bumps—on his chin, caused by strumming upon the latter with his heels whilst in the position shown in the photograph. The bump, which I had an opportunity of carefully examining for myself, might be truthfully translated by an astute phrenologist or

AMES, THE BONELESS WONDER.

physiognomist as indicating an extremely pliable disposition.

In the picture, Ames is seen performing his most extraordinary feat. An adjustable iron rod, terminating in a leather mouthpiece, is fixed to a massive table, and on this the acrobat raises his body over his head, resting his whole weight on his teeth, and folding his arms with an appearance of placidity he must be very far from feeling.

But, plainly, we cannot all be "boneless wonders." Not unto everyone is it given to perform such feats, and certainly not unto Mrs. Johnson, a lady of strongly marked individuality, whose portrait next appears. The last time I had the pleasure of meeting this substantial person was at Huber's Museum, in Fourteenth Street, New York, where she was in receipt of seventy-five dollars a week. Mrs. Johnson was a remarkably healthy woman, and one who exasperated her lecturer beyond everything by correcting him forcibly when in the midst of his harangue to the crowd. Like the less bulky members of her sex, she was amazingly fond of dress and jewellery. In the photograph she is wearing her favourite robe—acres of black silk, with raised flowers worked in gorgeous colours.

The most stringent regulations ever made by a flint-hearted agent could not keep Mrs. Johnson indoors; probably this is why her salary dwindled from 200 dollars a week down to a paltry seventy-five. She *would* assert herself—not a difficult thing, you would think, at any time—and she took long walks very early in the morning. Then, of course, with that superhuman energy that springs eternal in the breast of man when free shows are available, people got up early and followed her at a respectful distance. This latter was as it should be, for the great lady was of uncertain temper, and if she took it into her massive head to assault anyone (as she once did the unfortunate dog-faced man—himself no chicken), it would mean utter annihilation, Mrs. Johnson being 7ft. high and weighing 28 stone. Curiously, no one ever thought to ask why Mr. J. was not on the spot to share the glory and the seventy-five dollars.

THE FAT LADY, MRS. JOHNSON.

Side-Shows.

I.

By William G. FitzGerald.

THEY are of very ancient date. It has been stated that the various colossal skeletons that come to light from time to time are merely the remains of prehistoric side-shows—giants, in fact, that were in former times exhibited at one stone axe per "time." However this may be, side-shows have long flourished, and, doubtless, will continue to flourish so long as inquisitiveness remains a part of our nature.

Shows of all sorts thrive exceedingly on American soil—and coin. Barnum was a millionaire several times over during his wonderful career; and Adam Forepaugh had more money than he knew what to do with. Travelling shows in the United States are conducted on a tremendous scale. The staff may number hundreds, and then there are the human freaks (ever jealously guarded from the non-paying eye), the huge menagerie, and hundreds of horses of all kinds, from the *haute-école* Arab right down to bony "Jimmy," who drags a van.

From a Photo by] SPECIAL TRAIN BELONGING TO COUPÉ'S TRAVELLING SHOW. [*M. G. Greene, Atlanta, Ga.*

No wonder they require special trains! The photo. reproduced above shows the passenger part of one of these. The centre panel of the great Pullman car is adorned with a modest portrait of the proprietor of the show—or "director-general," as he loves to be styled. He probably owns the whole train, as well as the show, by the way. Advertisement being the very breath of the showman's nostrils, you will also notice lurid lithographs on the side of the car, so that the whole makes a stirring *ensemble* as the train enters a great terminus, with perhaps the bearded lady as engine-driver, and the pig-faced gentleman astride one of the buffers.

The born showman is so earnest in manner and gesticulation, so leathern of lung, and so profuse—not to say incoherent—in opulent adjectives before potential patrons, that he at length believes implicitly in every statement he himself makes. Such a one was Coxswain Terry, shrewdest of sailors, who owns the show next depicted. It was announced as "a 'air-raisin' pifformance"; and certainly it was a little uncanny, though not exactly up to the standard of the pictures hung outside. These depicted a gigantic individual, apparently in the last throes of death beneath a tropical sea, and surrounded by every conceivable (and inconceivable) denizen of the deep. Sword-fish and shark, whale and octopus—all were attacking him with staggering unanimity.

Visitors to this side-show see a tank containing 500 gallons of water—positively guaranteed not to burst and nearly drown the spectators, as similar tanks have often done. The water is heated by gas overnight to a temperature of about 90 degrees, and into it are thrown six or seven good-sized pythons or rock-snakes (some over 12ft. long), who protest fiercely against the whole thing. They would leave the water forthwith, were it not for the strong wire-netting on top of the tank.

Presently a man, young and scantily clad, appears at the back. He removes half the wire-netting and drops into the water among the snakes. They instantly twine themselves about his legs, his waist, his arms, and his neck; but some, more knowing than the rest, neglect him altogether, and endeavour to hurry out of the hated element.

UNDER WATER AMONG THE SNAKES.

A confederate mingles with the crowd in order to warn the submerged performer when one of the reptiles is half-way out; to help him when he is severely bitten (as he frequently is); and to render assistance when he is in danger of being strangled by a python about his throat.

The performance is one wild, whirling struggle with the writhing reptiles—sinking to the bottom from time to time with an armful of them, merely to drag them hither and thither to keep up the excitement and give patrons value for money. About once a fortnight, each snake takes a rest and a meal, the latter consisting of live rabbits, birds, and rats.

The baby, Thomas Sabin, whose portrait next appears, was a great blessing to his parents, who were people of no great weight, either in the literal or social acceptance of the term. For years he brought them ten pounds a week, his weight increasing, but his age almost standing still. He has a nice face, but few would care to dandle him on their knee. As we see him in the photo., this phenomenal baby is just turned two years of age, and weighs nearly *eight stone.* The child was born in Banbury, and was in no way remarkable for some considerable time. At length, however, little Tommy began to put on flesh so rapidly, that his parents, alarmed, sent for the local doctor, who in turn summoned a specialist from London. All this, of course, created some sensation, and in due time the inevitable showman came along with tempting offers.

It is more or less well known that vigilant agents are for ever scouring the universe, from Whitechapel to Central Africa, for

THE BIGGEST BABY IN THE WORLD.
From a Photo. by Hodge, Plymouth.

freaks of Nature—"refined freaks," as one showman remarked, whatever he meant by that. The famous "dime museum" is the habitat of human freaks; and America is the home of the dime museum. You will find one or more of these interesting institutions in every considerable town from Maine to California. The proprietor takes an empty shop or store in the principal street, rigs up a circular platform, and seats the freaks thereupon. Some waxworks or a cage of monkeys or lions are provided by way of adventitious free attractions; and perhaps there will be a "bijou theatre" at one side, in which fifteen minutes' performance is given at intervals; this latter, however, is an extra. But the freaks are the mainstay of the show. There they sit all day, beaming sympathetically on the inquisitive crowds who surge around them. There are fat ladies, Siamese twins, and skeleton men, bearded ladies and elastic-skinned people; giants and dwarfs; armless artists, and cave-dwelling pigmies; girls with hair of phenomenal length; people half black and half white; and countless other monstrosities whom to see is a nightmare.

Every half-hour the official lecturer clears his raucous throat and proceeds to deliver the history of each freak, with many an impressive flourish, whilst the freak himself (or herself) glares down with conscious pride on his throng of admirers. Such is the typical dime museum.

The skeleton man, next seen, has been the round of innumerable shows in the Old and New Worlds. His wife and son are photographed with him, and are in no wise abnormal. On the other hand, freaks—particularly midgets — often marry among themselves, mainly for business reasons.

The etiquette of the side-show holds a superabundance of clothing highly improper. Freaks *must* exhibit a good deal of their person *in puris naturalibus*, so as to do away with any suspicion of humbug. For the side-show cannot exist in an atmosphere of scorn and doubt; enthusiasm, energy, earnestness—these are the notes that herald success and fortune.

By no means the least curious of the American side-shows is the kiosk of the professional paper-tearer, which is seen in the next illustration. The entire façade of this elaborate little structure is made wholly

THE SKELETON MAN WITH HIS WIFE AND SON.
From a Photo. by Chas. Eisenmann, New York.

KIOSK OF THE PROFESSIONAL PAPER-TEARER.
From a Photo. by Robinson & Roe, Chicago.

of paper torn into shape by the Professor himself, who boasts of using no other implements whatever than his own ten fingers. This is certainly very wonderful when one looks closely into the photograph and studies the delicate lace-work; the arch and columns and ornaments, and the flower-pots and birds within—all made of paper torn with the fingers.

But this unique artist had a somewhat ignoble end in view; as a fact, he sold a patent blacking, using his stall and his handiwork as a lure for the unwary, who were ultimately almost forced to buy.

"Miraklus Con-t'nental Sensation. The Mawvel o' the Age. A wild, fiery Hafrican Elephant walkin' on the tight-rope, an' a dawncin' on a row o' bottles." Thus overwhelmingly was our next side-show announced to the expectant crowd. What the wild, fiery one did do is seen in the photograph; and it certainly is an interesting spectacle to see the enormous brute picking its way with patient care along the "bottles," which, as one may judge, are massive blocks of wood mounted on substantial planks. There is a platform at either end, and on to this the elephant steps with an unmistakable air of relief, after having accomplished the perilous passage.

There is still a mint of money in the side-show business. Tom Thumb received £150 a week, yet his presence (scarcely "services," since he did nothing but strut about the platform) was worth double that sum to his proprietor.

It was the famous freak-hunter, Farini, who introduced to the London public Zazel — "a beautiful lady shot from a monstrous cannon." Zazel was paid £100 a week at the Royal Aquarium. The cannon itself, I gather, was a French patent concern; it was made of wood, painted to resemble steel. Inside there was an ingenious arrangement of powerful india-rubber springs, which acted upon the plate on which Zazel herself stood. The lady got right into the cannon and lay upon her back, her feet resting upon the plate that was to propel

AN ELEPHANT WALKING ON BOTTLES.

"A BEAUTIFUL LADY SHOT FROM A MONSTROUS CANNON."
From a Photo. by the London Stereoscopic Co

her. The whole thing was made wonderfully impressive. The showman called for perfect silence at so serious a moment, and the band stopped playing. A flaming torch was applied to a fuse and there was a terrific explosion—*outside the cannon.* Simultaneously "the beautiful woman" flew out from the muzzle some thirty-five feet, and ultimately dropped into the net below.

There is one peculiarity common to all freaks and human curiosities. Directly they enter the show business, they assume another name—a name more or less appropriate or descriptive. Thus, midgets will be "billed" as Princess Topaz, or Little Dot, or Captain Tiny; and fat ladies as Madame Tunwate, or some such inelegant but suggestive cognomen.

"Knotella," the contortionist, is a case in point. His real name—like the birth of Jeames—is "wropt up in a mistry." However, this photograph proves that the man can throw himself into most amazingly bizarre postures. It is an interesting fact, by the way, that photography plays a very important part in the lives of professionals of this sort. Suppose they live in Vienna, and want an engagement in London. They give their best possible show in a photographer's studio, and then send a complete set of photos. to the London agents, supplementing this photographic record of their entertainment with a full written description. The agents, in turn, place the photos. before the managers of the variety theatres; and thus an engagement may be definitely fixed without the performer leaving his home in a distant part of Europe.

It is difficult to say whether male or female contortionists ("benders," as they call themselves) are the more successful in assuming strange and fearful attitudes; certain it is that Knotella is run pretty close by a charming young lady whose professional name is Leonora. Clad in

"KNOTELLA" DOING HIS WONDERFUL BACKWARD BEND.
From a Photo. by Wilkinson & Moor, Manchester.

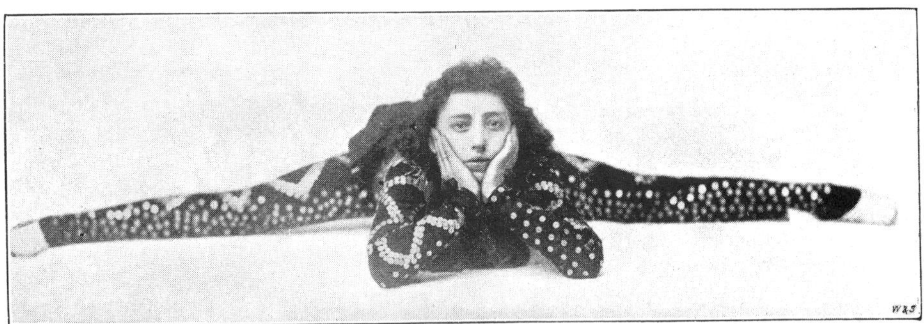

From a Photo. by] LEONORA AS "CONTEMPLATION." [*Meacham & Sabine, Youngstown.*

snaky, scaly tights, Leonora throws herself into postures that simply baffle description.

In the first photo. the lady is seen in an extraordinary attitude of quiet contemplation, her body hidden altogether. In the next

LEONORA POSING AS A "HUMAN BOAT."
From a Photo. by Meacham & Sabine, Youngstown.

she has formed herself into a kind of ship, with a decidedly prepossessing figure-head. This contortionist tells me she practises incessantly, and is for ever trying to devise some new and startling posture which, without being in any way repulsive to an audience, will yet demonstrate the marvellous pliability of the human frame.

The pony, lamb, and dog seen in the accompanying photograph are a diminutive trio, and they go through their performance without extraneous assistance of any sort. A highly ornamental kind of stall is provided for the pony, and, standing in this, he faces the audience. On a plush-covered canopy over his back stands the lamb, whilst the dog sits on a sort of third story above. Presently, out trots the pony for a gallop round, and as he passes the tier of canopies for the third time, the lamb skilfully leaps down on to his broad back. Then comes another round or two of this jockeying, and when the little dog thinks the public are in need of a new sensation, down *he* jumps on to the lamb's back, and round they all go, looking as if they really enjoyed it. In turn the riders watch their opportunity and regain their platforms, and at length the pony backs into the lower stall, to receive his share of well-merited applause.

Mr. John Chambers, the "Armless Wonder," when not side-showing, keeps a comfortable little shop at 697A, Old Kent Road. The famous Indian Armless Boy, who created such a sensation in America, didn't have to shave, or travel on the railway by himself, or use a latch-key, or put on boots, or read the daily papers, or write letters, or make himself useful in the house as becomes the father of grown-up girls. Mr. Chambers does all these things, and more. Never shall I forget his performance before

THREE PERFORMERS WHO GIVE A SHOW ON THEIR OWN ACCOUNT.
From a Photo. by G. Wacker & C. Knoth, Hamburg.

MR. CHAMBERS, THE ARMLESS WONDER, SHAVING HIMSELF WITH HIS FOOT.

a railway booking-office. He asked for the ticket, and while the clerk was getting it, the right laceless shoe was off, followed by the stocking, revealing a wondrously white, sensitive foot, with a wedding-ring on the second toe. Like lightning this foot was lifted and dipped into the low inside pocket of an Inverness cape, and next moment, simultaneously with the production of the ticket, the exact fare was "planked" smartly down on the ledge.

There is hardly a single thing which ordinary men do with their hands that Mr. Chambers cannot do with his feet. He owes the inception of his invaluable training to his mother, who, as she saw her baby kicking on the hearth-rug—as babies will—conceived the idea of teaching him to use his feet as other children do their hands.

The result of life-long practice in this direction is perfectly astounding. Look at Mr. Chambers shaving himself, in the first photograph. The plentiful lathering, the sure touch and sweep of the keen razor over throat and face—these must be seen to be realized. I have hinted that Mr. Chambers is useful in the house. He uses with his feet mallet and chisel, saw and hammer, as well as any expert carpenter; and he points with justifiable pride to floor-cloths laid, and meat-safes, writing-desks, and other domestic articles manufactured entirely by himself.

Chambers is one of a family of six boys, and all his brothers are perfectly formed. The second photograph shows this wonderful armless man having a little musical evening at home. He is playing the cornet, whilst his eldest daughter presides at the piano. I repeat, there is virtually nothing that Mr. Chambers cannot

A QUIET MUSICAL EVENING.

do with his feet. Mr. Chambers also conducts his own correspondence, business and private. That he writes a very creditable "hand" will be evident from the following specimen, which he was good enough to write specially for this article.

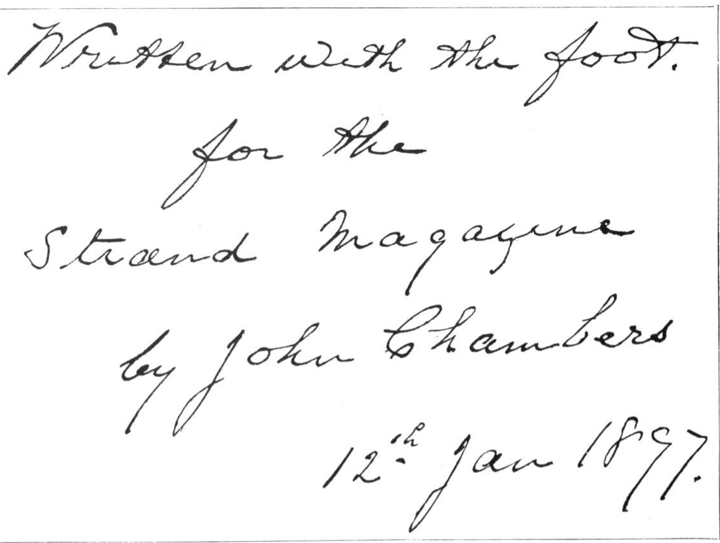
Written with the foot. for the Strand Magazine by John Chambers 12th Jan 1897.

SPECIMEN OF MR. CHAMBERS'S WRITING WITH HIS FOOT.

Kert Louw, the Bushman Chief, is the next side-show to figure in our gallery. Here is his story in brief. A great showman, who must be nameless, chanced to be exhibiting a Zulu troupe in London, when he was approached by a certain South African millionaire, financially interested in side-shows. "Why don't you bring over some pigmy earthmen?" suggested the millionaire; and the suggestion found favour in the sight of the showman. He accordingly dispatched an expedition, whose leader was instructed to proceed to Cape Town, and work northwards from there in search of the pigmy races. The expedition was assisted by the Cape Government officials. Said one of these latter: "Apply to Kert Louw, the Bushman Chief of the Kalahari Desert; he will get a whole tribe for you, if you like." But Kert Louw was not in favour at the time, and so was not easy to find. As a fact, a price of £100 was put on his head by the Cape Government, to whom he was something of a scourge by reason of mail robberies and murders on a huge scale.

But promises and guarantees at length brought the chief from his hiding-place, and he agreed to produce so many "earthmen" in return for a stated number of sheep and goats, and a quantity of tobacco, powder, and Cape "smoke," or vile brandy.

Thus the expedition was successful. In fact, it not only carried off the so-called earthmen, but it also managed to smuggle out of the country Kert Louw himself; and the Bushman Chief's photo. is here reproduced. Clad in unaccustomed garb, he became part of the show; and he only secured his release and return to his native wilds by a ruse quite in keeping with the cunning indicated in his villainous countenance. Having noticed that the showman-in-chief was passionately fond of diamonds, Kert Louw took him aside one day and assured him by all his gods that he knew of a diamond mine that would utterly efface the fame of Kimberley.

KERT LOUW—THE BUSHMAN CHIEF.

The showman subsequently announced to his subordinates that he was about to re-visit Africa, accompanied by the Bushman, on another freak hunt. So Kert Louw was taken out to the Cape in the gorgeous state-room of a Union liner, and conveyed up country in grand style—only to disappear from the showman's side and be lost in the wilderness. It was not a freak hunt, nor even a mine hunt—merely a wild-goose chase.

The three photographs next reproduced of Sadi Alfarabi, and his striking "business," give an excellent notion of what the great professional equilibrists of the world can accomplish. Sadi is a Russian by birth, and every single member of his family was an acrobat, each vying with the other in devising startling feats wherewith to take Europe by storm.

SADI ALFARABI ON THE TOWER.

In the first photo. we see Sadi standing on his hands on the summit of a miniature Eiffel Tower 30ft. high. A shaded oil-lamp is balanced on the back of his head; and as the point that supports him is movable, he revolves slowly on his perilous eminence. The second photo. shows the equilibrist performing a peculiarly difficult feat — walking on his hands on four billiard cues, his legs perfectly perpendicular in the air. He tells me that this hurts his hands exceedingly, and is likewise a severe strain on the muscles of the back. The third feat of the Russian performer shown here is considered the most difficult ever attempted by an equilibrist. It is really a very miracle of balancing. The chairs are in no sense trick chairs; they are not particularly light or frail, but solidity and weight are absolutely necessary to the accomplishment of such a feat. This photograph, as well as others, gives one an idea of the trouble which foreign speciality artistes take to insure that their photographs shall do them justice. There is the labour of dressing; the conveyance to the studio of all necessary "properties"; and last, but by no means least, the actual successful accomplishment of the feat, which must be sustained until after the crucial moment of uncovering the lens. And after all this the photos. may be utter failures! While I am on this subject, I may mention that on one occasion, in Buda Pesth, Sadi Alfarabi, whilst posing for the chair feat, incontinently collapsed in the photographer's studio. A fresh camera was afterwards necessary, likewise a fresh photographer.

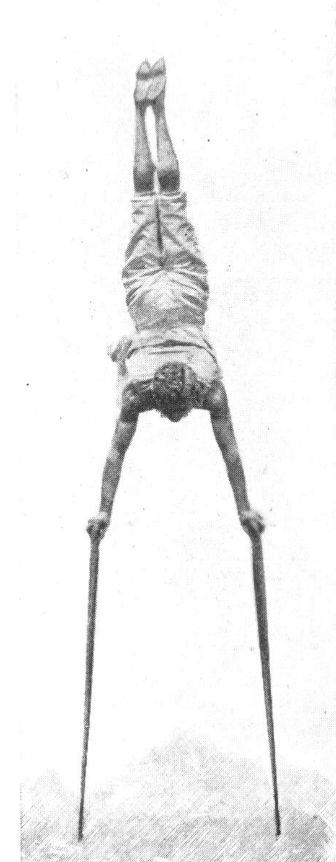

WALKING ON BILLIARD CUES.

A MARVELLOUS BALANCING ACT.
From Photos. by Lawson & Powers, California.

(To be continued.)

[I have quite a budget of grateful acknowledgments to make to the following well-known impresarios and entertainment caterers, for the loan of their interesting photos. reproduced in this article: Messrs. Warner and Co., of Wellington Street; Nathan and Summers, 10, Henrietta Street; W. B. Healey and Son, 17, Great Marlborough Street; J. Woolf, of "Wonderland," Whitechapel; and Read and Bailey, of the Agricultural Hall.]

Side-Shows.

V.

By William G. FitzGerald.

NOTHING can be more certain than that parody and travesty will follow a big boom in the entertainment world. And provided that the parody is really funny and clever, there is money in it. When the "strong man" craze was at its height, a certain relatively humble comedian conceived a really delightful and original idea. His only child—a sweet little girl of four or five years—was one day found alone in her bedroom doubling up her chubby right arm, lifting her tattered doll high into the air with tremendous pomp and circumstance, and generally giving an irresistible "strong man" show before a full-length mirror, with preternatural, big-eyed gravity. The father thought that if his baby-girl could give a similar show in public it would prove a great attraction. It did. And yet there was, after all, absolutely nothing in the thing; the infant went through certain motions in imitation of the orthodox strong man; and the people literally howled with delight—particularly as the tiny mimic's turn followed that of the real article.

TOM WOOTTWELL, THE MOCK "STRONG MAN."
From a Photograph.

This leads up to the "strong man" parody devised by Mr. Tom Woottwell, than whom no funnier fellow exists. The show indicated in the photo. here reproduced was screamingly comic. First, as to the costume of the mock "strong man." He is dressed in dilapidated old tights, which are supposed to be strained almost to bursting point at the arms and calves, owing solely to the abnormal muscular development of those parts. The calves are particularly funny—far less sinew than sawdust, however.

And observe the showman's leer as he strikes an attitude for the great feat of breaking a thick iron chain on the "muscles" of his arm. "Keep your eye on me, and you'll be astonished," he is saying. You would be, by the way, if you saw the next stage of the show. The man's mighty arm bends slowly but surely; his breath comes quick and short, and at the supreme moment the chain snaps asunder with an extraordinary uproar and flies right up into the wings—hauled up there, of course, by invisible wires.

The terrible strain proves too much for the great man; it "knocks the stuffin' out of him"—literally, for suddenly the "muscles" collapse and a thin stream of sawdust trickles on to the stage, leaving the audience convulsed with laughter.

The wonderful convolutions of which the human body is possible have already been dealt with in these articles. But it has been found that no matter how astounding may be the postures assumed, the ordinary contortionist show is apt to pall upon the fickle public. Therefore, of course, there arises an artist who devises an absolutely novel show. Here he is—"Marinelli, the Man Snake," and premier contortionist of the world. The extraordinary performance of this "reptile" is a veritable nightmare—a suggestion of Mr. H. G. Wells's wildest flight of scientific extravagance. The monster rears aloft his awful head,

MARINELLI, THE HUMAN PYTHON.
From a Photo. by Jos. Bscherer, Munich.

emitting horrible sounds hitherto unknown among the invertebrates; he drags his slow length erratically along the stage, and then suddenly coils himself up, twisting backwards and forwards like a mad thing.

Marinelli was once responsible for a pretty bill of damages. He was rehearsing by himself at a great theatre-circus in Frankfort one day, when a troupe of performing animals — elephants and horses chiefly — unexpectedly entered the ring, also for rehearsal purposes. The moment the animals set eyes on the huge "snake," they stampeded madly, literally bringing down the house with them. Fortunately, the only audience consisted of a few porters and trainers. Three valuable horses were so injured in the rush, however, that they had to be shot, and two elephants got out into the streets in a state of the wildest terror. And all this because the Human Python's silken and tinselled skin looked so dreadfully natural, to say nothing about his terrifying convolutions.

Trick-cycling shows we are all familiar with. Some crack experts ride tricycles, and others bicycles. There are others, again, who, contemning a multiplicity of wheels, perform all their wonderful feats on one solitary wheel, with which they seem able to do any conceivable thing. M. Noiset, however, the trick-cyclist whom we have chosen for this article, has gone still higher (or is it lower?) in the scale. He rides *half a wheel!* Of course, the angles are not sharp, but rounded. No one ever heard tell of round angles, perhaps, but then our cyclist's performance is likewise unique. You will notice that the machine is provided with unusually long and powerful cranks, which (to say nothing about the back-pedalling necessary) are very requisite for the forward movement, when the half-circle has run its course, and the flat side is about to come down on to the ground. This young artiste, when touring across Europe and America in the various variety theatres, always contrived to get up public races between himself and the local professional scorcher, invariably stipulating, however, for a nicely calculated start. They have wonderful

M. NOISET ON HIS SEMI-CYCLE.
From a Photo. by Otta Flach, Konigsberg.

MDLLE. MAZELLO ROSE AND HER PERFORMING PIGEONS.
From a Photograph.

business instinct, these fellows! Of course, this sort of thing created no end of interest and amusement, and made everybody agog to visit the theatre-circus and see the "semi-cyclist" go through the whole of his show. But fancy a race at Herne Hill between our interesting young friend and Mr. Shorland or Mr. Stocks!

The next interesting show to be dealt with is that given by Mdlle. Mazello Rose and her marvellous performing pigeons and doves. Bird shows, as a rule, are the dullest of entertainments—a vast quantity of glittering apparatus ("made in Germany") and a few mournful cockatoos going round and round under obvious protest and because they can't help it. Mdlle. Rose's show, however, is very different. Her pigeons are the quaintest little beggars imaginable, and can perform everything that dogs perform. An acrobatic pigeon sounds staggering, but these birds stand in rows and tumble at the word of command. They also have a kind of fair all to themselves, with swings, see-saws, and roundabouts, all going busily.

Finally, there is a sort of pantomime—a house on fire, lurid stage, miniature engines and escapes, and a gallant rescue by the perky bird seen on the lady's left, nearest her face. "Their intelligence is almost human," remarked the agent to me, almost tearfully, as he was describing the show; "and I believe," he added, somewhat inconsequently, sinking his voice impressively—"I *believe* she talks to them in pidgin-English."

The evolution of the under-water show was very gradual. Years ago, if a professional swimmer went into a glass-fronted tank of water (heated overnight) and then leered at the audience for one minute, he was hailed as a very Titan among entertainers. Then came more or less graceful passes, kiss-waftings, and gesticulations, which also impressed people mightily. Later on, some original fellow thought of tricks under water—picking up coins with the mouth, skipping, passing through a hoop, eating, and the like. The subaqueous drama depicted in our photo., however, is of quite recent date. The *dramatis personæ* are Professor Beaumont and his two daughters. This tragedy under

A TRAGEDY UNDER WATER.
From a Photo. by Adrian Smythe, Llandudno.

ONE OF THE MOST DIFFICULT BALANCING FEATS EVER ATTEMPTED.
From a Photo. by G. Bellisario, Cardiff.

water, as played by the troupe of professional swimmers here shown, is a most touching business. I am assured that during the performance there is "not a dry eye in the audience." I can well believe it. The players themselves, even, are a trifle damp. You see, the idea is that the heart-broken father, mad with grief at the death of his wife, and seeing his two daughters suffering the torments of slow starvation, resolves to take the lives of the hapless girls. It is not made clear why the family should be in this state of destitution, though their wardrobe certainly, and of course, necessarily, is rather scanty. However, the whole point of the thing lies in the fact that the drama is played under water, and that within three minutes. At the end of this time a moving object-lesson in resurrection is given, and father and daughters retire in the lime-light, snorting a little after their long immersion.

One of the original Girards is next depicted, having been photographed in the very act of performing one of the most difficult balancing feats that can possibly be performed. Comment upon this feat is a little superfluous, so well does the photograph explain it. At the same time one may demonstrate the apparent impossibility of the thing by taking two canes and two ordinary felt hats and trying the feat for oneself. This artist belongs to that class of Continental performers which makes it a practice to sandwich in between grotesque foolery many exceedingly difficult and fine feats of balancing and dexterity. These, in fact, sometimes miss fire, and go unappreciated by superficial observers, owing to the seemingly careless and airy manner in which they are executed, and the comicalities with which their accomplishment is interlarded.

The next curious show to figure in this article is the one given by Alphonsine, the "Premier Spiral Ascensionist." It is only at big places of entertainment

MADAME ALPHONSINE, THE "SPIRAL ASCENSIONIST."
From a Photograph.

—like the Royal Aquarium (where the accompanying photo. was taken) and the Crystal Palace—that this lady can give her show, for her apparatus is extensive, besides being peculiar. The manner of the ascent is sufficiently obvious. A pole, fully 100ft. high, is firmly fixed, having at its apex a small circular platform, or rest, 2ft. or 3ft. in diameter; this is the ultimate goal of the "ascensionist." The spiral pathway is next erected about the pole, and stayed from it by means of light steel girders. This curious roadway commences at the floor end with a slight inclined plane. Here is placed the ball, a hollow wooden one, about 2ft. in diameter. When everything is ready the lady appears; so does the lime-light—that absolute *sine quâ non* of the sensational show. Madame jumps on the ball, and simply impels it up the spiral way by a series of more or less graceful prances and jerks with her slippered feet. She stops at various stages of her curious journey, ostensibly to salute her admiring audience and challenge their applause, but really to have a moment's rest, for it is terribly hard work. One grieves to hear that Madame has had some bad accidents. Once—fortunately just when she had reached the extreme summit—the entire spiral way collapsed, leaving one to wonder, as in the case of the fly in the amber, how the lady "got there." This accident was due to the defective fastening of one of the stay-rods. Several times the ball has left the perilous track—jumped the narrow ribbon of iron that protects the edge of the spiral pathway. On such occasions Madame has been more or less seriously hurt.

SPINNING THE HUMAN TOP.
From a Photo. by Frank Johnston.

Alaska and Laure, who appear in our next production, are two grotesque French comedians; they sing, dance, knock each other about, and generally work very hard. The funniest, as well as the most original, item in their stage "business" is the one depicted in the photograph we have reproduced. This is the "Boy with the Human Top." The "Human Top," if you take the trouble to turn him right side up, looks as if he thoroughly enjoyed the situation. On the stage his head usually rests in a sort of wooden cap, padded, and revolving on a well-oiled ball-and-socket arrangement. His legs are sometimes spread out, his hands always; this is in order that he may spin readily and long. The owner of the Top—the "Boy," that is—occasionally spins his human plaything with his hands, but more often than not he winds around the Top's body about 50ft. of clothes-line. Presently he pulls this, and the Human Top begins to gyrate, slowly at first, but later on with dizzy rapidity. It is an automatic Top—one that greatly helps its owner in the sport. As a fact, the Top can spin himself, but not for long. Besides, the presence of the Boy and the action of the clothes-line—these are essential to the success of the show.

The next photograph reproduced shows Moung-Toon, one of the most wonderful jugglers that the East has produced. As might be supposed from his name, Moung is a Burman; and the story of his evolution as a showman is interesting. It seems the Burmese are born jugglers; they juggle with everything, even their finances and their police. Well, Moung was as a boy very fond of juggling, and he proceeded to perfect himself in several of the ordinary native school pastimes that were the delight of young Rangoon.

One day the inevitable entertainment agent arrived among the pagodas and soon got together a body of native jugglers, mainly

MOUNG-TOON, THE MARVELLOUS BURMESE JUGGLER.
From a Photo. by F. Cooper, Marseilles.

on behalf of one of the great London exhibitions. Now, Moung was among these, but after one season in England, he devised new feats for himself, and then severed his connection with the troupe. The result was that he made heaps of money, bought costly apparatus for himself, and aspired to a dresser of his own race. Why he should want a dresser is not obvious from the photo.; still, Moung saw it was the correct thing among "big" men, and besides, it was nice and convenient to have someone to hand up the balls and so forth.

The amazing part of Moung's show was that *he never touched with his hands the things which he juggled.* He used glass balls and balls made of strips of cane. These he would pick up from the floor with his prehensile toes and balance upon his instep. A jerk, and the ball was upon his knee; another, and it was on his shoulder. Then he would place a second ball on his other shoulder in the same way. By a quick movement of his body, the juggler would next cause the balls to rise in the air and fall behind his back; but before they could reach the ground, he had knelt down and received them on the backs of his knee-joints.

What is virtually the foremost animal show of the world is given by Mr. Seeth's forest-bred lions. Seeth himself, who can command the handsome salary of £150 a week, is seen in the accompanying curious photo. with a full-grown lion on his shoulders. One of the most curious items in the show is a big "merry-go-round," manned by lions, and pulled round by a pretty little pony. Each lion squats grumpily in a miniature sailing ship, and protests from time to time at the futility of the whole business. Mr. Seeth also drives his lions (which are really magnificent brutes) in a specially built chariot; and as he himself is attired as a Greek hero, the *ensemble* makes a very striking picture. Seeth is a powerful and fearless man, both of these qualities being evidenced by our photograph.

Little Zeretto, the child acrobat depicted in the accompanying illustration, is a remarkable example of the pliability of the human frame. Much nonsense has been written and spoken about the

MR. SEETH, WITH ONE OF HIS PERFORMING LIONS.
From a Photo. by Karoly, Nottingham.

ZERETTO, THE CHAMPION CHILD HIGH KICKER.
From a Photo. by Harry A. Webb, Philadelphia.

cruelty which enters into the training of stage children. Always providing that their trainers commence with the children at a very early age, it is not only possible gradually to make the little ones perform astounding acrobatic and other feats, but the youngsters themselves get to love their calling and take an interest in it, and in the devising of new items of business.

The child that figures in this photo. is positively as supple as ever it is possible to become. You will observe that the tamboureen is held by the mother as high as the little girl can reach. Well, she is able to touch this with either foot —surely the uttermost limit of the high kick!

We now come to an entirely different form of entertainment, after the manner of the late Chevalier Blondin — with variations. In the accompanying photograph we see the Brothers Weichmann performing the "Human Wheelbarrow" feat on a rope 110ft. high and 200ft. long. This is, of course, an open-air show, and one requiring a net that weighs nearly a ton. The rope, it will be seen, is steadied with guy-ropes from both sides. The Brothers Weichmann have a pretty original show. Besides the Human Wheelbarrow feat seen in the photo., they go through amusing and even startling antics as man-monkeys and kangaroos, effecting a complete change of costume and character on the high rope, possibly over a wide river at some country fête or gala. For this they receive from £80 to £100 on each occasion. Everything that is requisite for the performance of the various feats is kept in the aerial box or refuge seen to the right in the photograph.

From a] "THE HUMAN WHEELBARROW" ON THE HIGH ROPE. [*Photograph.*

SELECTED BIBLIOGRAPHY

Culhane, John, *The American Circus - an Illustrated History*, Henry Holt & Co., 1990
Lord Delfont, *Curtain Up! - The Story of the Royal Variety Performance* Robson Books, 1989
Fisher, John, *Paul Daniels and the History of Magic*, Jonathan Cape, 1987
Gilbert, Douglas, *American Vaudeville - Its Life and Times*, Whittlesey House, 1940
Green, Benny, *The Last Empires - A Music Hall Companion*, Pavilion, 1986
Jay, Ricky, *Learned Pigs and Fireproof Women - Unique, Eccentric and Amazing Entertainers*, Villard Books, 1986
Lamb, Geoffrey, *Victorian Magic*,Routledge & Kegan Paul, 1976
Leslie, Peter, *A Hard Act to Follow - A Music Hall Review*, Paddington Press, 1978
Louvish, Simon, *Man on the Flying Trapeze - The Life and Times of W.C. Fields*, Faber and Faber, 1997
Loxton, Howard, *The Golden Age of the Circus*, Regency House, 1997
Napier, Valantyne, *Act as Known - Australian Speciality Acts on the World Vaudeville/Variety Circuits* Globe Press, 1986
Read, Jack, *Empires, Hippodromes & Palaces*, The Alderman Press, 1985
Stein, Charles, *American Vaudeville as seen by its Contemporaries*, Alfred A Knopf, 1984
Weightman, Gavin, *Bright Lights, Big City - London Entertained 1830-1950*, Collins and Brown, 1992
Ziethen, Karl-Heinz, Allen, Andrew, *Juggling - The Art and Its Artists*, Werner Raush and Werner Luft, 1985